The Ontology of Language

The Ontology of Language
Properties, Individuals and Discourse

Chris Fox

CSLI Publications
Center for the Study of Language and Information
Stanford, California

CSLI Publications
Center for the Study of Language and Information
Leland Stanford Junior University
Printed in the United States
03 02 01 00 1 2 3 4 5

Library of Congress Cataloging-in-Publication Data

Fox, Chris, 1965–
The ontology of language : properties, individuals and discourse / Chris Fox.
p.cm. -- (CSLI lecture notes ; no. 105)
Includes bibliographical references and index.
ISBN 1-57586-233-6 (alk. paper) -- ISBN 1-57586-234-4 (pbk. : alk. paper)
I. Language and languages–Philosophy. 2. Semantics (Philosophy) 3. Discourse analysis. I. Titles. II. Center for the Study of Language and Information (U.S.) CSLI lectures notes ; no. 105.

P106 .F688 2000
401--dc21 00-024134

∞ The acid-free paper used in this book meets the minimum requirements of the American National Standard for Information Sciences – Permanence of Paper for Printed Library Materials, ansi z39.48-1984.

Visit our web site at
http://cslipublications.stanford.edu/
for comments on this and other titles, as well as for changes and corrections by the author and publisher.

For Alice and Helen

Contents

Preface

Over the past few years, I have been exploring various issues in the semantics of natural language within a property-theoretic framework. One question that constantly arises is as follows: why attempt to re-examine the semantics of linguistic phenomena in a relatively obscure framework, when most researchers in the field have ploughed longer and deeper furrows using more well-established formalisms?

There are certainly benefits to be had from expressing ideas in familiar and trusty frameworks, such as Montague's Intensional Logic, not least the economy of using a formal system that requires little or no introduction. However, just because a framework is familiar does not mean that it, and its associated methodologies, are beyond question. Criticism of a framework does not necessarily imply a criticism of any semantic analysis that may have been developed within that framework. Theories of natural language semantic phenomena can quite often be transposed between frameworks with little re-working.

A semantic theory should capture our basic intuitions concerning the nature of natural language propositions. Thus, the book begins by re-examining Aristotelean ideas about the nature of propositions, properties and individuals. The Property Theory presented axiomatises notions of proposition and truth in a way that is sympathetic to an Aristotlean view of properties and individuals. Further issues concerning the nature of individuals and discourse are then explored within this axiomatic framework.

When encountering a proposed ontology, we can strengthen the axioms of the theory to capture the desired behaviour. We should, however, be careful not to be tempted into producing the ontological equivalent of ghosts and ghouls: when given a choice between two theories with the same coverage, we should favour the one with the fewest ontological commitments and the weakest formal power. In considering the semantics of discourse, for example, we should perhaps be careful not to confuse the ontology required in presenting appropriate truth conditions with the machinery required to produce them.

Some of the material presented has appeared in different forms elsewhere: Chapter 3 and Chapter 4 are both adapted from my PhD thesis (Fox 1993). An earlier version of Chapter 4 was also presented at the Amsterdam Colloquium (Fox 1994b). Chapter 2 is derived from a section of a "FraCaS" project deliverable (Cooper et al. 1994) and closely follows Ray Turner's presentation of his axiomatisation of Aczel's Frege Structures (Turner 1988, Turner 1990, Turner 1992, Aczel 1980). It includes material adapted from some other works (Fox 1993, Fox 1994b, Fox 1998). The basic ideas from which Chapter 5 grew have also appeared elsewhere (Fox 1994a).

ACKNOWLEDGEMENTS

Discussions with the following people have helped me find the motivation to write this work, they are, in no particular order, Hans Kamp, Jan van Eijck, Josef van Genabit, Robin Cooper, Steve Pulman, Dick Crouch, Massimo Poesio. I am also indebted to Manfred Pinkal, who provided me with the opportunity to work in a stimulating research environment, and to Gennaro Chierchia, who gave helpful comments on my treatment of plurals and mass terms and on my analysis of intensional individuals.

Ray Turner suggested that I should write this book. My views on many of the underlying philosophical issues in semantics and logic have been illuminated and developed during invaluable discussions with him over the years.

Without the support and encouragement of my wife, Camilla, the work that became this book would never have been begun.

The first draft of the manuscript was prepared during an extremely difficult time for my family, with the very premature birth of my twin daughters. It is to them that this book is dedicated.

1

Introduction

What is the appropriate ontology of a formal semantic theory? Which notions should, or must, be taken to be primitive and which are derivative? As a starting point we could take the Aristotelean view. Paraphrasing somewhat, this is the view that there are two basic categories, that of individuals, and that of properties. Members of these categories may be combined by way of predication. In this ontology, predication is subject to certain constraints. Properties may be predicated of individuals and properties may be predicated of properties. In either case, a proposition results. However, individuals may not be predicated of individuals or properties.

Several questions may be raised about such an ontology. First, there are metaphysical questions concerning, in this case: the nature of propositions; what counts as an individual; what counts as a property; and whether it is appropriate to count the properties amongst the subjects of predication. Second, we may question whether such an ontology is adequate for all of the phenomena that arise in the formal analysis of language. Third, we may wonder whether a category can be eliminated, either by showing that it can be derived from other categories in the chosen ontology, or from some alternative ontology. For example, in the example of the basic Aristotelean ontology, we may question whether statements apparently involving properties and individuals may be reduced to statements that involve some other notions, and by so doing perhaps eliminate either the category of individuals, or that of properties. If we can do so, then the further question arises as to how we are to choose between competing ontologies.

From the formal, as opposed to metaphysical perspective, we also have to consider how best to characterise our chosen ontology, both with regard to the desired patterns of behaviour, and also with regard to whether a particular formalisation captures the spirit of the chosen ontology. We might, perhaps unwittingly, make use of a formal device that has the effect of rendering a category derivative, when metaphysical arguments suggest it should be primitive.

1.1 Individuals, Properties and Guises

Continuing our consideration of the Aristotelean ontology of individuals and properties, the first thing that we might question is the nature of individuals. Perhaps the paradigm case of individuals is provided by particulars. If we follow Strawson, then these would include those things that we can refer to directly by way of demonstratives: pointing at an object allows us to refer to it specifically (Strawson 1959).

Strawson extends the means by which we can refer to particulars to include expressions that contain within them a statement of some relationship that holds between the particular in question and other particulars to which we can already refer. We can use such relational expressions to refer to particulars that cannot be referred to directly by any demonstrative expression.

We might be tempted to take the mere act of physically pointing at some particular to be sufficient to refer to it. However, this cannot be right, even if we put aside the pragmatic problems of interpreting the act of pointing. Consider the act of pointing to a bench made out of wood: the act, in itself, is ambiguous; it may be the bench that is being pointed to, but how is that to be distinguished from pointing to a constituent part, or even the substance from which the bench is made? If these different attempts at pointing cannot be distinguished, they cannot be used to refer uniquely. Demonstratives, of whatever form, can only refer uniquely if they are accompanied, perhaps implicitly, by some indication of the salient aspect of the physical manifestation to which we are attempting to refer.

The relevant aspect may be thought of as the guise under which we are referring to the physical manifestation, or perhaps the role which it is fulfilling. It seems natural to associate guises with properties: we refer to the aspect of a physical manifestation of a particular which possesses the property in question. There is an element of intensionality here; it appears that the properties which hold of an individual can depend upon the guise under which we refer to it.[1]

The need to have properties to clarify the guise under which we denote a physical manifestation of a particular gives a strong argument in favour of taking properties to be at least as basic as individuals: to define prop-

[1] In Chapter 4 we will see how the results of one formalisation of such "intensional individuals," due to Landman (Landman 1987, Landman 1989) can be reproduced without introducing a new ontological category.

erties by way of sets of individuals requires that we first have the means to denote those individuals, but we cannot denote particulars, even with demonstratives, without first having available appropriate properties.

There are other, perhaps more familiar arguments for taking properties to be basic. Following Strawson, it just seems wrong to reduce a property to an extensional set-theoretic notion: we can know the intended meaning of a property without being acquainted with those objects that have that property, yet from a simple set-theoretic view, a property and the objects that have that property cannot be distinguished, and so being acquainted with the meaning of a property means we must be acquainted with the individuals that have that property, and know that it is those objects, and those alone, that have the property in question.

We may adopt a more complex set-theoretic view, where properties are equated with functions from possible worlds and individuals to truth values (Kripke 1959, Kripke 1963, Carnap 1947). But even here we can raise similar objections: to know the meaning of a property it seems that we must be acquainted with all the pairs of possible worlds and individuals that belong in the extension of the set that corresponds to the property.[2]

So the standard set-theoretic accounts of properties seem counterintuitive. We can also argue that they are formally inadequate. There are many examples of properties that are distinct, yet which have the same extension. For example, the properties 'being the Morning Star' and 'being the Evening Star' have the same extension, namely the planet Venus. However, historically it was acceptable to assert that one of these properties applies to an object seen in the morning sky whilst asserting that the other property did not. Our knowledge today allows us to infer that such assertions should not be made together. However, we can still distinguish two assertions that differ only on which of these two properties they contain. Hence, they must involve distinct properties. Indeed, as we shall see below, an analysis of statements of the form 'To be the Morning Star is to be the Evening Star.' is in danger of being vacuously true if the properties cannot be distinguished (Black 1944).

[2]We could be acquainted with the elements of a set by way of some characteristic function. If we define sets using characteristic functions, then there is a sense in which such a formalisation forms the basis of a property theory. We could say that the properties in question are actually defined by these functions, and not the sets that they characterise. If these function have an intensional identity criterion, then that would result in an intensional property theory. In set theory, there is no guarantee that characteristic functions are computable. If we were to restrict ourselves to those sets that have computable characteristic functions, then we would be restricting ourselves to the fragment of set theory which can be represented within PT (Chapter 2).

Set-theoretic treatments with possible worlds may be able to distinguish these properties by having them apply to different individuals in at least one possible world, even though they apply to the same individual in the real world. However, even this approach can be shown to be inadequate if the properties in question *necessarily* apply to the same individuals, as with "participles of exchange" such as 'being bought' and 'being sold'. These properties hold of exactly the same individuals, but the properties may be distinguished. We might have different attitudes towards the selling and buying of an object (Chierchia 1984). For example, we might view the selling of water as immoral, but the buying of it as a necessity.

This is an argument in favour of the view that properties should be taken as primitive. However, there is an alternative approach which does not require the abandonment of possible world semantics. We could allow the form of an expression to contribute to its own meaning, as with Cresswell's "structured meanings" (Cresswell 1985), and Carnap's "intensional isomorphism" (Carnap 1947) and related proposals (Lewis 1970, Cresswell 1975, Bigelow 1978). This idea can be traced back to Black's proposed treatment of the problem of analysis (Black 1944) that arises with statements such as:

> To be a brother is to be a male sibling.

where we wish to avoid equating this informative statement with:

> To be a male sibling is to be a male sibling.

This alternative proposal is to take the way in which a verbal and nominal expression contributes to the meaning of some statement as being an aspect of the meaning of that statement. If we accept that the meaning of a statement is obtained compositionally, then the way in which an expression contributes to the meaning of a statement is related to the syntactic nature of that expression.

It could be argued that to accept such an approach is to accept the view that the intensionality of expressions can be characterised as a syntactic issue; intensional equality-statements between expressions are concerned with form and not extension. In a sense, this is what is meant when we say that we take properties (and other expressions) to be primitive, where the notion of equality is that of equality between syntactic forms. It should also be noted that primitive properties are not inconsistent with possible worlds *per se.* The relevant point is that although possible worlds provide an appealing analysis of the metaphysical modalities of necessity and possibility, they do not naturally capture an appropriately fine-grained notion of intensionality. Arguments in favour of complicating a possible worlds analysis in order to account for the intensionality of language are also arguments in favour of an approach in which properties are primitive.

Some might object to the idea of primitive properties on the grounds that simply stipulating that they are undefined primitives does not shed any light on their nature, unlike a theory that reduces them to other independently motivated entities, such as functions from individuals to truth values. However, although it may yield some useful insights, it is not wise to adopt such a reduction if it makes the wrong predictions. The connection between properties and functions from individuals to truth values can effectively be regained when we consider the truth conditions of statements involving the predication of primitive properties.

In natural language, we seem to be able to predicate properties of properties, for example we can assert that "red is a colour," and we can have attitudes to properties as in 'John likes red'.[3] So properties can have the same role in statements as particulars, the paradigm case of individuals. This effect might be achieved without directly permitting properties to be individuals; we could have some individuals that correspond to the "nominalisations" of properties. However, there seems to be no immediately obvious ontological reason for adopting this position, so we might as well admit properties themselves into the class of individuals, as they can appear in statements in those places in which particulars occur as subjects.[4]

Clearly, these are not individuals that you can touch. They have a Platonic aspect to them, although there is no reason to assume that they have an existence that is independent of our conception of the world. We could think of them as denoting algorithms, or programs, which indicate whether or not an individual has the corresponding property.[5]

It also seems acceptable for propositions—which result from predi-

[3]In everyday language, we might use the expression 'being red', rather than 'red', when we wish to make clear that we are talking of a property, as in "The ball has the property of being red." This might be taken to suggest that 'red' is itself not a property. It is certainly the case that 'red' and 'being red' are distinct, as we would not claim that "being red is a colour." We take it that both can act as properties, the first is a simple property, the second is the property of having the property red.

[4]The Aristotelean ontology itself is silent on the issue of whether properties can appear as subjects. However, it certainly does not forbid it, and the nature of language suggests that good arguments would be needed if we were to do so.

[5]Indeed, there is a sense in which we can take algorithms to be the intensions of *all* expressions; in the theory that we adopt, intensions are terms in the untyped λ-calculus, and this calculus can be interpreted as a programming language (Barendregt 1984, Peyton-Jones 1986).

cating a property of an individual—to occur as subjects. For example, we have attitudes towards propositions, we may believe them, or know whether they are true or false. Such attitudes can be taken to express properties that hold of the proposition in question. If no reasons to take a more sophisticated view become apparent, then we might as well also admit propositions as individuals.[6]

We might also wish to consider other putative categories of individuals, such as events and places, but we shall leave them out of the present discussion.

It turns out that we can produce a theory that takes properties as basic notions using a formalisation that is weaker than set theory. One methodological principle that will be maintained is that we should avoid strengthening the basic ontology with more powerful notions unless absolutely necessary. For example, given a choice between addressing a phenomena by way of set theory or by way of some weaker alternative, we will choose the alternative.

1.2 The Methodology of Least Commitment

When presented with two alternative theories, one scientific criterion for assessing which is the better theory is to see which has the greatest predictive power. However, there are other ways of assessing theories. If two theories have a similar coverage, then we might instead favour the theory which has the fewest theoretical commitments. As an extreme example, a "scientific" theory that explains all but admits the existence of ghosts and ghouls is not to be envied. Even if those ghosts and ghouls are internal to the theory, and do not appear in the data or the conclusions, we would surely favour a theory that accounts for the same data without such supernatural help.

A theory which makes use of powerful devices can seem to lack the explanatory power of a weaker theory that covers the same data. In this way, an ontology which has the full power of set theory available perhaps explains less than a weaker theory with the same coverage. We can illustrate this with an example from the syntax of natural language; the fact that we can describe a significant fragment of natural language syntax using variants of context free grammars makes a stronger claim about language than noting that the syntax of the same fragment of natural language can be expressed within the more powerful class of transformational grammars.[7] From the perspective of scientific methodology, the

[6]As with properties, the Aristotelean ontology is silent on the issue of propositions as subjects.

[7]There are other parallels here. There are some syntactic phenomena which seem to require a more powerful formalism than that offered by context free grammars.

weaker theory makes a bolder claim because it is more susceptible to falsification; all other things being equal, it should then be preferred.

To summarise, given a choice between two similar theories, with a similar coverage of the relevant data, we should favour the simplest theory. The simplicity of a theory can sometimes be measured by its formal strength, in which case we should favour a weak theory over a more powerful one. Such a theory has greater explanatory power in the sense that it gives a better indication of the strength of the formal system that is required to explain the data. In essence, we are looking for the most constrained framework (one that allows us to prove the least) which, at the same time, has the flexibility necessary to achieve descriptive adequacy.

In this context, it is important to distinguish between the power of a formal theory, and its expressivity. We need a theory that is sufficiently expressive to allow us to represent the appropriate notions, preferably in a natural way, without being unnecessarily powerful. As an example, if we wish to predicate properties of properties then one approach would be to adopt a higher-order theory in place of a first-order theory. However, with certain restrictions, we can achieve the same ends within a suitably expressive first-order theory; we need not necessarily resort to a more powerful higher-order logic. Having a sufficiently expressive theory is a virtue, having an inappropriately powerful theory is not.

In cases where we have two theories of the same formal power, we should favour the one that has the weaker ontological commitment. As set theory is so powerful, we should not be surprised if can give a set-theoretic interpretation of a particular ontology. And just because we can do so does not mean this is then the intended interpretation of that ontology.

Although we talk only of a methodology of least commitment, there is implicit in this a complementary principle of "sufficient commitment"; in developing a theory we must be prepared to increase its formal and ontological commitments if that is required. We are interested in finding a theory whose ontological commitments and formal power are just sufficient to account for the data, and no more. This methodology will be used to decide the appropriate axiomatisations of various phenomena, such as the treatment of non-denoting definite descriptions and the atomicity of mass terms.

Similarly, there are semantic phenomena which might require a stronger theory than that to be presented here. Reference to set-theoretic objects in mathematical discourse could provide examples of such phenomena. The objective is then to see just how far we can go with a system that is weaker than set theory. There may even be ways around the difficulties, in this case by encoding the problematic mathematical objects as first-order individuals, for example.

1.3 Plurals and Mass Terms

One aspect of individuals that will be examined is the nature of plural objects and mass terms. These entail adding more structure to particulars, our paradigm case of individuals, so that we can consider collections of them as a new individual. For example, we need to be able to predicate properties "collectively" of the denotation of plural noun phrases, as in 'the men met'. We may question whether this needs a fundamental alteration to the ontology, or whether the required notions can be derived from existing notions.

To avoid adding new notions to the basic ontology, we could consider representing the appropriate groupings by way of properties. That is, we could consider denoting collections of objects, in the case of plurals, or collections of "stuff," in the case of mass terms, by the property which exclusively applies to that collection. This is certainly possible with a simple set-theoretic treatment of properties, where properties are equated with their extensions. That is, we could adopt the notion of "set" to provide the appropriate collections. In an ontology that already admits sets, this might be a conservative way of representing the appropriate structures of plurals and mass terms. But here, we wish to adopt the principle of using the weakest theory that can account for the data. All that we require in this case is some means of grouping objects together. This can be achieved by systems that are much weaker than set theory, such as lattice theory (Halmos 1963, Birkhoff 1967, Gratzer 1978).[8]

Within the formal framework to be presented, we can use properties themselves, in place of sets, as a way of denoting collections of individuals or "stuff." However, because we wish to divorce properties from their extensions, it may not then be appropriate to consider equating plurals and mass terms with uniquely identifying properties, as it is the extensions of properties that appear to possess a plural or mass structure, not the properties that they have. Following this reasoning, we shall then strengthen the category of individuals with the addition of definably complete lattices.

We adopt the methodology of least commitment; the theory is too

[8]Conventionally, lattice theory is presented using the language of set theory. In such a presentation, a lattice consists of a set and a binary relation with certain restrictions. Such relations in turn can be formalised as a set of pairs. Indeed, pairs themselves can be formalised as sets. Given these standard presentations, it might be thought puzzling to assert that lattice theory is weaker than set theory, when the formalisation of lattice theory seems to require set theory. The answer is that although standard formalisations of lattice theory use set theory, we can think of lattice theory as being defined independently of set theory by some collection of axioms. These axioms can be given a set-theoretic model. The standard presentations of lattice theory can then be seen as formalising these models of lattice theory. It is clear that lattice theory is the weaker theory, as classical set theory cannot be modelled within it.

weak to say anything about the truth conditions of statements involving non-denoting definite descriptors. This follows Strawson, and much subsequent work: a definite descriptor that attempts to make reference to a particular presupposes that there is some such particular, and that the truth of that presupposition is a condition on the "presupposing statement" having a truth value (Strawson 1959).[9]

With mass terms, the question of atomicity arises: whether the denotations of a mass terms have minimal parts. At least in everyday usage, mass terms can be treated as if they are non-atomic. But language does not become inconsistent with the acceptance of the atomic nature of physical matter. It seems that language can remain neutral with respect to atomicity. Here then, a weak position will be adopted whereby we do not presume that mass terms are, or are not, atomic. Rather, the objective will be to produce an ontology of mass terms that is consistent with both positions.

It might seem that dispensing with atoms would reduce our commitments compared with remaining neutral. This would be the case if atoms were taken to be ontologically primitive. An alternative perspective is to say that atoms are essentially no different in kind to any other particulars. Any difference lies in the relationship between putative atoms and other particulars, namely that atoms have no proper parts. On this view, a theory that asserts either that atoms do or do not exist is formally stronger than one that remains neutral, whilst having an indistinguishable ontology. All other things being equal, the methodology of least commitment then suggests that the neutral theory is to be preferred.

Another issue that we need to consider is whether mass terms are homogeneous, for example, whether all parts of the denotation of "water" are "water." This need not depend upon whether or not mass terms are atomic. For simplicity, we will adopt the view that mass terms are homogeneous: although they may be related to inhomogeneous constituents, they are not equated with those constituents.[10] This parallels the treatment of the so-called "group denoting" nouns, such as 'committee': there is a connection between a committee and its members, but a committee is not to be equated with them (Barker 1992).

---

[9]Strawson argues that reference to properties has no such presupposition.

[10]An alternative analysis would be to allow inhomogeneous mass terms, and use the guise (§1.1) under which we refer to a substance to indicate the relevant mode of division (Fox 1993, Fox 1998). In the case of count terms, the guise could be used determine not only what is being referred to, but also gives an appropriate criterion for counting. An anonymous reviewer suggests that further evidence of this position may come from the fact that, in some classifier languages, classifiers are needed not only with numerals, but also with demonstratives, so the indication of the guise under which something is referred to is required both to count and to demonstrate.

1.4 Discourse Representation

The final example considered in this work concerns "Discourse Representation Structures" (Kamp 1981, Kamp and Reyle 1993), which have been devised to give a formal analysis of natural language discourse. It could be argued that these structures are a new basic category in addition to individuals and properties (or perhaps a new category of individual). Here it is shown that we can treat at least some examples of discourse within the classical framework. On this account, Discourse Representation Structures can be seen to be a non-essential formal device used in the process of constructing appropriate representations, which can be eliminated.

Similar arguments apply to alternative "dynamic" theories in which a category of assignments is used to give a non-classical interpretation of the logical connectives in order to obtain the appropriate truth conditions for natural language discourse (Groenendijk and Stokhof 1990, Groenendijk and Stokhof 1991). We show that there is no need to abandon the classical interpretations of the logical connectives.

1.5 Summary

There are several reasons for producing a formal system that is not sympathetic to metaphysical considerations. These reasons include: the convenience, or familiarity of an alternative characterisation; technical difficulties that make it hard to produce a consistent system; and, perhaps, ignorance of such considerations. This work seeks, in part, to overcome these difficulties by presenting some ontological arguments—some in favour of adding new ontological categories, others against—together with formal systems that are sympathetic to the conclusions of these arguments.

Producing a definitive ontology that is adequate for natural language semantics is beyond the scope of this work. Here, the objective is merely to provide an illustration of an approach to deciding on appropriate aspects of such an ontology, and their formalisation.

In this work, a version of Property Theory is adopted that is perhaps the simplest basic semantic framework which is sympathetic to the onotological considerations. There have been various analyses of a range of semantic phenomena within Property Theory (Chierchia 1982a, Chierchia and Turner 1988, Kamareddine 1988, Ramsay 1990). Here, the primary aim is not to analyse a vast range of linguistic phenomena, rather we cover just a few examples, and try to weigh all of the ontological implications carefully.

2

Property Theory

Here, a simple theory of propositions, properties and truth is described. We shall refer to this theory as simply "Property Theory."[11] The main objective is to have a theory that is sympathetic to an Aristotelian view of the nature of properties and individuals. In the following chapters we will then go on to describe how this theory can be strengthened to account for individuals corresponding to the denotations of plurals and mass terms, and how it can be used to produce semantics for discourse and to refer to individuals under a "guise."

We are not concerned with the various philosophical debates surrounding the different variants of property theory. For example, we will avoid discussion of the appropriateness of modelling predication as function application (Bealer 1989). It may also transpire that the framework has to be strengthened in various ways to account for the nature of propositions and the types of terms within, for example, intensional contexts.

Here, the main concern is to present a simple framework that is sympathetic to some fundamental ontological concerns, and which can be used to express theories about semantic phenomena in natural language.

2.1 Motivation

The motivation for property theory involves issues in intensionality and types. A basic premise of property theory is that if we wish to obtain a highly intensional theory then propositions and properties should be taken seriously as primitive notions which are independent of any set-theoretic interpretation. Equality between propositions should be as weak as syntactic equality between their representations; propositions should only be equated if they have the same syntactic form.

[11]In general, we shall use 'property theory' to refer generically to theories of propositions, properties and truth, whereas both the capitalised 'Property Theory' and 'PT' will be used to refer to the particular theory presented here, as developed by Turner (Turner 1990, Turner 1992).

As we shall see, if we provide a purely syntactic characterisation of the class of propositions, then this syntactic view of equality is problematic; it can lead to an inconsistency via the logical paradoxes. These paradoxes arise from certain cases of self-application. The need to avoid the logical paradoxes is often taken as a motivation for using strongly typed theories which ban all instances of self-application on syntactic grounds. However, an alternative is to adopt a weak representationalist view where not all terms of the appropriate syntactic form represent propositions. This allows the formalisation of a weakly typed, highly intensional theory in which unproblematic instances of self-predication can be represented, together with universal properties, like self-identity, which are prohibited in strongly typed theories.

Types can be re-introduced into the theory as first-order predicates. These first-order types have much greater flexibility than those of strongly typed logics. The admissibility of unproblematic instances of self-predication is just one consequence of this flexibility; perhaps the more significant underlying advantage of such a theory is that we can develop typing rules that match the empirical behaviour of natural language, rather having to work around some given system of strong syntactic typing rules that exists for formal, rather than empirical reasons.

Property Theory is not an empirical theory about natural language semantics, except in so far as it provides a treatment of intuitions about propositions and truth, and gives rise to limits as to what can be expressed. There is a parallel with syntactic theory. Syntactic formalisms enable us to express grammars, just as Property Theory can be used to express semantic theories. Formalisms for syntax do not, by themselves, constitute a grammar, although they may limit what can be expressed within a grammar. They provide a framework in which to explore treatments of empirical issues. In the same way, Property Theory, and theories of propositions, properties and truth in general, provide a vocabulary for implementing semantic theories and a formal space in which to explore issues in natural language semantics. There is, however, one sense in which Property Theory might be a component of an empirical theory of meaning, in that it could be taken to characterise the computational device with which speakers are endowed as part of their linguistic competence.[12]

The version of property theory presented here adopts a first-order axiomatic approach to propositions and truth. The axioms are incomplete with respect to the proposition-hood, and hence the truth of, paradoxical

[12]This observation was made by an anonymous reviewer.

terms. In addition to providing a treatment of propositions, properties and truth, this axiomatic approach can be taken as a methodology for natural language semantics. Some basic intuitions will be captured by the way in which natural language phrases are represented in the theory. To cover additional phenomena, we can, if necessary, add definitions and axioms which are strong enough to capture the salient intuitions. In conjunction with rules such as *Modus Ponens* and Universal Generalisation, inferences in natural language are then mirrored by corresponding inferences in the representation. So, the theory can be strengthened to cover various semantic phenomena in a uniform framework. The axioms may remain incomplete with respect to problematic or controversial issues. In this respect, the weakness of the theory is a strength. In addition, the weak axioms do not impose requirements such as strong typing, which can create additional complications for the treatment of some semantic phenomena. Of course, whenever we add axioms that strengthen the theory, we must ensure that the resultant theory is consistent.

Let us consider in more detail the relevant issues in intensionality and types which have been used to motivate Property Theory. A theory is said to be intensional if two objects can be distinguished, even though they are equated under some other mode of analysis. Given two levels of interpretation, one level is more intensional (less extensional) than the other if it embodies a weaker sense of equality. In terms of a theory of sets, we might contrive two notions of equality: one, when we consider sets to be defined by the members they have; another, weaker equality, when we take sets to be defined by the procedure used to determine their members. The latter sense of equality gives rise to an intensional view of sets; sets which have the same members, and hence which would be equated in standard set theory, may be distinguished in this intensional set theory if the procedures used to determine their members are different.[13]

Intensionality is required in the semantics of propositional attitudes. The simplest view of propositions is perhaps to claim that they denote truth-values. However, an individual believes and knows propositions that are to be distinguished from mere truth-values. Further, if the equality relation between propositions is given by the equality between the

[13]Some might argue that being extensional is an essential feature of sets. A reply to this would be that sets can have whatever behaviour we chose to give them. There are other non-standard characterisations of sets (Aczel 1988, Jubien 1989). Perhaps the issue in question is whether the use of the term 'sets' is misleading. Here, the use of the term is intended to convey the fact that the usual set-theoretic operators are supported, and that these operators behave in the expected way, *modulo* the notion of equality.

denoted truth values, then, in classical logic, there would only be two propositions, corresponding to "true" and "false." The traditional approach is to say instead that a proposition is something which evaluates to a truth-value given a "state of affairs," or "world." In other "possible worlds," or states of affairs, it may evaluate to a different truth-value (Kripke 1963). Thus, a proposition is equated with the set of worlds in which it holds.

We may question whether such an approach is sufficiently fine-grained; if two propositions necessarily hold in the same states of affairs, then they cannot be distinguished. If an agent believes a proposition, she is committed to believing all of its logical consequences. We may not wish to characterise belief in this way. For example, all propositions in mathematics become equated. It seems too strong to say that if an agent knows some mathematical truth, then that agent knows all mathematical truths. Clearly we need to be able to distinguish mathematical propositions which are equated on a possible worlds analysis.

There are also problems for the representation of properties on this account: a property will be represented by a function from individuals to propositions. As discussed in Chapter 1, some properties, such as those of 'being bought' and 'being sold' may become equated, yet we might wish them to be different (Chierchia 1984).

Greater intensionality would be obtained if propositions were taken to be equal only if they are represented by the same syntactic object. This is a representationalist view of propositions. However, this approach is potentially problematic. If the assertion of a proposition is equivalent to asserting its truth, then it is possible to construct paradoxical statements. To illustrate this, if we maintain the following equivalences, which express the Tarski Biconditional for statements and predication:

$s \leftrightarrow$ It is the case that s.
$px \leftrightarrow$ It is the case that p holds of x.

and define a property R by:[14]

$Rx =_{\text{def}}$ It is the case that x does not hold of x.

then, from this definition, we can deduce that:

$RR \leftrightarrow$ It is the case that R does not hold of R.

but, from the Tarski Biconditional above, it follows that:

$RR \leftrightarrow$ It is the case that R holds of R.

[14]In this example, R is intended to correspond to Russell's property.

Thus, we obtain the contradiction:

It is the case that R holds of R.	$\leftrightarrow$	It is the case that R does not hold of R.

A solution to this problem would be to ban expressions of the form RR. This is one purpose of strongly typed theories. An object's type specifies the type of those objects to which it may be applied, and the type of the resultant object. If $f \in \langle a, b\rangle$ (that is f is of type $\langle a, b\rangle$) and $g \in a$, then $fg \in b$. In the semantics of natural language, the types might correspond to syntactic categories.

To avoid paradoxical assertions requires a stronger notion of types, where objects must belong to one, and only one type, and syntactically, objects can only be applied to arguments of the appropriate type. There must be no notion of equality (or containment) across the types. Such "monomorphic" types refer to higher order functions. Strong typing precludes the formation of expressions such as:

$$RR$$

because it cannot be typed: if we assume $R \in \langle S, prop\rangle$ (that is, R produces a proposition when applied to something of type S) then for RR to be a proposition, it must be the case that $R \in \langle\langle S, prop\rangle, prop\rangle$, but this means R belongs to more than one type.[15] This is the approach taken in a possible worlds style analysis, which we have rejected because it does not have sufficiently fine-grained intensionality.

However, if we are to adopt a theory in which propositions are equated only if they are represented by the same syntactic object, then the use of strong types to avoid the paradoxes may lead to other problems. To express representations of beliefs of the form:

Mary believes$_m$ P

the representation of 'believes$_m$' must be of the type $\langle S, \langle e, prop\rangle\rangle$, where $P \in S$, and $Mary' \in e$. We can say that 'believe$_m$' is in the meta-language of object language sentences of type S. To express:

John believes$_j$ that everything Mary believes$_m$ is true.

requires that 'believes$_j$' for John is in the meta-language for statements about Mary's beliefs. If, however, we also have the expression:

Mary believes$_m$ that everything John believes$_j$ is true.

then we cannot express the appropriate content: this last sentence requires that 'believes$_m$' is in the meta-language of sentences containing

[15] Chierchia notes that even in some strongly typed theories, such as Dynamic Montague Grammar, the paradoxes may accidentally be reintroduced in the semantics of dynamic binding (Chierchia 1991) (see Appendix A).

'believes$_j$', which contradicts the requirements of the preceding example. In other words, we can conclude from these last two sentences that 'believes$_m$' and 'believes$_j$' are higher than each other in the object/metalanguage hierarchy, which is inconsistent (Turner 1992).

The problem is created by the use of strong typing, which was introduced to avoid the logical paradoxes. However, there is an alternative way of avoiding the paradoxes, which is to give up the Tarski Biconditional:

$s \leftrightarrow$ It is the case that s.

We can achieve this by saying that only some of the objects in the language represent propositions. It is only for such objects that the biconditional holds. This could be characterised as *weak* representationalism. In such a theory, we have two basic types. These types carve out (i) those individuals that correspond to propositions, and (ii) those that correspond to true propositions, respectively. Alternatively, we could have two types corresponding to true and false propositions, respectively. In this alternative system, an individual would be a proposition if it was either a true or false proposition. Regardless of how we choose to formalise the theory, the key point is that not every individual will be a proposition.

Among its advantages, such a weakly typed theory allows the expression of universal properties (such as being self-identical), and the simple expression of gerunds and infinitives (Chierchia 1982a, Chierchia 1984). As an example of the latter, in the following sentences:

John likes to play tennis.
John likes playing tennis.

we might wish to take 'to play tennis', and 'playing tennis' to denote properties, or at least terms which are systematically related to the property denoted by the finite verb phrase in:

John is playing tennis.

If we have a weakly typed framework in which properties are taken to be just another kind of individual, then in:

John likes Mary.
John likes playing tennis.

the verb 'likes' can be represented by an object of the same type.

Chierchia notes that if we take 'is fun' and 'being fun' to denote essentially the same property, then:

Being fun is fun.

predicates a property of itself (or, from a Fregean perspective, it predicates a property of the "individual correlate" of itself). With this example, we have a legitimate instance of self-predication, which would be ruled out in a strongly typed theory.[16]

In summary, the theory of propositions, properties and truth to be presented here is an axiomatic theory. The axioms characterising propositions are deliberately too weak to prove that paradoxical terms are propositions. As mentioned before, an axiomatic approach provides a methodology for natural language semantics, in which the semantic theory can be strengthened till it is just strong enough to capture the desired intuitions, but no stronger. The axioms can be left incomplete with respect to controversial intuitions. As we shall see, the axiomatic theory also lends itself to the characterisation of felicitous discourse, where only a meaningful discourse can be taken to constitute a proposition. For example, a semantic theory could be constructed where the axioms of truth need never apply to sentences with false presuppositions.

2.2 PT: An Axiomatic Property Theory

The particular version of property theory to be introduced here is PT, Turner's axiomatisation of Aczel's Frege Structures (Turner 1990, Turner 1992, Aczel 1980). In a Frege Structure, a class of propositions and a subclass of true propositions are carved out of the class of arbitrary syntactic expressions: the arbitrary syntactic expressions are those of the untyped λ-calculus, and the classes of propositions and true propositions are defined by the first-order predicates P and T, respectively.

There are other formalisations of property theory, or, more generally, theories of truth and propositions (Kripke 1975, Gilmore 1974, Feferman 1984, Gupta 1982, Herzberger 1982, Cocchiarella 1979, Jubien 1989, Bealer 1982, Kamareddine 1992, Kamareddine 1993, Kamareddine 1995, Turner 1989). There are theories that avoid equating predication with λ-application, as this may prove problematic for some examples (Turner 1989, Bealer 1989). Some of the alternative theories are discussed briefly in §2.9.

In §2.4, a short example is given to illustrate how the paradoxes are avoided without imposing strong typing restrictions on the syntax of the representations.

[16] As already mentioned (page 12), perhaps the ability to represent self-predication is not the crucial point, rather it is the underlying flexibility of the weak typing which is a key advantage of this theory. The acceptability of some cases of self-predication is just one consequence of this flexibility.

2.2.1 The General Framework

PT can be thought of as a combination of two languages. The first is a language of terms, which consists of the untyped λ-calculus, embellished with logical constants. A restricted class of these terms will correspond to propositions. Some of the propositions will, further, be *true* propositions.

When propositions are combined appropriately using the logical constants, other propositions result. As an example, given the propositions t, s, the "conjunction" of these, $t \wedge s$, is also a proposition, where $\wedge$ is a logical constant. The truth of the resultant proposition will depend upon the truth of the constituent propositions. In this case, if t, s are both propositions, then $t \wedge s$ will be a true proposition if and only if t and s are true propositions. The class of properties consists of those terms that form propositions when applied to another term. In PT, the act of predication is modelled by λ-application.

One essential point to note is that the notion of equality is that of the λ-calculus. This means that propositions are not equated just because they are always true together, nor are properties equated just because they hold of the same terms (i.e. form true propositions with the same terms). In other words, PT is a highly intensional theory.

It is also important to note that the language in which these logical constants are expressed has no proof theory (except for the λ-calculus rules governing the equality of terms) and that the notions of being a proposition, or a true proposition, cannot be expressed within this language. That is the purpose of the second language embodied in PT; the language of well formed formulae (wff). Essentially, this is a first-order logic. The terms of this logic—the expressions that can appear as the arguments of predicates, and over which the quantifiers of the logic range—are expressions of the first language; the λ-calculus extended with logical constants.

The language of wff has two predicates, P for "is a proposition," and T for "is a true proposition." This gives the formal means for axiomatising the behaviour of propositions and true propositions. For example, the fact that two propositions can be conjoined to form a new proposition is formalised as follows:

$$\mathrm{P}(t) \mathbin{\&} \mathrm{P}(s) \rightarrow \mathrm{P}(t \wedge s)$$

We can express the fact that this proposition is true if and only if the conjuncts are both true by the axiom:

$$\mathrm{P}(t) \mathbin{\&} \mathrm{P}(s) \rightarrow (\mathrm{T}(t \wedge s) \leftrightarrow (\mathrm{T}(t) \mathbin{\&} \mathrm{T}(s)))$$

Note that axioms concerning T must be restricted so that only terms that are propositions are considered: we do not want to give truth conditions to terms that are not propositions.

The distinction between a wff which expresses the truth conditions of a propositional term, and the term itself, can be taken to be akin to that between extension and intension in Montague semantics (Montague 1973). In that theory, however, intensions are derived from extensions. As a consequence, the equality of intensions is that of the extensions, so the intensions of propositions will be equated if they are always true together, and properties (the intensions of predicates) will be equated if they always hold of the same objects. This is in contrast to PT, where the intensions are basic. Propositions in the language of terms may have the same truth conditions when T is applied, but this does not force them to be the same proposition, so we might have:

$$\mathrm{T}(s) \leftrightarrow \mathrm{T}(t)$$

but that does not mean that the terms are equal:

$$s = t$$

Similarly, in the language of wff, properties may hold of the same terms, yet they may be distinct. The λ-equality of terms is thus weaker than the notion of logical equivalence obtained when considering truth conditions in the meta-language.

2.2.2 The Formal Theory

The following presents a formalisation of the languages of terms and wff, together with the axioms that provide the closure conditions for P and T.

The Language of terms

Basic Vocabulary:

Individual variables:	$x, y, z, \ldots$
Individual constants:	$c, d, e, \ldots$
Logical constants:	$\vee, \wedge, \neg, \Rightarrow, \Xi, \Theta$

Inductive Definition of Terms:

(i) Every variable or constant is a term.
(ii) If t is a term and x is a variable then $\lambda x(t)$ is a term.
(iii) If t and t' are terms then $t(t')$ is a term.

The Language of Wff

Inductive Definition of Wff:

(i) If t and s are terms then $s = t, \mathrm{P}(t), \mathrm{T}(t)$ are atomic wff.
(ii) If φ and φ' are wff then $\varphi \mathbin{\&} \varphi', \varphi \vee \varphi', \varphi \to \varphi', {\sim}\varphi$ are wff.
(iii) If φ is a wff and x a variable then $\exists x \varphi$ and $\forall x \varphi$ are wff.

The theory is governed by the axioms that follow.

Axioms of The λ-Calculus

(α) $\lambda x(t) = \lambda y(t[y/x])$ y not free in t

(β) $(\lambda x(t))t' = t[t'/x]$

A variable x is said to be "bound" (that is to say, "not free") in a term t iff:

(i) $t = \lambda y(s)$ and $y = x$, or x is bound in s.

(ii) $t = ss'$ and x is bound in either s or s'.

The notation $a[b/x]$ is used to denote the expression that results from substituting b for all free occurrences of x in a.

The axioms (α) and (β) define the equivalence of terms. They are known as the α and β axioms of equality, respectively. When read as rewrite rules, from left to right, they are also known as α-reduction and β-reduction. We sometimes use subscripts (as in $=_\alpha$ and $=_\beta$) to indicate an application of the corresponding axiom of λ-equality.

The closure conditions for propositions are given by the following axioms:

Axioms of Propositions

(i) $\mathrm{P}(t)$ & $\mathrm{P}(s) \rightarrow \mathrm{P}(t \wedge s)$

(ii) $\mathrm{P}(t)$ & $\mathrm{P}(s) \rightarrow \mathrm{P}(t \vee s)$

(iii) $\mathrm{P}(t)$ & $(\mathrm{T}(t) \rightarrow \mathrm{P}(s)) \rightarrow \mathrm{P}(t \Rightarrow s)$

(iv) $\mathrm{P}(t) \rightarrow \mathrm{P}(\neg t)$

(v) $\forall x\mathrm{P}(t) \rightarrow \mathrm{P}(\Theta\lambda x(t))$

(vi) $\forall x\mathrm{P}(t) \rightarrow \mathrm{P}(\Xi\lambda x(t))$

(vii) $\mathrm{P}(s \approx t)$

These axioms effectively give well-formedness conditions for propositions. In other semantic theories, these might be given by the syntactic definition of the language.

Truth conditions can be given for those terms that are propositions:

Axioms of Truth

(i) $\mathrm{P}(t)$ & $\mathrm{P}(s) \rightarrow (\mathrm{T}(t \wedge s) \leftrightarrow \mathrm{T}(t)$ & $\mathrm{T}(s))$

(ii) $\mathrm{P}(t)$ & $\mathrm{P}(s) \rightarrow (\mathrm{T}(t \vee s) \leftrightarrow \mathrm{T}(t) \text{ v } \mathrm{T}(s))$

(iii) $\mathrm{P}(t)$ & $(\mathrm{T}(t) \rightarrow \mathrm{P}(s)) \rightarrow (\mathrm{T}(t \Rightarrow s) \leftrightarrow \mathrm{T}(t) \rightarrow \mathrm{T}(s))$

(iv) $\mathrm{P}(t) \rightarrow (\mathrm{T}(\neg t) \leftrightarrow \sim \mathrm{T}(t))$

(v) $\forall x\mathrm{P}(t) \rightarrow (\mathrm{T}(\Theta\lambda x(t)) \leftrightarrow \forall x\mathrm{T}(t))$

(vi) $\forall x\mathrm{P}(t) \rightarrow (\mathrm{T}(\Xi\lambda x(t)) \leftrightarrow \exists x\mathrm{T}(t))$

(vii) $\mathrm{T}(t \approx s) \leftrightarrow t = s$

(viii) $\mathrm{T}(t) \rightarrow \mathrm{P}(t)$

The last axiom states that only propositions may have truth conditions.

The intended interpretation of the term Θ (Ξ, respectively) in propositions of the form $\Theta\lambda x(t)$ ($\Xi\lambda x(t)$, respectively) is that every individual (some individual, respectively) has the property $\lambda x(t)$. In the language of terms, the notions of variable binding and quantification are treated separately, with all variable binding being performed by λ-abstraction. For simplicity, the quantified propositions $\Theta\lambda x(t)$ and $\Xi\lambda x(t)$ can be written as $\Theta x(t)$ and $\Xi x(t)$, where the λ-abstraction is implicit.

The axioms for $\Rightarrow$ may require some explanation. We could have had:

$$\begin{array}{l} \mathrm{P}(t) \,\&\, \mathrm{P}(s) \rightarrow \mathrm{P}(t \Rightarrow s) \\ \mathrm{P}(t) \,\&\, \mathrm{P}(s) \rightarrow (\mathrm{T}(t \Rightarrow s) \leftrightarrow (\mathrm{T}(t) \rightarrow \mathrm{T}(s)) \end{array}$$

but this is a little too weak when we consider the dependent types in PT (described below, §2.3.4). The chosen axioms are stronger in that they are "lazy" about the nature of the consequent s. In classical logic, if t is false then we know that $t \rightarrow s$ is true without considering s. In PT, if t is a false proposition, then not only do we not need to consider the truth of s, we do not even need to determine whether it is a proposition. With the term $t \Rightarrow s$, the axioms only require a proof that s is a proposition in the case that t is true.

Of course, if we require it, the weaker form of implication can be defined by $t \rightsquigarrow s =_{\mathrm{def}} \neg t \vee s$. If we have the stronger form of implication, we can define stronger forms of $\wedge$ and $\vee$ ($\vec{\wedge}, \vec{\vee}$) where there is no need to evaluate whether the second term is a proposition if the first term is a proposition and the truth of the entire term can be determined by it. In the case of $\vec{\wedge}$ we only need to show that the second term is a proposition if the first term is a true proposition. We can take the entire expression to be a false proposition if the first term is a false proposition. With the strengthened disjunction $\vec{\vee}$ we need to determine that the second term is a proposition only if the first term is a false proposition. If the first term is a true proposition, then the entire expression can be taken to be a true proposition. Formally, they can be defined as follows:

$$\begin{array}{lll} t \mathrel{\vec{\wedge}} s & =_{\mathrm{def}} & t \wedge (t \Rightarrow s) \\ t \mathrel{\vec{\vee}} s & =_{\mathrm{def}} & t \vee (\neg t \Rightarrow s) \end{array}$$

The basic theory presented here is very weak. The general approach for analysing new semantic phenomena is to amend the theory either definitionally, as is done when adding dependent type constructors (§2.3.4) or by strengthening it with more axioms and primitive notions, such as for mass term, plurals (Chapter 3) and events. This is, of course, in addition to obtaining appropriate representations for natural language expressions.

2.3 Definitions of Types

Here, we see how various types can be defined in the theory, which can include the concepts of quantifier, determiner, and function space. These can be used when giving a Montagovian-style analysis of natural language semantics (Montague 1973) in PT. In addition, definitions for dependent types in PT are presented, following Turner (Turner 1990). These operators feature in constructive type theory, such as Martin-Löf's Type Theory (MLTT) (Martin-Löf 1982, Martin-Löf 1984) and can be used in a constructive analysis of generalised quantifiers (Sundholm 1989), which are useful in the treatment of "donkey" sentences (Ranta 1991, Dávila-Pérez 1995, Turner 1997) (see Chapter 5 and Appendix B).

2.3.1 Basic Types

The notions of n-place relations can be defined recursively:

(i) $Rel_0(t) \leftrightarrow \mathrm{P}(t)$

(ii) $Rel_n(\lambda x(t)) \leftrightarrow Rel_{n-1}(t)$

We can write $Rel_1(t)$ as $\mathsf{Pty}(t)$ (where Pty stands for "property") and $\lambda x(t)$ as $\{x : t\}$. In keeping with this set-like notation, we can write $\mathrm{T}(tx)$ as $x\varepsilon t$, especially if t is a property. In the language of terms, we may write tx as $x\epsilon t$.

Sometimes, in place of $\forall x(\mathrm{T}(fx) \rightarrow \varphi)$ and $\exists x(\mathrm{T}(fx) \,\&\, \varphi)$, we will write $\forall x\varepsilon f.\varphi$ and $\exists x\varepsilon f.\varphi$, respectively. Similarly $\{x : fx \wedge gx\}$ will sometimes be written in the form of a separation type: $\{x\epsilon f.gx\}$.

Following Turner (Turner 1992) we can define both empty and universal properties:

$$\begin{aligned} \nabla &=_{\mathrm{def}} \{x : (x \approx x)\} \\ \Omega &=_{\mathrm{def}} \{x : \neg(x \approx x)\} \end{aligned}$$

These properties cannot be defined in a strongly typed theory.

2.3.2 Type Operators

We can give definitions for intersection $\cap$, union $\cup$, difference $-$, Cartesian product $\otimes$, disjoint union $\oplus$, and function space $\mapsto$ operators:

$$\begin{aligned} \cap &=_{\mathrm{def}} \lambda f \lambda g\{x : fx \wedge gx\} \\ \cup &=_{\mathrm{def}} \lambda f \lambda g\{x : fx \vee gx\} \\ - &=_{\mathrm{def}} \lambda f \lambda g\{x : fx \wedge \neg gx\} \\ \otimes &=_{\mathrm{def}} \lambda f \lambda g\{z : \Xi x \Xi y(z \approx \langle x, y\rangle \wedge fx \wedge gy)\} \\ \oplus &=_{\mathrm{def}} \lambda f \lambda g\{z : (\mathsf{fst}(z) \approx 0 \wedge f(\mathsf{snd}(z))) \vee (\mathsf{fst}(z) \approx 1 \wedge g(\mathsf{snd}(z)))\} \\ \mapsto &=_{\mathrm{def}} \lambda f \lambda g\{z : \Theta x(fx \Rightarrow g(zx))\} \end{aligned}$$

which trivially lead to the following theorems:

$$\begin{array}{lll}
z\varepsilon(t \cap s) & \leftrightarrow & z\varepsilon t \ \&\ z\varepsilon s \\
z\varepsilon(t \cup s) & \leftrightarrow & z\varepsilon t \vee z\varepsilon s \\
z\varepsilon(t - s) & \leftrightarrow & z\varepsilon t \ \&\ \sim z\varepsilon s \\
z\varepsilon(t \otimes s) & \leftrightarrow & \mathsf{fst}(z)\varepsilon t \ \&\ \mathsf{snd}(z)\varepsilon s \\
z\varepsilon(t \oplus s) & \leftrightarrow & (\mathsf{fst}(z) = 0 \ \&\ \mathsf{snd}(z)\varepsilon t) \vee (\mathsf{fst}(z) = 1 \ \&\ \mathsf{snd}(z)\varepsilon s) \\
z\varepsilon(t \mapsto s) & \leftrightarrow & \forall x(z\varepsilon t \rightarrow zx\varepsilon s)
\end{array}$$

where pairs $\langle \cdot, \cdot \rangle$ and the projection, or selector functions $\mathsf{fst}, \mathsf{snd}$ have their usual definitions:

$$\begin{array}{lll}
\langle x, y \rangle & =_{\text{def}} & \lambda z(z(x)(y)) \\
\mathsf{fst} & =_{\text{def}} & \lambda p(p\lambda xy(x)) \\
\mathsf{snd} & =_{\text{def}} & \lambda p(p\lambda xy(y))
\end{array}$$

so that:

$$\begin{array}{lll}
\mathsf{fst}\langle x, y \rangle & =_{\beta} & x \\
\mathsf{snd}\langle x, y \rangle & =_{\beta} & y
\end{array}$$

2.3.3 Natural Language Types

It is straightforward to define first-order types which correspond to the notions of determiner, quantifier and functional types in natural language semantics:

$$\begin{array}{lll}
\mathsf{Quant}(f) & =_{\text{def}} & \forall x(\mathsf{Pty}(x) \rightarrow \mathrm{P}(fx)) \\
\mathsf{Det}(f) & =_{\text{def}} & \forall x(\mathsf{Pty}(x) \rightarrow \mathsf{Quant}(fx)) \\
(R \Longrightarrow S)(f) & =_{\text{def}} & \forall x(Rx \rightarrow S(fx))
\end{array}$$

The semantic types of the representations of lexical items has to be declared in order to be able to prove that a well formed sentence is represented by a proposition.

2.3.4 Dependent Types

The dependent type operators Σ and Π of MLTT (Martin-Löf 1982, Martin-Löf 1984) can be defined in PT (Smith 1984, Turner 1990). In essence, when given two terms f, g of an appropriate type, both Σ and Π form new types. Both operators can be used in the analysis of discourse in MLTT (Sundholm 1989, Ranta 1991, Ranta 1994, Dávila-Pérez 1995), as in Appendix B. Later, in Chapter 5, it will prove useful to have a notion of these dependent type operators for a treatment of Geach's "donkey" sentences, and other anaphoric puzzles in PT.

A term h will be of the type Σfg if it is a pair $\langle a, b \rangle$, where the first element a is of type f, and the second element b is of the type ga. In the interpretation of natural language discourse, we can consider a as providing a context in which b is interpreted. Then the context for subsequent discourse will be $\langle a, b \rangle$.

A term h will be of the type Πfg if it is a function that takes terms a of type f, and produces terms of the type ga. Again, we can consider a as the context in which g is interpreted.

These type operators can be defined in PT as follows:

$$\begin{array}{lll} \Sigma & =_{\text{def}} & \lambda f \lambda g\{h : f(\mathsf{fst}(h)) \wedge g(\mathsf{fst}(h))(\mathsf{snd}(h))\} \\ \Pi & =_{\text{def}} & \lambda f \lambda g\{h : \Theta x(fx \Rightarrow gx(hx)\} \end{array}$$

These definitions support the following theorems:

If $\mathsf{Pty}(f)$ and $\forall x(x\varepsilon f \rightarrow \mathsf{Pty}(gx))$ then:

$$\begin{array}{l} \mathsf{Pty}(\Sigma fg) \\ \mathsf{Pty}(\Pi fg) \end{array}$$

and:

$$\begin{array}{lll} h\varepsilon\Sigma fg & \leftrightarrow & \mathsf{fst}(h)\varepsilon f \;\&\; \mathsf{snd}(h)\varepsilon g(\mathsf{fst}(h)) \\ h\varepsilon\Pi fg & \leftrightarrow & \forall x(x\varepsilon f \rightarrow hx\varepsilon gx) \end{array}$$

To paraphrase these definitions, $h\varepsilon\Sigma fg$ means that h is a pair, where the first component of the pair is an element ("proof," or "witness") of f, and the second is an element of g applied to that element of f. The expression $h\varepsilon\Pi fg$ means that h is a function which takes an element of f and gives a "proof" of g applied to that element of f. With both of these types, the evaluation of g is dependent upon the chosen element, or "proof," of f, just as in MLTT. In some sense then, the meaning of g depends upon the context created by f.

As a special case, if x is not free in g then the term $\Sigma f\lambda x(g)$ is equivalent to $f \otimes g$, and the term $\Pi f\lambda x(g)$ is equivalent to $f \mapsto g$.

2.4 The Paradoxes as a Category Mistake

Within PT, we can take the problematic "property" R, in the example on page 14, to be defined by:

$$R =_{\text{def}} \lambda x(\neg xx)$$

Now we can evaluate the term RR:

$$\begin{array}{lll} RR & = & (\lambda x(\neg xx))\lambda x.(\neg xx) \\ & =_{\beta} & \neg((\lambda x(\neg xx))\lambda x(\neg xx)) \\ & = & \neg RR \end{array}$$

At first glance this might appear to demonstrate a contradiction. However, these statements are concerned with the equality of terms, not the equivalence of propositions. To demonstrate the equivalence of propositions, and hence derive a contradiction, we need to apply the axioms of truth. But the axioms for T only apply to propositions. We can prove that Rx is a proposition only if we can prove that x is a property. As we cannot prove that R is a property, we are never in a position were we are obliged to consider the equivalence of RR and $\neg RR$.

PT thus avoids the paradoxes without banning self predication. To assume that paradoxical expressions are propositions, and to assume that R is a property, is to make a category mistake. Later, in Chapters 3 and 5, we will adapt this analysis to the treatment of non-denoting definites and pronouns.

2.5 INTERNAL DEFINABILITY

A predicate Q in the language of wff is said to be internally definable iff there is a property q such that:

$$\forall x(Q(x) \leftrightarrow x\varepsilon q)$$

That is, $\forall x(Q(x) \leftrightarrow \mathrm{T}(qx))$.

Note that neither T nor P are internally definable, as that would lead to a paradox (Aczel 1980, Turner 1990). For example, assuming that we can internally define T by the property $true'$, then the following holds:

1. $\mathrm{P}(true'(t))$, for all t, as $true'$ is a property.
2. $\forall x(\mathrm{T}(x) \leftrightarrow \mathrm{T}(true'(x)))$ from the definition of internal definability.
3. $\forall x(\mathrm{T}(\neg true'(x)) \leftrightarrow {\sim}\mathrm{T}(true'(x)))$ from the axioms of PT, given that $true'$ is a property.

Now we can define a term r as follows:

$$r =_{\text{def}} \lambda x(\neg true'(xx))$$

and consider the expression rr:

$$\begin{aligned} rr &= (\lambda x(\neg true'(xx)))\lambda x(\neg true'(xx)) \\ &= \neg true'((\lambda x(\neg true'(xx)))\lambda x(\neg true'(xx))) \\ &= \neg true'(rr) \end{aligned}$$

We can then deduce that:

$$\mathrm{T}(\neg true'(rr)) \leftrightarrow {\sim}\mathrm{T}(rr)$$

But $rr = \neg true'(rr)$, so we can deduce:

$$\begin{aligned} \mathrm{T}(\neg true'(rr)) &\leftrightarrow {\sim}\mathrm{T}(rr) \\ &\leftrightarrow {\sim}\mathrm{T}(\neg true'(rr)) \end{aligned}$$

which is a contradiction, and so T cannot be internally definable. Similar arguments can be made in the case of P.

However, predicates that do not lead to the internalisation of P and T can be internally definable. For example, we can introduce internally definable classes of individuals. Such classes will be used when notions of plural individual and natural language denotable individuals are introduced (Chapter 3), and with the structured individuals that arise in the treatment of discourse referents (Chapter 5). Types which are characterised by such internally definable predicates are also known as "small types" (Aczel 1980).

We can introduce internal analogues to P and T in PT, provided they cannot be shown to be properties. For example, we can have $\hat{p}, \hat{t}$ where:

(i) $\mathrm{P}(s) \rightarrow \mathrm{P}(\hat{p}s)$
(ii) $\mathrm{P}(s) \rightarrow \mathrm{P}(\hat{t}s)$
(iii) $\mathrm{P}(s) \rightarrow (\mathrm{T}(\hat{p}s) \leftrightarrow \mathrm{P}(s))$
(iv) $\mathrm{P}(s) \rightarrow (\mathrm{T}(\hat{t}s) \leftrightarrow \mathrm{T}(s))$

These terms behave like **S5** modalities (Turner 1990).

2.6 Model

Here, a simple domain-theoretic model of the λ-calculus is sketched, extended to model a Frege Structure (Aczel 1980). First of all we need a model for the λ-calculus. This can be used to build a model of PT.

2.6.1 A Model of the λ-Calculus

Following an existing approach (Scott 1973), we can build a model of the λ-calculus from Scott domains consisting of complete lattices. In the limit we have a domain D_∞ isomorphic to its own continuous function space, so $D_\infty \cong [D_\infty \longrightarrow D_\infty]$.[17] We can define mappings:

$$\Phi : D \longrightarrow [D \longrightarrow D]$$

and:

$$\Psi : [D \longrightarrow D] \longrightarrow D$$

That is, Φ maps objects of the domain D into continuous functions of $[D \longrightarrow D]$, and Ψ maps continuous functions of $[D \longrightarrow D]$ into objects of D.

When modelling the λ-calculus, we can use these mappings to change our view of a λ-term. We can take a term to be either a continuous function, or an argument of the appropriate type for some other continuous function. This mirrors the fact that in the untyped λ-calculus, terms can appear freely as both functions and arguments.

Definition 2.1 *A* Scott Model *is a triple* $\mathcal{D} = \langle D, \Phi, \Psi \rangle$ *with* D *a domain and* Φ, Ψ *as above.*

[17] Continuous functions are functions that have "fixed points"; they can effectively be approximated by some finite iteration. In essence, this means that they are computable functions.

The terms of λ-calculus can be interpreted in such a structure (by $\mathcal{I}[\cdot]$) relative to both an assignment function g, which assigns elements of D to variables, and an interpretation function i, which assigns elements of D to constants. The function $g[d/x]$ is the function g except that d is bound to x. Reference to $\mathcal{D}$ is dropped in the following, and i is assumed to be fixed:

$$\begin{aligned}\mathcal{I}[x]_g &= g(x)\\ \mathcal{I}[c]_g &= i(c)\\ \mathcal{I}[\lambda x(t)]_g &= \Psi(\lambda d.\mathcal{I}[t]_{g[d/x]})\\ \mathcal{I}[t(t')]_g &= \Phi(\mathcal{I}[t]_g)(\mathcal{I}[t']_g)\end{aligned}$$

2.6.2 A Model of PT

Following Aczel:

Definition 2.2 *A model for* PT *shall be taken to be a Frege structure* $\mathcal{M} = \langle \mathcal{D}, T, P\rangle$ *where* $\mathcal{D}$ *is a model of the λ-Calculus and*

$$\begin{aligned}T &: D \longrightarrow \{0,1\}\\ P &: D \longrightarrow \{0,1\}\end{aligned}$$

Where T *and* P *satisfy Aczel's structural requirements (Aczel 1980), repeated below.*[18]

The characteristic functions T and P provide the extensions of the truth predicate, and the proposition predicate, respectively. The axioms for P are verified by the following structural requirements:

(i) if $P(\mathcal{I}[t]_g) = 1$ and $P(\mathcal{I}[s]_g) = 1$, then $P(\mathcal{I}[t \wedge s]_g) = 1$;
(ii) if $P(\mathcal{I}[t]_g) = 1$ and $P(\mathcal{I}[s]_g) = 1$, then $P(\mathcal{I}[t \vee s]_g) = 1$;
(iii) if $P(\mathcal{I}[t]_g) = 1$ and $P(\mathcal{I}[s]_g) = 1$ whenever $T(\mathcal{I}[t]_g) = 1$, then $P(\mathcal{I}[t \Rightarrow s]_g) = 1$;
(iv) if $P(\mathcal{I}[t]_g) = 1$ then $P(\mathcal{I}[\neg t]_g) = 1$;
(v) if $P(\mathcal{I}[t]_g) = 1$ for all x, then $P(\mathcal{I}[\Theta\lambda x(t)]_g) = 1$;
(vi) if $P(\mathcal{I}[t]_g) = 1$ for all x, then $P(\mathcal{I}[\Xi\lambda x(t)]_g) = 1$.
(vii) $P(\mathcal{I}[t \approx s]_g) = 1$

The axioms for T are supported by the following:

(i) if $P(\mathcal{I}[t]_g) = 1$ and $P(\mathcal{I}[s]_g) = 1$, then $T(\mathcal{I}[t \wedge s]_g) = 1$ iff $T(\mathcal{I}[t]_g) = 1$ and $T(\mathcal{I}[s]_g) = 1$;
(ii) if $P(\mathcal{I}[t]_g) = 1$ and $P(\mathcal{I}[s]_g) = 1$, then $T(\mathcal{I}[t \vee s]_g) = 1$ iff either $T(\mathcal{I}[t]_g) = 1$ or $T(\mathcal{I}[s]_g) = 1$;

[18] Aczel's paper uses a different notation to that adopted here.

(iii) if $P(\mathcal{I}[t]_g) = 1$ and $P(\mathcal{I}[s]_g) = 1$ whenever $T(\mathcal{I}[t]_g) = 1$, then $T(\mathcal{I}[t \Rightarrow s]_g) = 1$ iff either $T(\mathcal{I}[t]_g) = 0$ or $T(\mathcal{I}[t]_g) = 1$ and $T(\mathcal{I}[s]_g) = 1$;

(iv) if $P(\mathcal{I}[t]_g) = 1$ then $T(\mathcal{I}[\neg t]_g) = 1$ iff $T(\mathcal{I}[t]_g) = 0$;

(v) if $P(\mathcal{I}[t]_g) = 1$ for all x, then $T(\mathcal{I}[\Theta\lambda x(t)]_g) = 1$ iff $T(\mathcal{I}[t]_{g[d/x]}) = 1$ for all $d \in D$;

(vi) if $P(\mathcal{I}[t]_g) = 1$ for all x, then $T(\mathcal{I}[\Xi\lambda x(t)]_g) = 1$ iff $T(\mathcal{I}[t]_{g[d/x]}) = 1$ for some $d \in D$;

(vii) $T(\mathcal{I}[t \approx s]_g) = 1$ iff $\mathcal{I}[t]_g = \mathcal{I}[s]_g$;

(viii) If $T(\mathcal{I}[t]_g) = 1$ then $P(\mathcal{I}[t]_g) = 1$.

This last requirement states that the function T characterises a subset of P. Thus the terms have a subclass consisting of terms that correspond to propositions. This subclass, in turn, has a subclass of terms corresponding to the true propositions.

The language of wff can now be given truth conditions:

$$
\begin{array}{lll}
\mathcal{M} \models_g s = t & \text{iff} & \mathcal{I}[t]_g = \mathcal{I}[s]_g \\
\mathcal{M} \models_g \mathrm{T}(t) & \text{iff} & T(\mathcal{I}[t]_g) = 1 \\
\mathcal{M} \models_g \mathrm{P}(t) & \text{iff} & P(\mathcal{I}[t]_g) = 1 \\
\mathcal{M} \models_g \varphi \,\&\, \psi & \text{iff} & \mathcal{M} \models_g \varphi \text{ and } \mathcal{M} \models_g \psi \\
\mathcal{M} \models_g \varphi \vee \psi & \text{iff} & \mathcal{M} \models_g \varphi \text{ or } \mathcal{M} \models_g \psi \\
\mathcal{M} \models_g \varphi \rightarrow \psi & \text{iff} & \mathcal{M} \not\models_g \varphi \text{ or } \mathcal{M} \models_g \psi \\
\mathcal{M} \models_g \sim\varphi & \text{iff} & \mathcal{M} \not\models_g \varphi \\
\mathcal{M} \models_g \forall x\varphi & \text{iff} & \text{for all } d \in D,\ \mathcal{M} \models_{g[d/x]} \varphi \\
\mathcal{M} \models_g \exists x\varphi & \text{iff} & \text{for some } d \in D,\ \mathcal{M} \models_{g[d/x]} \varphi
\end{array}
$$

A wff φ of PT is valid in a model $\mathcal{M}$ iff $\mathcal{M} \models_g \varphi$ for all assignment functions g.

2.7 Syntax-Semantics Interface

There are many possible approaches to the representation of natural language (NL) semantics in PT. Perhaps the most obvious is to adapt Montague Semantics, as described in "The Proper Treatment of Quantification in Ordinary English" (PTQ) (Montague 1973). In the next section, we sketch Turner's static PTQ-style treatment (Turner 1992). Chierchia offers an alternative that deals with some discourse phenomena by embodying ideas from Dynamic Montague Grammar (Groenendijk and Stokhof 1990) in a variant of PT (Chierchia 1991) by generalising the model for abstraction and application (see Appendix A). In Chapter 5 and Appendix C, a different analysis is presented, where dependent types are used in the analysis of the truth conditions of the quantifiers, as in the constructive semantics for natural language (Sundholm 1989, Ranta 1991, Dávila-Pérez 1995, Turner 1997). However, unlike the constructive theories, this analysis is classical, and unlike Chierchia's proposal, it gives a dynamic theory with no change to the model.

In implementing theories of natural language semantics in PT, the basic approach is to find a compositional representation of sentences as terms. The axioms for P and T can then be used to find the truth conditions of felicitous sentences. In order to achieve the desired truth conditions with some phenomena, such as plurals and mass terms, it is necessary to add more axioms, and new distinguished terms. For the PTQ fragment, no new axioms are required.

If we adopt the methodology of least commitment, we should prefer theories that do not require additional axioms (or, theories where the axioms can be shown to be eliminable, and any new terms are merely syntactic sugar) over those that require a genuine strengthening of the logical framework.

The freedom that an axiomatic approach gives may seem a heavy responsibility: it is possible to create an inconsistent theory with some apparently simple and desirable additions. However, no semantic framework can guarantee the construction of only consistent theories. All theories may result in unwanted consequences (indeed, as mentioned above in §2.1, Property Theory is intended to address some of the unwanted consequences of Montague's Intensional Logic and its possible worlds models, as well as those of syntactic treatments of propositional attitudes). One methodology, which can help avoid inconsistency, is to adopt the weakest axioms possible to obtain the desired effect. If the additional axioms are mainly concerned with truth conditions, and are guarded with requirements that relevant terms are propositions, then the chances of accidentally reintroducing the paradoxes are reduced.

PT provides no specific inference theory other than first-order theorem proving with λ-equality. In a particular application, there may be methods that can be employed to reduce the complexity of the inference process, and perhaps make it fully decidable. The basic axioms of the theory concerning propositions, P, and truth, T, can typically be implemented as Horn clauses. Provided that statements governing which terms constitute propositions, and true propositions, reflect the form used in the antecedents of the axioms, then the the theory is decidable for those terms which match the axioms "syntactic" coverage, and simple proofs need not be computationally complex. Of course, in the general case the full power of first-order theorem proving is required.

2.8 PTQ-LIKE INTERPRETATION

We will sketch how a PTQ-style treatment carries over to Property-theoretic semantics (Turner 1992, Chierchia and Turner 1988, Kamareddine 1988, Chierchia 1991). The essential difference, compared to the standard Intensional Logic version of PTQ, is that all terms in PT are already intensional, so there is no need for the operator $^\wedge$ which is used in PTQ to derive intensions from extensions (Montague 1973).

The semantic representation of a sentence is an intensional term. If this term can be shown to correspond to a proposition via the axioms for P, then its truth conditions can be found using the axioms for T. As an illustration, the sentence:

Every boy laughed.

could be represented by the term:

$$\Theta x(\mathit{boy}'x \Rightarrow \mathit{laughed}'x)$$

This can be obtained by an appropriately annotated grammar. In itself, this term is independent of any truth conditions. To find the truth conditions of the sentence, we must first show that the term representing it is a proposition, that is:

$$\mathrm{P}(\Theta x(\mathit{boy}'x \Rightarrow \mathit{laughed}'x))$$

This is an expression in the language of wff. According to the axioms for P, this will hold if:

$$\forall x(\mathrm{P}(\mathit{boy}'x) \rightarrow \mathrm{P}(\mathit{laughed}'x))$$

This can be proved if the terms *boy'* and *laughed'* have been declared to be properties. In other formalisms, proving that the representation forms a proposition corresponds to checking that the expression meets certain syntactic constraints. However, the use of a semantic notion of well-formedness, rather than a syntactic notion, is what allows PT to avoid the paradoxes without resorting to strong typing.

If the sentence is a proposition, then its truth conditions are given by:

$$\mathrm{T}(\Theta x(\mathit{boy}'x \wedge \mathit{laughed}'x))$$

According to the axioms, this holds if and only if:

$$\forall x(\mathrm{T}(\mathit{boy}'x) \rightarrow \mathrm{T}(\mathit{laughed}'x))$$

We can produce the appropriate representations using the interpretations of the words given in Table 1.

The grammar should be arranged so that the representation of the noun phrase 'every boy' is produced by applying the representation of

Word	Category	Representation
every	determiner	$\lambda p\lambda q(\Theta(px \Rightarrow qx))$
a	determiner	$\lambda p\lambda q(\Xi(px \wedge qx))$
boy	noun	*boy′*
laughed	verb (intransitive)	*laughed′*

TABLE 1 The Lexicon

'every' to that of 'boy', giving:

$$\lambda p\lambda q(\Theta(px \Rightarrow qx))(\mathit{boy}')$$

which, by β-reduction, is equivalent to:

$$\lambda q(\Theta(\mathit{boy}'x \Rightarrow qx))$$

The final representation of the sentence, 'Every boy laughed' is then found by applying the meaning of the noun phrase to that of the verb, giving:

$$\lambda q(\Theta(\mathit{boy}'x \Rightarrow qx))(\mathit{laughed}')$$

which reduces to:

$$\Theta(\mathit{boy}'x \Rightarrow \mathit{laughed}'x)$$

which is what was wanted.

We must be able to show that this representation is a proposition. We can do this by assigning appropriate first-order types to the basic representations. The nouns and intransitive verbs are just properties, that is $\mathsf{Pty}(\mathit{boy}')$ and $\mathsf{Pty}(\mathit{laughed}')$. The type Pty (§2.3.1) corresponds to the Montagovian type $\langle e, t\rangle$.

As is conventional, we can call the representation of a noun phrase a "quantifier," which has type Quant (§2.3.3). Such quantifiers yield propositions when given a property. We can define this behaviour by the following:

$$\mathsf{Quant}(f) =_{\text{def}} \forall x(\mathsf{Pty}(x) \rightarrow \mathrm{P}(fx))$$

This corresponds to the Montagovian type $\langle\langle e, t\rangle, t\rangle$.

The determiners 'a' and 'every' can be assigned their own type, which we shall call Det (§2.3.3). Terms of type Det form terms of type Quant when given a property.

$$\mathsf{Det}(f) =_{\text{def}} \forall x(\mathsf{Pty}(x) \rightarrow \mathsf{Quant}(fx))$$

This corresponds to the Montagovian type $\langle\langle e, t\rangle, \langle\langle e, t\rangle, t\rangle\rangle$

We can see that the term $\Theta(\mathit{boy}'x \Rightarrow \mathit{laughed}'x)$ can now be shown to be a proposition.

Montague's higher-order type spaces correspond to function spaces.

These can be constructed in this first-order framework using the following definition (§2.3.3):

$$(Q \Longrightarrow R)(f) =_{\text{def}} \forall x(Q(x) \rightarrow R(fx))$$

Asserting that the predicate $(Q \Longrightarrow R)$ holds of a term corresponds with stating that the term belongs to the type $\langle Q, R \rangle$ in Montague's system.

Unlike that system, we do not need to use types to impose rigid, hierarchical well-formedness conditions to avoid the paradoxes. Also, there is no need for an intension forming operator $^\wedge$, or the related pseudo-type s that appears in Montague Semantics.

This brings us to the representation of intensionality and transitive verbs. Transitive verbs require a Quant to form a term of the same type as an intransitive verb, that is, they will be of type $(\mathsf{Quant} \Longrightarrow \mathsf{Pty})$.

In the truth conditions of sentences such as 'A man seeks a unicorn' we do not want to claim that there is a unicorn. We can follow Montague's approach to this, and have 'seek' take the representation of 'a unicorn' as one of its arguments, giving the representation

$$\Xi x(man'x \wedge seeks'(\lambda q(\Xi y(unicorn'y \wedge qy))x))$$

Assuming that man' and $unicorn'$ are properties, and $seeks'$ is of type $(\mathsf{Quant} \Longrightarrow \mathsf{Pty})$, then this will have the truth conditions:

$$\exists x(\mathrm{T}(man'x) \;\&\; \mathrm{T}(seeks'(\lambda q(\Xi y(unicorn'y \wedge qy))x)))$$

Unlike in Montague Semantics, the representation of 'a unicorn' is already intensional, so we do not need to apply an intension forming operator to it in order for it to be appear as an argument to $seek'$.

Transitive verbs that do have an existential commitment can be treated in a way that parallels that for Montague Semantics. We can, for example, give the verb 'find' the semantics $\lambda r \lambda x(r(\lambda y(find'xy)))$, so that the sentence, 'A man finds a unicorn' has the representation:

$$\Xi x(man'x \wedge \Xi y(unicorn'y \wedge find'yx))$$

Assuming that man' and $unicorn'$ are both properties, and $find'$ is a two place relation, this will have the truth conditions:

$$\exists x(\mathrm{T}(man'x) \;\&\; \exists y(\mathrm{T}(unicorn'y) \;\&\; \mathrm{T}(find'yx)))$$

The treatment of other phenomena, such as relative clauses, and "quantifying-in" can also be carried over from the Montague framework.

Not all sentences will express propositions. As an example, the axioms should not allow the representation of:

> This sentence is false.

to be a proposition, otherwise the theory would fall foul of the paradoxes.

As we have seen with the verb 'seek', not all logical constants in the representations of sentences will be interpreted as logical connectives in the truth conditions. As a final example, the sentence:

Mary believes that every boy laughed.

might be represented by the term:

$$\mathit{believe}'(\Theta x(\mathit{boy}'x \Rightarrow \mathit{laughed}'x))\mathit{mary}'$$

If this is a proposition, then in its truth conditions T will not apply to 'every boy laughed':

$$\mathrm{T}(\mathit{believe}'(\Theta x(\mathit{boy}'x \Rightarrow \mathit{laughed}'x))\mathit{mary}')$$

This corresponds to the idea that the object of a belief is an intensional proposition, not a truth value, or set of possible worlds.

2.9 Other Approaches

Probably one of the earliest logical theories of properties arises in Frege's work on the logical foundations of arithmetic. His formalisation of properties was extensional; two properties were to be equated if they applied to the same individuals. Unfortunately, Frege's theory was inconsistent, as it was possible to derive a paradox.

Russell sought to avoid the paradoxes from which Frege's theory suffered by way of a theory of types. His theory can also be thought of as logical theory of extensional properties, but free from the paradoxes.

In Montague's work, his original conception was that the semantics of natural language was to be modelled within set theory. In a sense, his Intensional Logic was merely an aid to the process of mapping between natural language and set theory, and it could be eliminated. However, Intensional Logic proved to be of interest in itself. It provides a logical theory of intensional properties and propositions.

Modern theories of properties are effectively an extension of this line of development, whereby the objective is to formalise a highly intensional theory of properties and propositions. In some cases, an additional goal is to explore theories with weaker typing requirements, so that self-predication is permitted for example, without re-introducing the paradoxes.

The theory presented here is Turner's axiomatisation of Aczel's Frege Structures (Turner 1992, Aczel 1980), and is based on the theories of properties by Chierchia and Turner (Turner 1987, Chierchia and Turner 1988). Aczel's work is an explicit attempt to produce a consistent version of Frege's formal theory. Turner's work was originally motivated by the desire to explore formal systems in which self-predication is permitted.

This is not the only theory that has sought to formalise a notion of fine grained intensionality or permit felicitous cases of self-predication. Cocchiarella presents a second-order property theory (Cocchiarella 1979), and Kamareddine has developed a form of property theory that allows an element of higher order quantification (Kamareddine 1992, Kamareddine 1993). This might be used to address an issue in the semantics of propositional attitudes (Turner 1997). Bealer discusses various issues concerned with property theory (Bealer 1982). Kamareddine presents a theory which appears to have various property theories as special cases (Kamareddine 1995). Turner has explored some of the formal connections between theories of properties and truth, and theories of modalities (Turner 1989).

An alternative to logical theories of properties is presented by set theory. Again, the issue of the appropriate level of intensionality arises. Possible worlds construals of properties, as used in Montague's set-theoretic model of Intensional Logic, provide a more intensional model than the simpler analysis which takes properties to be sets of individuals. However, although possible worlds provides an appealing analysis of some modalities, it is not at all clear that it gives an adequate account of intensionality.

Jubien developed an intensional set theory (Jubien 1989), where the axiom of extensionality is removed. We can model fine-grained intensionality by pairing the sets that correspond to the extensions of properties with identifiers. Properties with the same extension may then be distinguished by way of the associated identifier. This can be seen to be related to Cresswell's structured meanings (Cresswell 1985) and similar theories.

The issue of self-application has also been considered within a set-theoretic setting. Aczel's non-wellfounded set theory gives an analysis of felicitous self-predication (Aczel 1988). As with Jubien's theory, Aczel's theory is based on standard Zermelo-Fraenkel set theory but with one axiom removed. Note that standard set theory does allow self-predication, it is just that all expressions of the form $x \in x$ are judged false.

Although we can obtain some of the formal results that are required for natural language semantics, it is arguably simpler just to take properties as primitive rather than apply various fixes to set theory.

A somewhat orthogonal approach to the logical and set-theoretic analyses of properties is provided by constructive type theory, exemplified by the theories of Martin-Löf (Martin-Löf 1982, Martin-Löf 1984), which have been used for the representation of natural language semantics (Sundholm 1989, Ranta 1991, Ranta 1994, Dávila-Pérez 1995). Whereas the logical and set-theoretic approaches both have an essentially classical view of properties and propositions, the constructive theories have their roots in a different philosophical tradition, known as intuitionism. In constructive type theory, we can view properties as types. Depending upon how equality is defined, it may be possible to have two types with the same elements without being committed to the equality of those types. This would give rise to intensional properties. In constructive type theories, propositions are also taken to be types, indistinguishable in kind from properties. The elements of these propositional types can be taken to correspond to proofs of the proposition. Even if two propositions are always true together, if their proofs can be distinguished then the propositions need not be equated.

Type theory, and some of the variants of property theory mentioned here, are discussed by Turner (Turner 1997). Stalnaker gives a strong defence of possible worlds approach to intensionality (Stalnaker 1984). Thomason presents a strongly typed theory with fine-grained intensionality (Thomason 1980).

3

Plurals and Mass Terms

Standard interpretations of natural language nominal expressions have them denoting or quantifying over objects in a domain of ordinary, singular individuals. This is not generally sufficient to cope with plurals and mass terms. In both cases we need to strengthen the representation language by adding a new class of terms that have a structure which captures our intuitions about the denotations of plurals and mass terms. Before formalising an appropriate ontology we must make our intuitions explicit, both to obtain the required behaviour, and to be confident that any additional ontological commitments are indispensable.

3.1 Plurals

In this section we discuss the justifications for adding a new kind of term to the ontology of natural language semantics which correspond with collections of individuals that are denoted by plural expressions. Following well established arguments, the existing machinery of basic terms, propositions, logical connectives and quantifiers is shown to be inadequate for the semantics of plurals.

The plural terms could be represented using sets of singular individuals. However, a weaker lattice-theoretic treatment can also model their behaviour, where simple, singular individuals are represented by atoms in the lattice, and plurals are represented by the "joins" of singular individuals. Following the methodology of least commitment (Chapter 1, §1.2) a set-theoretic treatment seems to be an unmotivated strengthening of the theory when the weaker lattice-theoretic approach is available.[19]

We can also adopt the methodology of least commitment to account

[19]Both the imposition of a lattice-like structure on individuals, and the uninterpretability of non-denoting descriptions, mentioned in the next paragraph, have been defended by Ojeda (Ojeda 1993). He also defends the atomlessness of mass terms, which we discuss later, in §3.2.

for non-denoting terms (Strawson 1950) and formulate the theory so that, when appropriate, statements involving non-denoting terms cannot have their truth evaluated.

There have been proposals to allow explicit groupings within those terms corresponding to collections in order to account for reciprocal statements as in 'The pigs and cows were separated from each other'. These proposals require that the representation of the collection of pigs and the representation of the collection of cows constitute formally distinct "groups" within the term representing 'the pigs and cows'.

We will review Schwarzschild's arguments against the explicit representation of such groups (Schwarzschild 1991, Schwarzschild 1992). Instead, groups can be seen as an artifact of the structured nature of discourse. A group is then some salient collection of objects in the context of the discourse. Rather than adding additional structure to the static representations of collections, groups can be recovered from undifferentiated collections by way of contextually salient properties.

If Schwarzschild's arguments are accepted, then the ontological commitments required to address these "group" phenomena are then reduced to those of discourse theory. In turn, it seems that we can devise ways of representing discourse phenomena without any adding any new basic classes of objects to our ontology (Chapter 5).[20]

Groups have also been proposed in the representation of plural collective nouns such as 'committees'. As we shall see, the need for groups in this case is also questionable.

3.1.1 DISTRIBUTIVITY AND COLLECTIVITY

Some sentences with plural and conjoined nouns can be represented with ordinary individuals. For example, from the sentence 'John and Mary die', it is possible to infer that 'John dies and Mary dies', effectively distributing the verb over the conjunction. Similarly with syntactic plurals, when we say 'the boys died', we interpret this distributively, so that it is roughly equivalent to 'every boy died'. Verbs that always have this behaviour are said to be "distributive."

It is also possible to infer 'John and Mary die' from 'John dies and Mary dies'. Verbs that have this behaviour are said to be "cumulative." Sentences involving verbs that are both cumulative and distributive can

[20]Limits on space and time, however, preclude any detailed demonstration of how group phenomena can be treated in a theory of discourse.

Krifka has proposed a treatment of group phenomena in discourse which makes use of parametrised individuals (Krifka 1996). If parameterised individuals are represented by way of functions, then this could be taken as further support for the view that no additional ontological commitments are required to address group phenomena.

always be represented in terms of ordinary (singular) individuals. However, there are cases where this is not possible. For example, the verb "meet" is not distributive. Given the sentence 'John and Mary met', it is not legitimate to say 'John met and Mary met'. The verb 'meet' is said to be "collective." With syntactic plurals, as in 'the boys met', it is usual to interpret this as a collective activity (or perhaps a collection of collective activities). Similarly, if "John and Mary bought a boat together" the boat was bought by the "collection" or "sum" consisting of both John and Mary. To represent such collective readings, the terms of a formal representation language must be enriched to represent plural objects.

We can show that collective verbs, like 'meet', are cumulative: from 'the boys met and the girls met', we may infer 'the girls and the boys met'. The conclusion is weaker than the antecedents—more circumstances may satisfy the final sentence than satisfy the first. Cumulativity is a property of many, but not all, verb phrases. Taking an example from Schwarzschild (Schwarzschild 1991), if we have:

> The students in Mr. T's shop class are all of the same sex.
> The students in Miss Murphy's home economics class are all of the same sex.

we cannot then infer:

> The students in Mr. T's shop class and the students in Miss Murphy's home economics class are all of the same sex.[21]

Given that we seem to need terms that represent collections of individuals, a compositional treatment of these phenomena should be able to explain the relationship between collective and distributive interpretations of sentences. Distribution should not only have its occurrence restricted to certain properties, but it should also be restricted to an appropriate level: if John danced, it does not imply that John's intestines danced. This inference is normally blocked by assuming that individuals, like John, are atomic, and independent of their physical parts, at least with respect to distributive inferences. The theory will remain silent as to the nature of the relationship between individuals and their physical manifestations.[22]

---

[21]Perhaps the conclusion is acceptable if 'are all of the same sex' is interpreted as distributing over the conjunction. The strong sense of non-cumulativity in this example might be attributed to the presence of an implicit existential quantifier, introduced by the phrase 'the same sex', that outscopes the subject noun phrase. That is, we might interpret 'N are all of the same sex' as entailing 'there is a sex which all of N have'.

[22]At best, the nature of this relationship seems to be both vague and context

Typically, theories that seek to account for the behaviour of conjoined nominals and plural nouns allow individuals to be joined in some fashion to create new plural objects, or "sums." So, the representation of 'John and Mary' is some plural object that is the "sum" of the individuals 'John' and 'Mary'. This sum can then be the argument of the representation of a verb such as 'meet' or 'die'.

Bartsch and Bennett (Bartsch 1973, Bennett 1975) amend the extensional treatment of semantics so that terms may be individuals, as before, or sets. Thus, if the "meaning" (denotation) of the word 'boys' is the set of a, b, c:

$$[\![\text{boys}]\!] = \{a, b, c\}$$

then:

The boys bought a boat.

is translated into:

$$\exists x(\mathit{boat}'(x) \ \& \ \mathit{bought}'(\{a, b, c\}, x))$$

which can be paraphrased by: "there is a boat, and a, b, c collectively bought it."

There is a problem with this analysis; many words must now be multiply ambiguous depending on whether individuals, or sets appear in a particular argument position. There would then be four representations for 'bought', but 'who bought the boat?' does not seem intuitively to be ambiguous.

Subsequent authors have tried to improve upon this approach by taking singular and plural terms to be objects of the same type. It is, for example, possible to "elevate" the representation of singular terms to singleton sets (Landman 1989, Scha 1981). Schwarzschild takes an alternative route of equating singleton sets with their members, so $a = \{a\}$. This he calls "Quine's innovation" (Schwarzschild 1991). Such a structure of sets and singleton sets models a complete atomic Boolean algebra (Halmos 1963, Birkhoff 1967, Gratzer 1978).

We can of course use a Boolean algebra directly, rather than a model of it. Conjunction between definite noun phrases can then be modelled by the "join" operator in the Boolean algebra. This operator allows the sum of two terms to be created. The definite descriptor can be interpreted by the supremum operator[23] of the Boolean algebra as used by Link, for example (Link 1983). This is summarised in Table 2.

---

dependent (Jubien 1997, Chapter 9).

[23]Alternatively, the definite descriptor could be modelled by an operator that picks the greatest element in the extension of the predicate. Singular nouns can be represented by predicates that range over atoms in a Boolean algebra, and plural nouns

Natural Language	Representation Language	Set-theoretic Interpretation	Lattice-theoretic Interpretation
John	j'	$\{j'\}$	j'
John and Mary	$j' + m'$	$\{j'\} \cup \{m'\}$	$j' \sqcup m'$
the men	$\sigma x(men'x)$	$\{x : x \in men'\}$	$\bigsqcup_{x \in men'} x$

TABLE 2 Interpretations of Plurals

The sentence:

John and Mary met.

would be represented by:

$$met'(j' + m')$$

which can then be given either a set-theoretic or a lattice-theoretic interpretation.

It might seem desirable to represent the sentence:

John and Mary died.

directly as:

$$died'(j') \;\&\; died'(m')$$

The distinction between the collective and distributive readings would then effectively reside in the scope of the conjunction. With the collective reading, conjunction would have narrow scope; it is within the scope of the representation of the verb phrase. In the distributive example, it would have wide scope; outscoping the representation of the verb phrase. This is sometimes presented as a "type-lifting" phenomena. The operator + is interpreted as collective term formation. The distributive reading is obtained by "lifting" the type of terms to generalised quantifiers (roughly speaking, j' is lifted to $\{p : j' \in p\}$); and the conjunction of these quantifiers is then interpreted as set intersection (Partee and Rooth 1983, Lønning 1989). This is equivalent to taking distribution over conjoined noun phrases to be a variety of ellipsis, where:

John and Mary died.

is analysed as a reduced form of:

John died and Mary died.

---

by predicates that range over the elements of the Boolean algebra that are generated by the atoms in the extension of the corresponding singular property. If a predicate has no extension, then there is no greatest element, and if there is more than one element in the denotation of a singular predicate p, then 'the p' is badly formed, as again there is no greatest element (Scha 1981).

Ellipsis occurs with other categories, as in the noun phrase:

> the man and woman

where the determiner distributes over the conjunction.[24] Distributive inferences with noun phrases are more general than this, as they can involve plural nouns, as in:

> The men died.

The scoping ambiguity could be generalised to cover the implicit conjunction present in plural nouns (Lakoff 1970).[25] Representing the collective-distributive distinction in this way results in collectively read noun phrases always having narrow scope. With examples that only use intransitive verbs, this might not seem problematic. However, with the following sentence:

> Five insurance associations gave a $25 donation to several charities.

it is possible to obtain an interpretation where 'five insurance associations' is given a collective interpretation, which outscopes a distributive interpretation of 'several charities', so that each charity received $25, but there are only five associations (Roberts 1988). This suggests that the distributive v. collective readings should not, in general, be equated with wide v. narrow scope interpretations, and that collections of individuals are things in themselves, and not a simple artifact of scoping. That is, we *must* introduce plural objects into our ontology to account for the behaviour of sentences involving plural noun phrases. It may still be legitimate to treat distribution over conjunction as part of a theory of ellipsis, rather than exclusively in a semantic theory of plurals and mass terms. If collections of individuals are not scoping artifacts, it should, at least in principle, be possible to quantify over them. However, universal quantification over arbitrary collections has an impact on the logical

[24]This ellipsis can be treated syntactically: in categorial grammars, these scoping effects are accounted for using "type-lifting" (or "type-raising"), echoing Partee and Rooth's semantic analysis (Dowty 1988, Partee and Rooth 1983).

[25]On a quantifier scoping account of the collective-distributive distinction, we might represent the collective interpretation by having the verb phrase outscope (the intension of) the noun phrase. The distributive interpretation would arise when the verb phrase has narrow scope. For example, $\exists x(men'x \ \& \ die'x)$ would represent 'some men died', whereas the sentence 'some men met' would be represented by $met'(\lceil\lambda p\exists x(men'x \ \& \ px)\rceil)$, where $\lceil\lambda p\exists x(men'x \ \& \ px)\rceil$ is the intensional representation of 'some men'. With a strongly typed semantic theory, the types of the verb phrase, and/or noun phrase would have to be altered, so that the representation of the noun phrase can appear as an argument of the verb phrase. The representation of the noun phrase in the distributive representation is said to be "lifted" to produce the collective representation.

complexity of the representation. We shall return to the issue of scoping, lifting and logical complexity later in this chapter (§3.1.4, §3.1.5 and §3.1.8).

If the difference between collectively and distributively read sentences is not, in general, a scoping effect—residing in the relationship between the interpretation of the verb phrase and noun phrase—then the question arises as to whether the distinction resides in the semantics of the verb phrase, or that of the noun phrase. If we follow Link's account (Link 1984, Link 1991a), the distinction is in the predicate representing the verb phrase. According to this view, some predicates are always distributive, such as *died'*. The sentence:

John and Mary died.

could be interpreted as:

$$died'(j' + m')$$

As 'died' is taken to be distributive over the conjoined noun phrase, then it holds of the conjuncts, and it is possible to infer that:

$$died'(j') \;\&\; died'(m')$$

For predicates that can be read ambiguously as either collective, or distributive, an operator ^{D} is optionally used to mark a predicate as being read distributively. So, if we represent the verb phrase 'bought a boat' with the predicate *bab'*, the sentence:

John and Mary bought a boat.

could be represented as one of:

$$bab'(j' + m')$$
$$^{\mathrm{D}}bab'(j' + m')$$

where from the latter, it is possible to infer that *bab'* holds of the individuals, or atoms of the sum, thus entailing:

$$bab'(j') \;\&\; bab'(m')$$

If it is legitimate to run the inference the other way, so that from:

$$p(x) \;\&\; p(y)$$

we can infer:

$$p(x + y)$$

then the verb (or predicate) is said to be cumulative. In some theories an operator distinct from ^{D} (* for example) is used to indicate that the predication arose out of cumulative behaviour (Lønning 1989, Link 1991b). Given:

$$bab'(b') \;\&\; bab'(j' + m')$$

we may infer:

$$^{*}bab'(b' + j' + m')$$

which is indeterminate as to which parts the unadorned property applies.

Verbs (or predicates) which are both fully distributive and cumulative (like 'died') are said to be "homogeneous": their cumulative and distributive forms may be equated.

Many of the treatments of plural objects follow broadly similar lines. Lønning seeks to provide a unified framework in which to compare these different approaches (Lønning 1989). He takes the "standard" approach to be typified by Leonard and Goodman, Massey, Link and Scha (Leonard and Goodman 1940, Massey 1976, Link 1983, Link 1987, Link 1991b, Scha 1981). These all assume the associativity, symmetry and idempotence of conjunction. This, as Lønning points out, is not universally accepted. In §3.1.4 and §3.1.5 we discuss in more detail the issue of associativity, and whether it is appropriate when we consider the "intermediate" distributive readings which lie between the extremes of the fully distributive and fully collective. In addition, there is some dispute about whether there should be a "bottom element" in the representation, which is a part of all individuals. Such an element arises naturally in the usual axiomatisation of appropriate lattice-theoretic models.

3.1.2 Bottom, Non-denoting Terms, and Presupposition

In a Russellian treatment, we could say that "non-denoting" definite descriptors, like 'the present king of France' denote the bottom element—indeed, this would be the natural consequence if a Boolean algebraic model were adopted—and predication of the bottom element leads to falsity. This can be viewed as a simple formal treatment of presupposition with definite descriptors: any true predication of a term presupposes that the term exists, if the term does not exist, then any (atomic) predication of it cannot be true.

The problem of non-denoting terms is not peculiar to a theory of plurals. However, in giving terms an appropriate structure to represent plurals, the notion of a bottom element arises, and we have to decide whether this corresponds to the extension of non-denoting terms. If it does, then we have to consider how we are to axiomatise the behaviour of expressions in which it occurs. Here, we do not attempt to give a fully fledged theory of existence presuppositions, but seek to give the weakest characterisation that could be strengthened to encompass a notion of "projection" which permits us to say, felicitously, "Either France is a republic, or the present king of France is bald," for example (Beaver 1997, Levinson 1983, van der Sandt 1988).

We might decide to assign 'false' to any sentence containing a predication of a non-existent, or non-denoting term, so both 'the present king of France is bald' and 'the present king of France is not bald' are false sentences (Lønning 1989). This is a contradiction in classical logic, as it can be seen to involve an assertion of the form $A \mathbin{\&} \sim A$. Such a contradiction could be avoided if we reject bivalence—so expressions need not be just either true or false—and say that these sentences are "not true," as opposed to "false." Intuitively, this idea corresponds to the fact that a term's existence can be presupposed by both positive and negative attributions of properties.

We could follow Blau, and adopt a non-classical logic which explicitly rejects bivalence by adopting three truth values, the value 'unknown' being assigned to predication of non-existent terms (Blau 1981). An alternative is to adopt a free logic, where such terms "denote elsewhere" and are thus not available for predication within the theory (van Fraassen 1966, Link 1991a). Or we could decide that there should not be a bottom element (Massey 1976, Bunt 1985, Link 1991a). This would have the effect of excluding non-denoting terms from the theory.

The issues concerning bottom; non-denoting terms; and the logical aspects of presuppositions with definite descriptors are taken up in the next section, where we present a property-theoretic analysis. Bivalence will be rejected simply by virtue of the fact that, in Property Theory, not every expression corresponds to a proposition. The law of excluded middle will still hold for those expressions that are propositions. In this proposal, we have an algebraic structure of natural language denotables. Bottom exists, and is part of all such terms, but it is not itself denotable (or at least, we cannot prove that it is). In general, natural language predication of a non-denoting term does not provably result in a proposition.[26]

3.1.3 PT$^{\mathfrak{P}}$: PT WITH PLURAL TERMS

To represent sentences involving plurals in PT, we can add summation and supremum operators to the language of terms and axiomatise a Boolean structure, following Link (Link 1991a). However, there is no restriction on term formation in PT, so we have to consider whether we want, require, or allow, a Boolean/mereological structure to involve *all* terms. It seems appropriate to have such a structure only amongst those terms which represent denoting natural language nominals. This can be achieved by restricting the scope of the relevant axioms. To have

[26]This account has the potential to be compatible with a formal theory of presuppositions (Fox 1993).

a Boolean structure on all terms is an unmotivated and unnecessary strengthening of the theory.[27]

Link uses a free logic as he wants all his terms to correspond to plural objects: he does not want any term to correspond to non-denoting definite descriptors (Link 1991a). If he dealt with "non-denoting" terms by making them denote a bottom element, and bottom was in the language of terms, then this would be like saying that there is a term which "does not exist," but which is a part of all other terms. The only other option—in order to maintain a one-to-one correspondence between natural language denotable objects, and terms in the representation language—is to say that non-denoting terms genuinely do not denote in the theory, and there is no bottom element. Both of these requirements would be met if we used a free logic with strict equality. In PT, however, we already have a range of terms which cannot correspond to objects referred to by natural language: the language of terms includes objects formed by arbitrary λ-abstraction and application, of which only some will be of interest.[28] We also have a theory designed to cope with the paradoxes. It is possible to deal with the intuitively much simpler kind of category mistake that appears to occur with non-denoting noun phrases within the existing theory, without producing a free version of PT.

It would seem that in natural language there is no object which we consider to be a part of all other objects. However, we must be careful of restricting the representation language—the formal theory—because of a restriction in the language being represented; that would be to presume that all legitimate terms in the formal theory must play a part in the representation of natural language. It will be possible to construct a bottom element using the supremum operator and inequality.[29] It goes

[27] An additional reason for having only a subclass of terms with a Boolean structure becomes apparent when considering the model theory of PT. A model of PT can be constructed using a lattice theoretic model for the λ-terms (Turner 1990). It is convenient to use the ordering and join in this lattice to model the summation and supremum operators. If, however, we give a Boolean structure to all terms, it is not possible to do this: no model of the λ-calculus could then be constructed (M. Henson, PC).

Note that the terms we are talking about here are those of PT, not those of natural language; to say that we do not have a Boolean structure over all terms of PT is not in conflict with any desire to formalise a universal Boolean structure over natural language terms, as discussed by Keenan and Faltz (Keenan and Faltz 1985).

[28] It is the objective of Frege Structures, axiomatised by PT, to carve out those terms of logical interest, and give them structure. Similarly, when PT is used for the representation of natural language, the formal theory delineates those terms of interest in the semantics of natural language, and gives them structure. There is no reason for all terms to correspond to natural language denotable objects.

[29] Namely, the supremum of an empty property: $\sigma x(x \not\approx x)$.

against the untyped nature of PT to impose conditions on syntactic well-formedness beyond those of the basic untyped λ-calculus, so we cannot eliminate this term from the theory on syntactic grounds.

Within models of PT, the existence of a bottom element is mathematically convenient. It might be thought that mathematical convenience should be overridden if it goes against the methodology of least commitment, but this is to assume that the theory must be complete with respect to such models. We take it that the role of a model of PT is merely to demonstrate consistency; there is no requirement that the theory be complete with respect to a model.

We assume that a bottom element is to be distinguished from other particulars only by way of its relationship to them, and not by way of its ontological category. So, rather than stating that bottom does not exist, we should prefer a theory that allows us to prove as little as possible about it, on the grounds of formal simplicity.[30] The question should then not be whether there is a term corresponding to a bottom element, or whether it appears in some model of the representation language, but rather, how such a term features in the semantics of natural language, if at all.

If the theory contains a bottom element, we may wonder whether any natural language term can denote it. We might view denotable objects as pieces of information. When such objects are conjoined, then the information in them is combined. The ordering relation is then an information ordering. Bottom is merely an absence of information. We could use the bottom element to represent non-denoting definite descriptors. However, this has the undesirable consequence that all non-denoting terms are equated (Parsons 1970, Parsons 1975). Non-denoting definite descriptors do, indirectly, convey information. Namely, they are informative with regard to the preconceptions of a person who creates an utterance which involves them. They give an indication of the relevant presuppositions required to make sense of the utterance. The existential presuppositions depend upon the non-denoting descriptor. The representation language should not then force a collapse of all non-denoting terms. Indeed, it can be argued that the theory should not necessarily force a collapse of *denoting* terms with the same extension. This issue is discussed in Chapter 4.

Regarding non-denoting nominals, as the part-whole structure is intended to represent denotable terms, it seems clear that they should not be represented by such terms (or, more weakly, we should not be able

---

[30] A similar argument can also be used in the case of atomic mass terms (Chapter 1, page 9).

to prove that they are represented by such terms). Within propositions representing natural language sentences, we are only interested in quantifying over denotable terms. If "everyone went to the party," we should not be able to conclude that "the present king of France went to the party." It also follows that we should not be able to prove that bottom is a denotable, as it does not represent a denotable term.

As discussed above (§3.1.2), with a sentence involving non-denoting terms we could take the Russellian view, and say that predication of a non-existent object gives rise to falsity, or we could reject bivalence, so that such statements are neither true nor false (Blau 1981). In PT we already reject bivalence: not all terms correspond to propositions that are true or false. Unlike three-valued accounts of propositions, this is not at the expense of classical theorems, such as the law of excluded middle: if a term corresponds to a proposition, then it must be true or false, but truth values are only held by propositions. To prevent truth or falsity being assigned to sentences involving non-denoting terms, we can claim that they are not propositions (though they may have the form of propositions), or, more weakly, we cannot prove that they are propositions. This theory, especially the weaker view, allows for a certain degree of presupposition modelling. If we model question answering as a proof production process (De Roeck et al. 1991), then when attempting to prove 'the present king of France is bald' the proof will fail, because we cannot even prove that this is a proposition. The reason for its failure is that there is no present king of France.[31] So, the helpful answer to 'is the present king of France bald?' would be 'there is no present king of France'.[32]

[31]Note that this does not deal with generics, such as 'the unicorn has a horn', which are not within the remit of the formal theory under discussion. If a treatment of generics is added, the arguments concerning 'the present king of France' will still hold on both generic, and non-generic readings, as there is no *kind* (Carlson 1977) corresponding to that noun phrase. Mythological terms, as in 'Pegasus is a horse' may be more problematic.

[32]This may be too weak: as has been indicated by Strawson, there are sentences involving non-denoting terms, to which some find it acceptable to ascribe a truth value. This is typified by passive constructions such as 'The exhibition was visited by the present king of France' which some take to be a false proposition, unlike 'The present king of France visited the exhibition' (Strawson 1964). One argument is that the existence presupposition only occurs for definite descriptors which are in the "foreground," or "active," in some sense. The theory below does not preclude a strengthening of the axioms to allow propositionhood to be proved in such cases, should a suitable formal theory of the foreground/background distinction be forthcoming. A simple-minded response could be to give a Russellian, quantificational representation of passive definite descriptors, or to allow the passive form of 'visit' to form propositions with terms that are not provably denotable. A tentative treatment of some of these examples is offered elsewhere (Fox 1993, Chapter 10).

As can be seen, adopting the various views advocated produces the effect of a free logic, without raising the question of what it means not to denote within a theory. Natural language predication of non-denoting definite descriptors is consigned to the same dustbin as other unhelpful constructions, such as the paradoxical sentences. It just becomes another case of a sortal category mistake. As discussed in Chapter 2, Property Theory avoids the paradoxes by having axioms that are too weak to prove that they are propositions. We adopt the same weak approach with regard to whether non-denoting definite descriptors denote bottom, and to the result of predication of a non-denoting term.

It could be argued that paradoxical sentences, such as "This sentence is false." and sentences involving non-denoting definite descriptions like "the King of France" are meaningless for different reasons, and that these distinctions should be reflected in the theory. We take it that the distinction is meta-theoretic; although meaninglessness in both cases is characterised by an inability to prove that the respective representations are propositions, they can be distinguished by the way in which such a proof fails.

This is no different from formal grammar, where expressions are simply classified into those that are syntactically well formed and those that cannot be show to be well formed. By itself, the rules of a formal grammar do not attempt to classify expressions according to the reasons that they fail to be well formed. However, at the meta-level it is sometimes possible to classify ill-formed expressions according to the way in which attempts to prove syntactic well-formedness fail.

We are now in a position to strengthen PT (§2.2) with plural terms. For simplicity of presentation, we will use the term 'plural' in an improper sense, so that it can refer both to proper plurals and singulars.

Language of plural terms

To the basic vocabulary of terms is added:

Predicative constant:	$\mathfrak{p}$
Operative constants:	$+, \sigma$

It is intended that $\mathfrak{p}$ will hold of plural terms. It corresponds to a "small type" (§2.5) so it is safe for this to appear in the language of terms. The term $+$ is the summation operator. The term-forming interpretation of definite descriptors makes use of σ. The term $\sigma\lambda x(t)$ will be used to represent that object which is the sum of objects y such that $\mathrm{T}(t[y/x])$; that is, it denotes the sum of the terms that have the property $\lambda x(t)$. As with the quantifiers, the explicit binding operator λ may be omitted, leading to the simpler notation $\sigma x(t)$.

The language of wff is unchanged, and the theory is governed by the axioms of the λ-calculus as before, together with PT's axioms for propositions and truth.

Further Axioms For $\mathrm{PT}^{\mathfrak{P}}$

The summation operator + is intended to be the semantic analogue of natural language conjunction of nominal terms. To mirror the effect that in many cases natural language conjunction is symmetric, that is:

John and Mary met.

has the same import as:

Mary and John met.

the operator + is also taken to be symmetric.

Axiom 3.1 *The summation operator is symmetric.*

$$a + b = b + a$$

In general, however, natural language conjunction is not symmetric; consider sentences involving the word 'respectively'.

In English, we can say:

John and Mary are husband and wife (respectively).

whereas we would not say:

Mary and John are husband and wife (respectively).[33]

Schwarzschild suggests that this asymmetry can be accounted for in the "dynamic" component of meaning (Schwarzschild 1991, Schwarzschild 1992). That is, the term denoted by the conjoined noun phrase is the same, irrespective of the order of the conjuncts, but the linear order has an effect on the discourse structure. In the example above, the terms 'Mary' and 'John' become available for anaphoric reference, and the order in which they become available may be recorded in the representation of the discourse structure. The 'respectively' construction can then be interpreted at the meta-discourse level. Thus, it is acceptable to take summation to be symmetric in this static theory.

If ordering is to be ignored, then:

John and Mary and Harry

refers to the same complex term as:

---

[33]Note that it sounds odd to native speakers if we say "Mary and John are wife and husband (respectively)." This might suggest that there is some patriarchal noise in the data. However, there is clearly an asymmetry in the conjunction with "respectively" constructions.

Harry and Mary and John

The next axiom, taken together with the symmetry of +, allows any permutation of summed terms to be equated by making + associative.

Axiom 3.2 *The summation operator is associative.*

$$a + (b + c) = (a + b) + c$$

As alluded to above (§3.1), non-associative summation has been used to capture intermediate distribution, but, as we shall see in more detail below (§3.1.4 and §3.1.5), such a treatment of these readings is inadequate.

The operator + can also be made idempotent. This is perhaps harder to exemplify in natural language. The idea is that:

John and John

just refers to the same individual as:

John

Clearly, we never say 'John and John', when both terms refer to the same individual, as it is redundant. Perhaps we might refer to:

John and the judge

when John is the same person as the judge. Then, if we know that John is the judge, the sentence:

John and the judge are 42.

has the same import as:

John is 42.

Axiom 3.3 *The summation operator is idempotent.*

$$a + a = a$$

In Chapter 4, we will encounter cases where we might not wish to equate the representations of 'John' and 'the judge'. This will not undermine idempotence.

Definitions in the theory do not strengthen it, they merely allow otherwise complex axioms and statements to be expressed more clearly. The following definition provides the notion of one term being part of another:

Definition 3.1

$$t \leq s =_{\text{def}} (t + s = s)$$

We can define an internal analogue of this:

Definition 3.2

$$t \ll s =_{\text{def}} (t + s \approx s)$$

From this definition we can obtain the following theorems:

$$\mathrm{P}(t \ll s)$$
$$\mathrm{T}(t \ll s) \leftrightarrow t \leq s$$

The predicative constant $\mathfrak{p}$ is intended to be a property that characterises the (provably) denotable plural terms.

Axiom 3.4 *The term* $\mathfrak{p}$ *is a property.*

$$\mathrm{P}(\mathfrak{p}t)$$

For simplifying the expression of axioms, a predicate $\mathfrak{P}$ is defined in terms of the "small type" $\mathfrak{p}$.[34] It will be used later, in axioms that restrict supremum formation to just plural terms.

Definition 3.3 *Predicate* $\mathfrak{P}$.

$$\mathfrak{P}t =_{\text{def}} \mathrm{T}(\mathfrak{p}t)$$

If we take two count nominals and conjoin them, the result is a new count nominal. Reflecting this in the representation, we can have the following closure condition on denotable plurals:

Axiom 3.5 *The sum of two plurals is itself a plural.*

$$(\mathfrak{P}a \;\&\; \mathfrak{P}b) \rightarrow \mathfrak{P}(a + b)$$

Note that we cannot have $\mathfrak{P}(a + b) \rightarrow (\mathfrak{P}a \;\&\; \mathfrak{P}b)$ as it cannot be guaranteed that the unrestricted parts of a plural are plural.

We want to generalise sum formation so that we can form the supremum of a set of individuals in $\mathfrak{P}$, where the set is characterised by the extension of a property of plural terms. The term σ is intended for this purpose. The language of terms does not restrict how this operator may combine with other terms, although we are only interested in its behaviour when combined with properties whose extension is contained within the terms characterised by $\mathfrak{P}$. The following axiom is indifferent as to whether there is a bottom element, and whether such an element is a plural. It is also indifferent as to what a "non-denoting" definite descriptor denotes. It is important to realise, however, that this axiom

[34] We might like to think of $\mathfrak{P}$ taking the role of E in Link's theory (Link 1991a).

is deliberately too weak to justify saying that a non-denoting definite descriptor is a plural. This axiom also remains silent as to whether the supremum of a property with a mixed extension is a plural.

Axiom 3.6 *If a property has an extension, and that extension is contained within the domain of plurals, then its supremum is also a plural.*

$$\forall p((\mathsf{Pty}(p) \mathbin{\&} \forall x(\mathrm{T}(px) \rightarrow \mathfrak{P}(x)) \mathbin{\&} \exists x(\mathrm{T}(px))) \rightarrow \mathfrak{P}(\sigma x(px)))$$

This is intended to correspond to a notion of lattice-theoretic completeness in the domain of plurals. However, true completeness would require that the supremum of any arbitrary set of plurals is a plural. This is only expressible if we have genuine second-order quantification over arbitrary sets. In PT, a "set" is a collection of objects that form the extension of some property; we can only quantify over these "definable" sets. This axiom thus expresses the weaker notion of definable completeness (Lønning 1989, Link 1991a), which, as we can see, can be stated within a first-order framework.

Our approach to the so-called "non-denoting" definite descriptors could be parodied by saying that we do not have an approach. In particular, the result of attributing a natural language property to a non-existent term should not be a statement that is true or false. Instead, it should be a term that cannot be proven to have a truth value. As propositions have truth values, this suggests that the result of such an attribution should not be a proposition. This effect can be achieved by having the denotation of "properties" that arise in the representation of (the plural part of) natural language restricted to a class of terms that only form propositions when predicated of terms that are provably plural. We shall adopt a weaker view which defines a class of terms that cannot be *proven* to produce propositions when attributed to non-plural terms (or rather, terms that are not provably plural):

Definition 3.4 *A term is a plural property if it forms propositions when applied to a plural term.*

$$\mathsf{Pty}_{\mathfrak{P}}(p) =_{\mathrm{def}} \forall x(\mathfrak{P}x \rightarrow \mathrm{P}(px))$$

This is consistent with a proof-theoretic treatment of helpful answers (De Roeck et al. 1991): a tableau-style proof concerning the sentence 'the present king of France is bald' will fail with an unclosed branch corresponding to the fact that we cannot prove that 'the present king of France' is a denotable plural. The weak closure condition on plurals given in the previous axiom mean that we cannot prove that 'the present king of France' is a denotable plural because there is no present king of

France. This corresponds to the feeling that the sentence 'the present king of France is bald' sounds odd precisely because there is no present king of France.

Corresponding to singular count nominals, a class of atomic plural terms can be defined. These are plural terms that have no proper plural parts:

Definition 3.5 *Atoms are the least plurals which are not part of all plurals.*

$$\mathfrak{A}t =_{\text{def}} \forall x((\mathfrak{P}x \mathbin{\&} x \leq t) \rightarrow (x = t)) \mathbin{\&} {\sim}\forall x(t \leq x)$$

As it is a "small type," atomicity can be internalised:

Definition 3.6 *(Internal atomicity.)*

$$\mathfrak{a} =_{\text{def}} \lambda t(\Theta x((\mathfrak{p}x \wedge x \ll t) \Rightarrow x \approx t) \wedge \neg\Theta x(t \ll x))$$

This definition gives the following theorems:

$$\mathrm{P}(\mathfrak{a}t)$$
$$\mathrm{T}(\mathfrak{a}t) \leftrightarrow \mathfrak{A}t$$

We can define forms of the quantifiers, and supremum operator, restricted to denotable count terms:

Definition 3.7

$$\forall x\varepsilon\mathfrak{P}.\varphi =_{\text{def}} \forall x(\mathfrak{P}x \rightarrow \varphi)$$

Definition 3.8

$$\exists x\varepsilon\mathfrak{P}.\varphi =_{\text{def}} \exists x(\mathfrak{P}x \mathbin{\&} \varphi)$$

Using these quantifiers, we have a logic where free variables range over all terms, and quantified variables range over denoting count terms; if we restrict ourselves to these bounded quantifiers, then we effectively have a free logic.

These quantifiers can be given internal analogues:

Definition 3.9

$$\Theta x\epsilon\mathfrak{p}.t =_{\text{def}} \Theta x(\mathfrak{p}x \Rightarrow t)$$

Definition 3.10

$$\Xi x\epsilon\mathfrak{p}.t =_{\text{def}} \Xi x(\mathfrak{p}x \mathbin{\vec{\wedge}} t)$$

where $(a \vec{\wedge} b) =_{\text{def}} a \wedge (a \Rightarrow b)$, as in §2.2.2. We need this stronger form, rather than just $\wedge$, so that we can show that $\Xi x \epsilon \mathfrak{p}.t$ forms a proposition for all x (as required for the axioms of truth to be applicable), even if t only forms a proposition when x is a plural. Note that in the universal case, the axioms for $\Rightarrow$ are already strong enough.

A restricted supremum operator can also be defined:

Definition 3.11

$$\sigma x \epsilon \mathfrak{p}.px =_{\text{def}} \sigma x(\mathfrak{p}x \vec{\wedge} t)$$

Again, we need to use $\vec{\wedge}$ in the right side of this definition. This is because we can then show that term, $\lambda x(\mathfrak{p}x \vec{\wedge} t)$, is a property when $\lambda x(t)$ is a property of plurals, which allows us to prove $\mathfrak{P}(\sigma x \epsilon \mathfrak{p}.t)$ (provided its extension is not empty) by way of Axiom 3.6.

The remaining axioms help to characterise $\mathfrak{P}$ (and hence $\mathfrak{p}$) and σ. If the nominals 'the workers' and 'the bosses' are not the same, it is surely because they are constituted by different individuals. This idea is generalised in the following axiom:

Axiom 3.7 *Different plural terms have different atoms as parts.*

$$\forall xy \varepsilon \mathfrak{P}.(x \not\leq y \rightarrow \exists u \varepsilon \mathfrak{P}.(\mathfrak{A}u \ \& \ u \leq x \ \& \ u \not\leq y))$$

Later, when looking at Landman's intensional individuals, we will see how nominals may have the same extension, yet have different import, so 'the workers' and 'the bosses' may be ascribed different properties, even if they were to be constituted of the same individuals (Chapter 4).

The operator σ is intended to capture the meaning of the definite determiner 'the'. The noun phrase 'the men' is taken to refer to the collection of all men (should it exist). Any individual man must be part of this collection:

Axiom 3.8 *All plural terms having a property must be part of the supremum of plural terms having that property.*

$$\forall p \forall y \varepsilon \mathfrak{P}.((\mathsf{Pty}_{\mathfrak{P}}(p) \ \& \ \mathrm{T}(py)) \rightarrow y \leq \sigma x \epsilon \mathfrak{p}.px)$$

As any individual man is part of the collection of humans ("the humans"), it follows that the collection consisting of all men ("the men") is also part of the collection of humans:

Axiom 3.9 *If all plural terms which have a property p are part of some other plural term y, then the supremum of terms having p must also be part of y.*

$$\forall p \forall y \varepsilon \mathfrak{P}.((\mathsf{Pty}_{\mathfrak{P}}(p) \ \& \ \forall x \varepsilon \mathfrak{P}.(\mathrm{T}(px) \rightarrow x \leq y)) \rightarrow \sigma x \epsilon \mathfrak{p}.px \leq y)$$

The final axiom of this theory is intended to capture the notion that a collection of individuals is dependent upon the individuals concerned: should we take different individuals, then we would have a different collection. There is no sense in which:

John and Mary and Harry

can be the same term as:

John and Mary

This restriction can be achieved by noting that 'Harry' is also part of 'Mary and Harry', which in turn is part of the larger term. Thus 'Harry' takes part in the "generation" of the larger term, and is not part of it contingently. Generalising, when an individual is part of a collection of terms having some property, it must either be because it has that property, or is part of a term that does:

Axiom 3.10 *Different atoms have different suprema.*

$$\forall p \forall u \varepsilon \mathfrak{P}.((\mathsf{Pty}_{\mathfrak{P}}(p) \,\&\, \mathfrak{A}u \,\&\, u \leq \sigma x \epsilon \mathfrak{p}.px) \rightarrow \exists z \varepsilon \mathfrak{P}.(\mathrm{T}(pz) \,\&\, u \leq z))$$

We can define a "collective" operator * and a "distributive" operator ^{D} (Lønning 1989, Link 1991b):

Definition 3.12 *The collective operator.*

$$^* =_{\mathrm{def}} \lambda p \lambda t (t \approx \sigma x (px \wedge x \ll t))$$

Definition 3.13 *The distributive operator.*

$$^{\mathrm{D}} =_{\mathrm{def}} \lambda p \lambda x (\Theta u (\mathfrak{a} u \wedge u \ll t \Rightarrow pu))$$

From these definitions we can infer the following:

$$\begin{array}{lll}
\mathsf{Pty}_{\mathfrak{P}}(p) & \rightarrow & \mathsf{Pty}_{\mathfrak{P}}(^*p) \,\&\, \mathsf{Pty}_{\mathfrak{P}}(^{\mathrm{D}}p) \\
\mathsf{Pty}_{\mathfrak{P}}(p) \,\&\, \mathfrak{A}t & \rightarrow & (\mathrm{T}(^{\mathrm{D}}pt) \leftrightarrow \mathrm{T}(pt)) \\
\mathsf{Pty}_{\mathfrak{P}}(p) \,\&\, \mathfrak{A}t & \rightarrow & (\mathrm{T}(^*pt) \leftrightarrow \mathrm{T}(pt)) \\
\mathsf{Pty}_{\mathfrak{P}}(p) & \rightarrow & (\mathrm{T}(^{\mathrm{D}}pt) \leftrightarrow \forall u(\mathfrak{A}u \,\&\, u \leq t \rightarrow \mathrm{T}(pu))) \\
\mathsf{Pty}_{\mathfrak{P}}(p) & \rightarrow & (\mathrm{T}(^*pt) \leftrightarrow t = \sigma x(\lambda x(\mathfrak{p}x \wedge px \wedge x \ll t)))
\end{array}$$

The top element—the plural of which all others are a part—can be defined as follows:

Definition 3.14 *The top element* $\top$ *of the plurals is the supremum of all plural terms.*

$$\top =_{\mathrm{def}} \sigma x \epsilon \mathfrak{p}.(x \approx x)$$

The complement of a plural term—the supremum of plural terms that are not part of a given plural term—can also be defined:

Definition 3.15 *The complement $\overline{s}$ of the supremum s of plurals having the property p is the supremum of plurals not having the property p.*

$$\overline{\sigma x \epsilon \mathfrak{p}.t} =_{\text{def}} \sigma x \epsilon \mathfrak{p}.\neg t$$

As this is definitional, a bottom element $\bot$—the term that is a part of all plural terms—can be defined as $\overline{\top}$, but it cannot be proven that $\mathfrak{P}\bot$.

It is possible to make $+$ definitional; observe that any plural a can be given as the supremum $\sigma x \epsilon \mathfrak{p}.(x \approx a)$, allowing us to define $+$ by way of the following equality:

$$\sigma x \epsilon \mathfrak{p}.px + \sigma x \epsilon \mathfrak{p}.qx = \sigma x \epsilon \mathfrak{p}.(px \vee qx)$$

This equality is a consequence of the axioms given. If it is definitional, the axioms governing $+$ are satisfied.

To implement the formal semantics of natural language in a Montague style using PT we can follow the account due to Turner (Turner 1992), as sketched in Chapter 2. The predicates P, T can be viewed as characterising types in the language of terms. These types can be enriched with $\mathsf{Det}, \mathsf{Quant}$ corresponding to those terms which represent natural language determiners and quantifiers, respectively (§2.3.3). Their definitions, and that of the function space predicates, are repeated here:

$$\begin{array}{lll} \mathsf{Det}(f) & =_{\text{def}} & \forall x(\mathsf{Pty}(x) \to \mathsf{Quant}(fx)) \\ \mathsf{Quant}(f) & =_{\text{def}} & \forall x(\mathsf{Pty}(x) \to \mathrm{P}(fx)) \\ (P \Longrightarrow Q)(f) & =_{\text{def}} & \forall x(P(x) \to Q(fx)) \end{array}$$

Thus those objects which give propositions when predicated of quantifiers are of type $(\mathsf{Quant} \Longrightarrow \mathrm{P})$.

For the semantics of natural language in $\mathrm{PT}^{\mathfrak{P}}$ we can produce a restricted set of types, constrained to plurals:

Definition 3.16

$$\mathsf{Det}_{\mathfrak{P}}(f) =_{\text{def}} \forall x(\mathsf{Pty}_{\mathfrak{P}}(x) \to \mathsf{Quant}_{\mathfrak{P}}(fx))$$

Definition 3.17

$$\mathsf{Quant}_{\mathfrak{P}}(f) =_{\text{def}} \forall x(\mathsf{Pty}_{\mathfrak{P}}(x) \to \mathrm{P}(fx))$$

The function space predicates can be defined as before:

Definition 3.18

$$(P \Longrightarrow Q)_{\mathfrak{P}}(f) =_{\text{def}} \forall x(P(x) \to Q(fx))$$

A model of PT extended with plurals can be constructed by taking a lattice-theoretic model of λ-calculus (Scott 1970), and using this to form the basis of a Frege Structure (Aczel 1980). A sub-lattice of the model for the λ-terms can be strengthened to form a complete Boolean algebra. In the model, being a plural corresponds to being in this Boolean algebra. The summation and supremum operators can be interpreted as the join and supremum operators of the lattice. Details of the model are given in §3.4.

We now have incorporated the intuitions behind Link's plural logic into PT. This completes the analysis of the ontology for extensional, non-group denoting plurals in a property theoretic setting.

Now we can go on to consider some arguments about the particular choices made in this formalisation, and whether we should add additional structure to the ontology in order to account for reciprocals and other phenomena.

3.1.4 Associativity, Reciprocals and Structured Groups

There are readings of sentences which call into question the associativity of the conjunction of nouns. Some verbs can be ambiguous between distributive and collective interpretations. From the sentence 'John and Mary bought a boat' we might conclude either that they bought a boat together, or separately. When there are more than two members of a collection, then there may be further readings, depending upon how the parts of the collection are grouped. From the sentence:

> John, Mary, Peter and Sharon bought a boat.

it is not clear how many boats were bought. There could be as many as four (the distributive reading, which can be marked by using the word "each"), or as few as one (the collective reading), or some number in between. These other readings may be termed "intermediate distributive readings." In general, we could think of there being a range of readings with the distributive and collective as the two extremes.

At first sight, it might seem desirable to add structure to the representations of collections in order to indicate the relevant sub-collections. If we are concerned with ontological issues, then we must consider the arguments for and against adding such structured sums to our ontology of individuals.

If structure is to be added to indicate the relevant objects to which a property should distribute, then perhaps a similar structure could be used to indicate the relevant sub-collections involved in reciprocal statements, the difference being that the reciprocal property does not distribute down to these sub-collections (unless they are collections of structured collections), but instead indicates some relationship between them.[35] If we take the reciprocal sentence:

> (Wellington and Blüchner) and Napoleon fought against each other at Waterloo.

only the indicated "bracketing" of the noun phrase matches the historical facts (Hoeksema 1983). In the semantics of sentences involving reciprocals, the various representations obtained by this explicit bracketing of the noun phrase are sometimes termed "structured group readings."

Typically, proposals for representing structured groups effectively involve the use of non-associative brackets, or non-associative conjunction—which has the effect of introducing non-associative brackets—sometimes together with an associative conjunction, although this can introduce an ambiguity in the interpretation when there is no intuitive justification.

Hoeksema proposes a non-associative conjunction (Hoeksema 1983). However, he does not consider plural definite descriptors nor a distributive operator.

Link obtains structured and intermediate distributive readings by taking conjunction to be ambiguous between $x + y$ and $\langle x\rangle + \langle y\rangle$ (Link 1984), where $\langle\cdot\rangle$ are non-associative brackets. Some over-generation can be avoided if this new non-associative conjunction is n-ary, occurs at just one level, and always has wider scope than the standard, associative conjunction. However, such a theory can still over-generate; with collective predicates we can produce redundantly structured arguments (Lønning 1989).

Others have taken the definite descriptor as ambiguous between x and $\langle x\rangle$ (Hoeksema 1987, Landman 1987, Landman 1989, Roberts 1987). But the definite descriptor is not usually taken to be ambiguous when not conjoined—although there are exceptions (Landman 1989)—as over-generation can occur (Hoeksema 1987). Distribution also goes wrong with an unambiguous +: distribution across $\langle x\rangle + \langle y\rangle$ reaches the terms $\langle x\rangle$ and $\langle y\rangle$ whereas it is usually required to reach x and y (Landman 1989).

Lønning proposes a type-lifting solution which seeks to avoid overgeneration (Lønning 1989). Conjunction is then ambiguous between collective term conjunction, and conjunction of terms "lifted" to quantifiers (Partee and Rooth 1983).

Many of these proposals cannot easily cope with cases where there is a conjoined verb phrase, and the noun phrase is to be interpreted dis-

[35] In the general case, the intuitive meaning of reciprocals is often unclear, and does not lend itself to some easy reduction, although some progress has been made in this area (Dalrymple et al. 1998).

tributively with respect to one verb phrase and collectively with respect to the other. For example:

Ray and Tess awoke early and met in the ballroom.

is equivalent to:

Ray and Tess awoke early.
Ray and Tess met in the ballroom.

where the first sentence is read distributively, and the second is read collectively (Schwarzschild 1991). This might suggest that there is an ambiguity in the the verb phrase as well as the noun phrase, so that the collective verb phrase can be "type-lifted" to accept a structured noun phrase, and so ignore that structure.

If adding more structure to the representation of conjoined nominals did account for all the relevant data, then that would be a good reason for strengthening the ontology of plural terms. However, attempts at obtaining structured group readings and intermediate distribution by positing an ambiguity in conjunction fail to account for sentences such as:

Rodgers, Hammerstein and Hart wrote musicals.

where the intended interpretation is:

Rodgers and Hammerstein wrote musicals together, and
Rodgers and Hart wrote musicals together.

The formal reason is that an ambiguous conjunction can only account for ambiguity amongst partitions[36] of the collections of individuals, whereas the correct reading here requires the entire noun phrase to be taken as ambiguous between the possible covers[37] or more accurately, minimal covers[38] of the collection of individuals referred to (Gillon 1992).

Consider the representations of reciprocals: an ambiguous conjunction cannot account for the intended reading of the following:

Despite their current membership of the common market, only 45 years ago, *Germany and England and France and*

[36] In set-theoretic terms, a partition of a set S is a set P of non-empty subsets of S where members of P are disjoint, and the union of the members of P is S. The partitions of $\{a,b,c\}$ are $\{\{a,b,c\}\}$; $\{\{a,b\}\{c\}\}$; $\{\{a\},\{b,c\}\}$; $\{\{a,c\},\{b\}\}$; $\{\{a\},\{b\},\{c\}\}$.

[37] A cover is a more general than a partition: there is no requirement for members of a cover to be disjoint. The covers of $\{a,b,c\}$ will include its partitions, and $\{\{a,b\},\{b,c\}\}$; $\{\{a,c\},\{b,c\}\}$; $\ldots$; $\{\{a,b\},\{b,c\},\{a,b,c\}\}$; $\ldots$ for example.

[38] A minimal cover M of a set S is a smallest set of non-empty subsets of S which cover it. For example $\{\{a,b\},\{b,c\}\}$ and $\{\{a,b,c\}\}$ are both minimal covers, but covers such as $\{\{a,b\},\{b,c\},\{a,c\}\}$ and $\{\{a,b,c\},\{b\}\}$ are not minimal as they each have proper subsets that are covers of the original set.

> *Italy were fighting against each other* in one of the worst wars in history.

The alignment of forces cannot be captured by any bracketing of the subject noun phrase (Schwarzschild 1992). This observation brings into question the need for adding additional structure to the representation of plural terms. The appropriate groupings might instead be seen as an artifact of the context—either salient world knowledge, or the structure of the preceding discourse—which then licenses some distributive inferences but not others. We shall look at these arguments in more detail to confirm whether or not adding additional structure to our ontology of plural terms is an appropriate way of accounting for the data.

3.1.5 AGAINST GROUPS

Although some of the above examples do seem to require us to consider covers of plural terms, we should be cautious of complicating the nature of plural terms to account for this. For example, we might take some sentences to be ambiguous between distributive and collective readings, and take the intermediate readings to be subsumed by the collective reading. The collective representation would then be ambivalent as to the possible intermediate distributive readings. This view has support from the fact that it is possible to disambiguate the distributive and collective readings, with words like 'together' or 'each', but there is no convenient means of marking a sentence so that a particular intermediate distributive interpretation is favoured. The structured group readings of reciprocal sentences would similarly be subsumed by a collective representation.

Schwarzschild presents arguments against elaborating the structure of the noun phrase. He uses the following example to show that intermediate distributive readings exist, and that the exact nature of the reduction of such readings is context dependent:

> "Imagine a situation in which two merchants are attempting to price some vegetables. The vegetables come in various varieties and they are piled in baskets. To determine their price, the vegetables need to be weighed. Unfortunately, our merchants do not have the appropriate scale. Their grey retail scale is very fine and is only meant to weigh a few vegetables at a time. Their black scale is coarse, meant to weigh small truckloads. Realising this one of the merchants truthfully says:
>
>> The vegetables are too heavy for the grey scale and too light for the black scale.

> In order to save space in our explanation, let us reword his utterance:
> a) The vegetables are too heavy for the grey scale.
> b) The vegetables are too light for the black scale.
> [The sentence (a)] is false on its distributive reading ... It is true on its collective reading but that is not what the merchant intended. [The sentence (b)] is false on the collective reading ... It is true on its distributive reading, but again that is not what the merchant intended to say. The physical arrangement of the vegetables in the baskets suggests a plurality-cover of the vegetables with the cells of the cover corresponding to basketsful of vegetables. [The original utterance] is true and informative on the intended intermediate distributive reading reading because the verb phrase is true of every member of that cover." (Schwarzschild 1991)

He suggests that we might like to consider all verbs as being considered distributive with respect to some contextually determined cover (Schwarzschild 1991).[39]

Schwarzschild observes that perhaps it has been considered important to give some structure to the representation of nominals because there does seem to be some import taken from the choice of nouns. If "the animals" are just "the cows" and "the pigs," then:

> The cows and the pigs were separated.

seems to suggest something different from:

> The young animals and the old animals were separated.

In a null context—where there are no prior statements about the manner in which the animals were separated—the former suggests separation took place by species: "the cows were separated from the pigs," whereas the latter that the separation was by age (Schwarzschild 1992). The question is whether this aspect of the import of these sentence should be construed as some inherent part of the meaning of conjoined noun phrases. However, with some verb phrases, such as 'filled the barn to capacity', it is intuitively the case that the sentences:

> The animals filled the barn to capacity.
> The cows and the pigs filled the barn to capacity.
> The young animals and the old animals filled the barn to capacity.

[39]This is perhaps at odds with the evidence that the fully distributive form can be easily disambiguated using such terms as 'each'.

have the same import. If the noun phrase is given a different structure in each case, then the verb phrase must have homonyms, or "lifted" forms, so that when the verb phrase applies to 'the animals', the lifted form applies to any structured representation of them. In sentences where there are both structured and unstructured interpretations of one noun phrase, as in:

> The young animals and the old animals arrived from different places and filled the barn to capacity.

the noun phrase could be given a structured representation, and the unstructured property 'filled the barn to capacity' can apply to the structured nominal by using a lifted form. According to Schwarzschild, the reverse of this phenomenon also exists, so that if a verb phrase applies to a structured nominal, then a "lowered" homonym of the verb applies to the unstructured nominal. If we have:

> The cows and pigs were separated.

then it is the case that:

> The animals were separated (by species).

We might prefer to utter the first sentence to indicate directly that the animals were separated by species (according to some Gricean maxim of quantity), but the adjunct 'by species' would cancel this maxim.

We can consider how these lifting and lowering operations might iterate. Lifting a lifted predicate results in a lifted predicate. Lowering a lowered predicate results in a lowered predicate. Lowering a lifted predicate results in the original predicate, if it is not a higher-order predicate.[40] The more complex case is the lifting of a lowered predicate: such a predicate may apply to a group whose structure does not reflect the appropriate interpretation. If the animals were separated according to species, then we have:

> *original, unshifted predicate:*
> The young animals and old animals were separated.
> *lowered predicate:*
> The animals were separated (by age).
> *lifted lowered predicate:*
> The cows and the pigs were separated (by age).

However, if something is separated by age, it is separated. Thus it is the case that "the cows and pigs were separated," although the mode of separation is not indicated. The argument is that there might be

[40]Otherwise it is a null predicate, as is a lifted higher-order predicate, according to Schwarzschild's definitions.

times were it is appropriate to utter a sentence with the lifted lowered predicate: the different structure of the nominal may be appropriate for some other conversational reason. Schwarzschild presents an example where there are four lawyers, two defence and two prosecution, and one of the defence lawyers is a woman, the rest are men. We might utter one of the following:

> *original, unshifted predicate:*
> The defence lawyers and the prosecution lawyers used to fight each other in court every day.
> *lowered predicate:*
> The lawyers used to fight each other in court every day.
> *lifted lowered predicate:*
> That woman and those three men used to fight each other in court every day.

In some circumstances, it might be most appropriate to utter the final, lifted lowered reading, when identifying the individuals concerned (Schwarzschild 1992). The lifted lowered predicate also allows partitions of the conjoined noun phrases not obtainable with a structured conjunction.

The ambiguity—the distinction in meaning—that structured nominals allow us to represent requires us to make verbs ambiguous in a manner that can only be expressed if structured nominals are adopted. The ambiguity between the various lifted and lowered verbs does not appear to have any motivation other than to recover the meanings otherwise lost by the structured representation of nominals, and that ambiguity is not even expressible unless structured nominals are adopted. There is no means of indicating the desired reading of the verb phrase with regard to the various homonyms. When it is possible to elaborate on the intended interpretation of a verb phrase, by adding adjuncts, such as 'separated *by age*' then there is no need for a structured representation of the nominal. This can be taken as evidence that the various homonyms, created by lifting and lowering, do not represent a genuine ambiguity, but are just an artificial requirement of the belief that the static representation of conjoined nominals must be structured.

Considering the structured readings of nominals themselves, if it is assumed that they exist, then all predicates (derived from verb phrases) are potentially ambiguous. There is then no unambiguous predicate which can test the non-coreference of nominals such as 'the cows and the pigs' and 'the old animals and the young animals'. Schwarzschild suggests that the real difference between the meanings of such nominals is not in their static interpretation, but in their effect upon the discourse. The noun phrase 'the cows and the pigs' is given a static interpretation corresponding to 'the animals', but in the discourse itself, two further objects become available for anaphoric reference, namely 'the cows' and 'the pigs', in that order. In a null context these additional referents can provide a clue as to the means by which the animals are separated in 'the cows and the pigs were separated'. This could tie in with a dynamic treatment of 'respectively' constructions[41], as in:

> George and Mike are running with Dan and Lloyd respectively.

where the record of the linear order, required to interpret the sentence, is an aspect of the discourse and not the referents (Schwarzschild 1992). The evidence for this is that intersentential inferences are sometimes needed to recover the relevant reduction, as in the following example:

> "The first book is 2,000 pages long and it barely fits in the book bag. The second one is only 20 pages long, you can put it in your pocket. I refer to these as the fat book and the skinny book respectively."

as opposed to:

> "I refer to Miller's books as the fat book and the skinny book respectively."

which is difficult to interpret in a null context such as when appearing as the first sentence of a discourse (Schwarzschild 1991).

This suggests that some variety of anaphora resolution can be used to recover the appropriate "groups"; the discourse provides the properties which partition the subject denotation as appropriate. The sentence:

> The animals were separated.

can be treated as elliptic for:

> The animals were separated by n.

where n is a noun denoting a family of properties, such as 'age', 'sex' (as opposed to 'by female', 'by 10 years old'). Some mechanism allows the appropriate family of properties to fill in the missing adverbial phrase. So, the difference between:

> The cows and the pigs were separated.
> The animals were separated.

is that the former, in a null context, provides the source of the missing family of properties indicating the relevant partition (Schwarzschild 1992).

[41] Including 'correspondingly', 'analogously', 'equivalently', and 'in that order'.

These arguments support the view that we do not need to complicate the ontology of plural individuals; the data should be accounted for by using an appropriate theory of discourse.

Sentences such as 'the cows and pigs were separated from each other' are reciprocal in nature. There have been various proposals for trying to determine the truth conditions of reciprocal sentences (Fiengo and Lasnik 1973, Hintikka 1974, Langendoen 1978, Barwise 1979, Higginbotham 1981, Westerståhl 1987, Roberts 1987, Lønning 1987a, Lønning 1989, Heim et al. 1991, Gillon 1992, Dalrymple et al. 1998). However, we shall not consider them here; the essential point is that if such reductions require reference to groups or covers, then Schwarzschild's arguments can be used against representing them explicitly in the static ontology of plurals.

One issue that arises in the analysis of reciprocals and intermediate distribution concerns the question of how much can be communicated in natural language.[42] Dalrymple *et al.* propose a "Strongest Meaning Hypothesis," whereby a reciprocal statement is taken to denote the strongest proposition that is consistent with the non-linguistic context (Dalrymple et al. 1998). According to this view, such sentences do not then communicate the full strength of their intended meaning; they do not, by themselves, allow us to construct a model that satisfies them. We can only give them appropriate truth conditions when we already have non-linguistic constraints on their possible models.

Krifka's treatment of plural anaphora by way of "parameterised sum individuals" appears to have a similar behaviour (Krifka 1996). According to his treatment, sentences involving collections of individuals and anaphoric references to sub-collections require us to have a consistent model of the appropriate partitions, or covers, of the collections for the duration of the discourse. However, the discourse need not indicate the appropriate covers of the collections by itself. Again, such an analysis gives constraints on the models that can make the discourse true, but does not directly communicate what that model is.

If this view is accepted, then although the examples that Krifka addresses seem to require a notion of a group within a collection, the natural language expressions do not communicate what these groups are. Thus the collections that are denoted by the natural language statements do not carry an indication of the appropriate groupings within them.

---

[42]Lønning raises this issue when considering the logical power required of a semantic theory (Lønning 1989).

Before finally rejecting the need to add groups to the ontology of plural terms, we should look at transitive verbs and collective nouns, to confirm that there are no additional arguments in their favour.

3.1.6 Transitive Verbs

In general, it is not always obvious what readings are available for sentences involving transitive verbs; we should be cautious about stating the truth conditions of sentences such as 'three men carried four pianos' (Roberts 1987). Even when the intuitively acceptable readings of a sentence are obvious, they may be so dependent on the specific example that it is not clear how we can go about obtaining them systematically. Scha analyses sentences like:

600 Dutch firms have 5000 American computers.

in terms of "cumulative readings." The cumulative reading of this sentence entails that there are exactly 600 Dutch firms, and 5000 American computers (Scha 1981). Partee shows that these cumulative readings, where neither quantifier is within the scope of the other, are really a sub-class of the collective readings with two or more noun phrases (Roberts 1987). Link suggests that we might wish to consider transitive verbs as distributive on one or both arguments (Link 1991b). Others have also considered the phenomena of distributivity with two or more arguments of a verb at the same time (Scha 1984, Scha and Stallard 1988, Krifka 1996, Lasersohn 1998).

It would seem that giving a general compositional or reductive strategy for interpreting sentences with transitive verbs is as problematic as reducing the meanings of reciprocals, with the added complication of quantifier scoping effects. Roberts believes that the natural interpretation of Scha's cumulative sentences is the "group-group" interpretation, and that readings where the verb is taken to be distributive on one or both arguments are often highly marked, as with noun phrases containing the word 'each'. The suggestion is that with Scha's cumulative examples, reciprocals, and multiple definite plural noun phrases, any particular reductive analysis is not part of the truth conditions, but is implied by various pragmatic factors (lexical, contextual or general)—except in the case of reciprocals, where the reciprocal itself may contribute a distributive element (Roberts 1987).

However, this does not necessarily mean that we can dispense with all readings that seem to require the ability to pick out groups within collections. Although the exact relationships between members of collections may not be critical in the analysis of single sentences, it may become important when we consider discourse. Consider the example:

> Three students wrote five articles.
> They sent them to a journal.

We may interpret both sentences cumulatively. However, given a particular model of the relationship between the students and the articles that they were involved in writing, then it can be argued that there is a reading of the second sentence where each student, or group of students, sent just those articles that they were involved in writing. This has been called the "correspondence reading" (Elworthy 1995). In effect, the verb in the second sentence distributes into the salient groups of the first sentence.

We may question whether these readings exist independently of the cumulative readings. Krifka proposes a theory of parameterised individuals to account for such readings as these, as well as readings for transitive verbs that distribute into either argument when marked with 'each' (Krifka 1996). He uses an example something like the following to motivate the independent existence of the correspondence reading:

> Three students wrote three articles.
> They each sent them to a journal.

The argument is that there is an interpretation of this example where both sentences are satisfied by the same model, where each student wrote exactly one article, and sent that article to a journal. If we accept that there are such readings distinct from the cumulative reading, then we must be able to ensure that, in this case, the groupings of students and articles are preserved over the discourse.

It should be noted that Krifka's theory is essentially a theory of discourse. The structures that preserve the appropriate groupings are part of a rich representation of the discourse structure. The interpretation of the discourse may impose constraints on models that seek to satisfy them. Subsequent discourse may effectively rule out certain models. It appears that the representation of nominals need not—perhaps cannot—directly convey which of these is the appropriate model. This, arguably, can be taken to support the view that there is no need to add group structures to our static ontology of plural objects.

Note that in the formal theory of §3.1.3, we are only concerned with finding an appropriate ontology for plural terms. No attempt is made to represent the distributive and collective readings of sentences with transitive verbs, together with all the attendant problems of quantifier scoping, but the preceding arguments show that we do not need to countenance strengthening the ontology to account for these examples.

3.1.7 COLLECTIVES AND INTENSIONALITY

Landman uses structured nominal expressions to analyse the representation of collective nouns (Landman 1989).[43] As we wish to determine whether or not we need to add structure to our representations of plurals, we should see whether an analysis of collective nouns really does require it.

Examples of collective nouns are 'committee'; 'bunch'; and 'forest', as in 'a committee of men'; 'a bunch of flowers'; and 'a forest of trees'. They appear to allow several objects to be grouped into one. In British English, they can have plural number agreement in their singular form. In American English, the singular collective nouns (at least when they appear without an 'of' phrase) have singular agreement. Some speakers of English allow either number agreement with the collective nouns or the underlying objects, depending upon which objects seem most relevant, even when the underlying objects are not presented in an explicit 'of' phrase.

We might try to adopt an extensional analysis in which the committees are each equated with the sum of their members. This immediately leads to some difficulties. If we say "the committees were founded this year" it seems that we have to take 'were founded' to be distributive, in order for it to follow that each of the committees was founded this year. However, it is the committees that were founded, not the members. If we equate committees with the sum of their members, we would have to find some way of avoiding the conclusion that "each of the members of the committees was founded this year." One possibility would be to group the members in a manner akin to that used in some proposals for the analysis of intermediate distributive readings (Landman 1989) (§3.1.4).

There are occasions when we seem to be able to use a collective nominal to refer to the underlying objects, as in "There was a bunch of flowers. The bunch was red." meaning that the flowers in the bunch were red.[44] This might appear to support the equation of a collective

[43] These are sometimes confusingly referred to as "group" or "group denoting" nouns—perhaps because of proposals to represent their denotations with groups—leading to some ambiguity in the term 'group' as used in the literature. Nouns represented by grouped sums are also sometimes called "group denoting." Further adding to the confusion is the denotation of the word 'group' itself, which should probably be taken to name atoms, as argued by Barker (Barker 1992).

[44] As mentioned above, with a singular collective noun, some native speakers take the number agreement of the verb to indicate whether it is the collective itself, or the underlying objects that are being referred to. For these speakers, 'the bunch was p' implies that the bunch, as a whole, had the property p; however, 'the bunch were p' implies that the individuals within the bunch each had the property p. The num-

with the sum of its constituent elements.

A formal reason for supporting the extensional view of collectives is given if we consider a representation using complete atomic Boolean algebras (Lønning 1989): if we treat the copula as denoting equality, then:

John and Mary are a couple.

cannot be represented by an expression of the form:

$$john' + mary' = c'$$

unless, 'a couple' actually refers to a sum. Clearly, this can also be construed as a counter-example to the notion that the copula should be represented by equality.

As mentioned in arguments above (§3.1.5), doubt has been cast upon the need for an explicit, compositional, reductive representation of intermediate distributive readings. If we dispose of such readings by allowing them to be subsumed by collective readings, then we are left with the problem of representing the groups that occur with collective nouns. However, the use of theories originally designed for intermediate distribution and structured reflexives to explain the semantic behaviour of collectives is only appropriate if we accept the extensional view of these objects.

There are strong arguments against the extensional analysis. As observed by Bennett and others, two different committees may have exactly the same members, but still be different committees and have different things predicated of them (Bennett 1977). If the committees necessarily have the same members, then even an extensional approach with possible worlds cannot deal with this. A committee must be more than its members. To say that a committee meets is different to saying that the members of a committee meet: when a committee meets, all of the members need not be present.[45]

An additional argument against the identification of collectives with sums of individuals is that certain things can be predicated of a collection which cannot be predicated explicitly of the sum of underlying individuals, as exemplified by the following:

---

ber agreement of received British English, and the remaining ambiguity with plural collectives should make us cautious of trying to obtain some semantic generalisation from this. Lønning argues that for a theory of the semantic representation of plurals, the semantic arguments should have the most weight (Lønning 1987a). Syntactic evidence of number agreement should only be taken as secondary evidence.

[45]As collectives admit these apparent counter-examples, they may be akin to generic terms.

The group of boys has five members.
The boys have five members.

Also, collective nouns themselves can be pluralised, and ascribed collective properties (Chierchia 1982a):

The groups have 214 members, altogether.[46]

In the formal semantics of natural language, it is important to obtain the appropriate inferences. However, it can be hard to discern those inferences that are part of the logical behaviour of language from those that are contingent on extra-linguistic knowledge.

It is also difficult to see how far words like 'group' and 'member' should have their meanings tied up in the logical vocabulary of the semantics. In this respect, a weak theory which does not equate the object language terms 'group' and 'member' with primitive notions in the semantic theory, is better than a stronger one which does.

It is possible to allow committee-like collectives to be represented by atomic terms which, although related to their underlying "members," would not have to be equated with each other should they have the same underlying make-up. This intensional treatment of collectives can be divorced from the theory associated with intermediate distribution. We can take committee-like objects to be distinct if they could possess distinct properties. A function f can relate such a group to the sum of its underlying individuals (Barker 1992). When ascribing a property to a collective x in natural language, there is then a potential ambiguity as to whether the property applies to the collective x itself, or to the underlying objects fx. Dölling has a similar approach in a mereological framework, where he takes the meaning of 'the group of children met' to predicate 'met' of some group which is "constituted" by children (Dölling 1990).[47]

The existence of strong arguments against an identification of the extension of collective nouns with the sum of the individuals that "constitute" the collection surely means that, in general, the identification should not be made. Instead, we could say that a sentence like:

The group of boys met.

has an "extensional" distributive reading which is equivalent to the explicit distribution in:

[46]This could be a poor example, as its correct interpretation might depend upon the semantics of 'altogether'.

[47]It might be the case that whenever we encounter noun-phrase which refers to a plurality, such as 'the boys', we implicitly introduce an atomic term corresponding to something like 'the group of boys'.

The members of the group (of boys) met.

The arguments for and against equating the denotations of committee-like terms with their associated members applies also to ordinary individuals and their mereological parts. So that distribution works correctly, we assume that the representations of singular nominals are atomic, so a human, for example, must be atomic, as should individual windows and window parts. Yet it is true that a hand must be, in some sense, part of a human, and that a window part is part of a window, but humans, and windows, have a continuity of existence transcending that of their parts, or the matter that constitutes those parts. Some of these issues are examined in §3.2. These senses of "part-of" echo the relationship between committees and their members; we take a committee to be an atom that is systematically related to other atoms, namely, the committee members.

Again, it seems that in accounting for collective nouns, we should be content to have plurals in our ontology that lack the additional baggage of groups.

3.1.8 Logical Complexity

If we wish to exploit the weakest theory that accounts for the data, then clearly we should favour a first-order theory (like PT) over a second-order or higher-order one. We may question whether this is appropriate, or even whether it is possible. In particular, the axioms of a complete Boolean algebra are only expressible within a second order language, because the axiom of completeness requires us to quantify over all sets.[48]

Quantification over arbitrary collections of terms requires at least a second-order language. Such languages have an incomplete proof theory. If we admit quantification over arbitrary collections of objects, we must then face the issue of incompleteness in the proof system. It could be the case that the interpretations of natural language are, in practice, restricted. Depending upon the nature of such restrictions, we might only require a second order logic that has a general model, and which is therefore effectively of just first-order power (Orey 1959, Lønning 1989). This might arise if natural language does not require universal quantification over arbitrary collections. However, we would also need to consider the restrictions on the representation of negation and existential quantification to ensure that universal quantification over arbitrary collections does not arise indirectly.

[48]The axiom of completeness in a complete Boolean algebra requires that all subsets X of the algebra B must have a least upper-bound $\bigsqcup X$ in B ($\forall X \subseteq B, \bigsqcup X \in B$). This is second order, because we are quantifying over all of the sets X that are subsets of B. The essence of this axiom is captured by Axiom 3.6, although not in its full, second-order force.

In PT, we quantify over properties which can be expressed in the untyped λ-calculus, not sets. In effect, we only quantify over those collections which form the extension of some definable property. The completeness axiom of Boolean algebra then becomes completeness with respect to *definable* sets, as opposed to arbitrary sets (Axiom 3.6). This means we have an appropriate structure within a language of only first-order power.

Although the framework adopted automatically limits us to a first-order theory, we will still consider the circumstances whereby a more powerful formalism can be effectively restricted to first-order power. For an apparently second-order logic to be effectively first-order, there must be no genuine case of universal quantification over all possible sets, or collections. But Link suggests that there may be such examples in natural language (Link 1987):

> (All) competing companies have common interests.
> (All) children of the same age stick together.

Taking the first example, it is intended to be read as:

> Each collection of companies, such that they are competing, have common interests.

that is, we are quantifying over all subsets of competing companies. It is possible that such examples can only be given a dispositional, or generic, interpretation (Lønning 1989). This becomes clearer if we consider replacing 'all' with 'most':

> Most competing companies have common interests.
> Most children of the same age stick together.

where it cannot be the case that most collections of children stick together. If this is so, then Link's examples do not support the view that the representation language must be genuinely second-order.[49]

Roberts discusses the representation of non-logical quantifiers like 'most', 'few', and 'many' in some detail (Roberts 1987). If we take the sentence:

> Few people agree (with each other) on this issue.

the representation of 'agree' must take a collection as its argument. If this is paraphrased as "there are few groups of people who agree with each other on this issue," then it would seem that there is quantification

[49]In Link's example, even if it were the case that we really do quantify over all subsets of individuals satisfying the nominal predicate, it should be emphasised that this does not necessarily mean that the semantics must be genuinely second-order. As mentioned before, if there are only a subset of all possible sets over which we quantify in this way, then the semantics can be given a general model, and is effectively no stronger than a first-order theory (Orey 1959).

over arbitrary sums. This cannot be the correct interpretation. If there are four individuals a, b, c, d and the first three agree, then there are four collections of individuals that all agree: $a+b$; $a+c$; $a+b+c$; $b+c$, and seven collections of individuals that do not all agree: $a+d$; $b+d$; $c+d$; $a+b+d$; $a+c+d$; $b+c+d$; $a+b+c+d$. Thus the sentence is incorrectly taken to be true, according to this analysis.[50] For the example in question, Roberts notes that what is at issue is the cardinality of the maximal collection of people who agree. Determiners like 'few' then give rise to restricted quantification, not arbitrary quantification, over collections. However, there are examples that call this analysis into question. If there were a hundred people, and fifty pairs of matching sweaters, then the sentence:

Few people are wearing matching sweaters.

would be true on the suggested translation, as a maximum of two people would be wearing a matching pair. In this case we may require quantification over sums that are pairs (Roberts 1987). One conclusion that might be drawn from some of these problems is that, in general, no formal unpacking is possible. However, it does appear to be the case that such determiners do not give rise to quantification over arbitrary collections. In a later work, Link seems to support Lønning, suggesting that the noun phrase 'most competing companies' should be read as 'in most of the situations where we have a group of competing companies' (Link 1991a).

Even if universal quantification over arbitrary collections is disallowed, there is a potential problem with existential quantification over collections (stemming from indefinite noun phrases) if the scope of negation effectively gives rise to quantification over arbitrary collections. For the behaviour of natural language semantics to be limited to first-order power when represented within a second-order formalism, then restrictions would need to be imposed on the scope of negation in natural language sentences involving collectively read noun phrases (Lønning 1989).

We shall assume that, at least for most purposes, natural language semantics can be treated in a first-order framework. By adopting a first-order theory of properties, apparently second-order axioms are naturally restricted to first-order power. For example, the axiom of completeness in the plural domain becomes weakened to one of *definable* completeness. We need not then consider how the interpretations of sentences have to be restricted so that, given a second-order representation language, the semantics are effectively of only first-order power.

Using a first order representation language does mean that there can be no quantification over arbitrary objects. We may question whether

[50] Roberts attributes this argument to Angelika Krazter.

this is appropriate for, say, the semantics of vernacular mathematics, where we can make reference to higher-order objects. One means of avoiding this problem, at least in some cases, is not to equate, for example, the terms 'set' and 'member' with the notions $\{\cdot\}$ and ε used in the model, but instead to treat them as referring to first-order objects in the model. This may still be inadequate if we wish to deal with all of classical mathematics.

3.1.9 LATTICE THEORY AND INTENSIONAL SETS

Lattices can be modelled in set theory (Halmos 1963, Birkhoff 1967, Gratzer 1978). Landman shows how we can analyse plurality using a standard set-theoretic structure in place of lattice theory (Landman 1987, Landman 1989). As we have seen in §2.3.1 and §2.3.2, an intensional notion of set can be defined within PT, together with appropriate set-theoretic operations. It then seems reasonable to ask why we do not define an appropriate structure for plural terms using this notion of set. Indeed, if such an approach could be taken, then it might have the advantages of producing a simpler theory with fewer ontological commitments.

Terms involving the plural operators might be mapped to set-theoretic expressions as follows:

$$\begin{array}{rlll} t+s & \text{becomes} & t \cup s & =_{\text{def}} \lambda x(tx \vee sx) \\ \sigma x(t) & \text{becomes} & \{x : t\} & =_{\text{def}} \lambda x(t) \\ t \leq s & \text{becomes} & t \subseteq s & =_{\text{def}} \Theta x(tx \Rightarrow sx) \end{array}$$

It would then be necessary to formalise the closure conditions of denotable plurals ($\mathfrak{P}$) and the notion of a property of plurals ($\mathsf{Pty}_{\mathfrak{P}}$) with these new interpretations of the plural operators. This is complicated somewhat because there is a distinction between a simple singular individual (t), and a singular individual in the set-theoretic structure ($\{x : x \approx t\}$).

If properties of denotables are taken to be meaningful only when applied to elements of the set-theoretic plural structure, then the interpretation of $\sigma x(p)$ has to be changed. This is because elements of the property p will be intensional sets. To mirror the effect of the lattice-like structure, the supremum of p should be the supremum of the underlying individuals, not the supremum of the sets of individuals that are in the extension of p. The supremum $\sigma x(p)$ would then have to be interpreted as $\{x : \Xi y(p[y/x] \wedge y(x))\}$ so as to "flatten out" the structure of p's extension before forming the supremum.

Even if we can find a way through these complications and manage to find an appropriate model for $\mathfrak{P}$, there seems to be a fatal flaw with this set-theoretic plural structure. Plural terms are equated when they are founded on the same singular individuals, so $\sigma x(p) = \sigma x(q)$ when p and q are true of the same individuals. However, if we implement this operator by way of intensional sets, then $\sigma x(p) = \sigma x(q)$ is equivalent to $\lambda x(p) = \lambda x(q)$. But within PT, these expressions are equated on the grounds of λ-equality. Thus, if we try to avoid introducing the new term σ into PT by building the desired structure using intensional sets, then the notion of equality between pluralities is weaker than what is required; plural terms can only be equated if we refer to them in the same way. As we shall see in Chapter 4, there are occasions when we may wish to have something like this weaker notion of equality between natural language denotable terms, however it does not seem appropriate that this be our *only* notion of equality between such terms.

We could seek to remedy this by defining a notion of extensional equality $\approx_\eta$, where $\mathrm{T}(p \approx_\eta q)$ iff $\forall x(\mathrm{T}(px) \leftrightarrow \mathrm{T}(qx))$. But this cannot be made definitional, because we must ensure that p, q are properties for these truth conditions to make sense. So, in place of a definition, we require that $\approx_\eta$ be a new logical constant that is governed by an axiom of the form:

$$\mathsf{Pty}(p) \;\&\; \mathsf{Pty}(q) \rightarrow (\mathrm{T}(p \approx_\eta q) \leftrightarrow \forall x(\mathrm{T}(px) \leftrightarrow \mathrm{T}(qx)))$$

It seems that this is not a great simplification of the theory; we have merely replaced the constant σ by $\approx_\eta$, and have to play tricks with the nature of our properties in order to reproduce the desired plural structure.

The next part of this chapter is concerned with axiomatising an ontology that is suitable for representing the denotation of mass terms, as well as plurals. One issue concerns whether such an ontology should be atomic. Again, we can adopt the principle of least commitment, and develop a theory where the axioms are not strong enough to decide this point.

3.2 MASS TERMS

We begin this section by reviewing some of the various proposals for a formal analysis of natural language mass terms. Much of the essence of this review is taken from Bunt's work on mass terms (Bunt 1985).

Mass terms can be seen to refer to quantities of substances over which there is some part-whole relationship. In this sense, their ontological treatment can parallel that of plurals. Indeed, the only difference appears to be that there are discrete objects which underlie plural collections, to which we can refer using singular expressions, whereas, arguably, mass terms do not appear to have a discrete basis.[51] What we can do is axiomatise a part-whole structure which is open as to whether there are denotable atoms or not. This structure could be used for both mass terms and plurals. It would then be a contingent fact of plural nouns that they are founded on corresponding singular expressions.

The theory presented here assumes that the denotations of both count nouns and mass terms are homogeneous. This seems quite acceptable with plurals. We probably do not wish to equate the singulars on which they are based with the sum of their physical parts; it is not the case that if you chop off your arm, you cease to exist and a new one-handed person is born in your place. We could try and equate count individuals with some extensional space-time envelope, but this would surely be a derivative notion that presupposes we can already denote the individual whose space-time envelope we are trying to capture.[52]

With mass terms, things are not always so clear cut. In some of the literature there is a tendency to assume that substances referred to by mass terms are equated with their physical, and ultimately atomic extension. If we reject this equation, then we are free to decide whether or not our ontology of mass terms is atomic, independently of our sophisticated knowledge of physical science.

However, even if we reject the equation of substances with their physical extension, we still have to consider whether substances are homogeneous. For example, does 'muddy water' refer to an homogeneous substances, or should it have parts that are the substances "mud" and "water"? We can argue that this is akin to collective nouns such as 'committee', where there is an intimate relationship between a committee and its members, but that the part-of relation in the semantic theory is not the appropriate one with which to model it.

Sentences involving mass terms seem to be able to support entailments similar to those that occur with plurals. There are cumulative inferences:

Water is liquid
Oil is liquid
———
∴ Water and oil are liquid

and apparently distributive inferences:

Water is liquid
———
∴ Hot water is liquid

As with plurals, problems can arise because of the existence of generic

[51] In classifier languages, even this distinction may be in doubt.

[52] Jubien provides a clear discussion of the alternative perspectives on this issue (Jubien 1993, Jubien 1997).

readings for some of the examples. Again, we are primarily concerned with non-generic readings: readings that do not permit apparent counterexamples.

Quine defines mass terms as those objects that are cumulative, and do not "divide their reference" (Quine 1960). That is, mass terms do not indicate, by themselves, what their minimal parts might be, nor which non-minimal parts are appropriate. This is relevant to distributive inferences, as there are no *prima facia* appropriate parts to which we can restrict the distribution of a property. It could be taken as an argument against the use of an extensional mereology: in an extensional mereology the part-of relation would correspond with "physical part of." Clearly a word like 'water' does not apply to sub-atomic particles that are a physical part of water. There is little point in having a part-whole structure if the part-of relation cannot capture the relevant mode of division.

Quine distinguishes the use of mass terms before and after the copula (sometimes referred to as the "nominal" and "predicative" uses of mass terms, respectively). He claims that the use of a mass term after the copula results in the ascription of a property. The sentence:

This puddle is water.

would then result in the property $is \cdot a \cdot bit \cdot of \cdot water'$—or just $water'$, when there is no confusion between the predicative and nominal use of the term—being ascribed to the puddle. Before the copula, he treats mass terms on a par with proper names:

Water is a liquid.

attributes the property $is \cdot a \cdot liquid'$ to that object named 'water'. In the light of more recent work on generics, we may consent to this if the sentence is given its natural generic interpretation. However, Quine apparently is not attempting to give an account of generics. He does not take the object named by 'water' as some intensional "kind" (Carlson 1977), but as the single sprawling object that is the water of the universe.

An alternative to Quine's proposal would be to interpret 'water' as such an object both before and after the copula. The copula could then be interpreted as *part-of* ($\leq$), so that the sentence 'this puddle is water' is represented by:

$$this \cdot puddle' \leq water'$$

rather than:

$$water'(this \cdot puddle')$$

The former represents 'water' as a term rather than a property. As Bunt notes, the reason why Quine does not choose this representation for mass terms after the copula is that the interpretation of the copula as a part-of relation gives rise to distributive inferences, since the part-of relation is transitive. If 'this puddle is water' is true, then, on the suggested interpretation, every part of this puddle would also be water, including the non-watery parts, such as the physical atoms. Quine would equate the truth conditions of $x \leq water'$ with those of $water'(x)$ only when considering those x that are not too small to count as water. This problem arises if we adopt an extensional ontology for mass terms, and have no formal means of limiting distribution to the *relevant* parts.

Quine's proposal has been extensively criticised. Burge notes that Quine has no treatment of mass terms that occur neither before nor after the copula (Burge 1972), as in:

Phil threw snow at Bill.

Further, Quine does not establish a logical connection between the predicative and non-predicative uses of mass terms (Moravcsik 1973), thus he is unable to account for inferences of the form:

This puddle is water
Water is wet
———————————
∴ This puddle is wet

nor that "water is water" (Pelletier 1974). We might question whether we want the above inference to follow by virtue of the representation of the sentence rather than by virtue of some contingent behaviour of the predicates in question. For example, given the sentences: 'this house is concrete' and 'concrete is made by mixing portland cement, aggregates and water', we might be cautious of concluding that 'this house is made by mixing portland cement, aggregates and water'.[53]

Moravcsik gives two proposals for the treatment of mass terms (Moravcsik 1973). In one, he proposes that the object m_{sp} that is referred to by a mass term m after the copula is the "whole" consisting of objects that are not too small to count as the substance in question. According to this 'x is water' would be represented by:

$$x \leq water_{sp}{}'$$

This has the effect of limiting the distributive inferences to the appropriate parts. As all its parts are water, then it is the case that:

$$water_{sp}{}' \leq water'$$

Bunt notes that this proposal solves the wet puddle puzzle. It does not solve the "water is water" puzzle, however, as mass terms before the

[53]In both examples there seems to be ellipsis in the use of the copula ('This puddle is *constituted of* water', 'This house is *made of* concrete') which might effect the inferential behaviour.

copula are still interpreted *à la* Quine. This statement would correspond with the assertion that all the parts of water are part of the "whole" consisting of parts not too small to count as water:

$$water' \leq water_{sp}'$$

Unless we choose an ontology in which there cannot be such parts, then this results in a contradiction by way of the antisymmetry of $\leq$: the "whole" of parts not too small to count as water would be the same thing as the water itself. For this account to work, it is not possible for "wholes" to form objects that are sums of their parts, and have a uniform, transitive part-of relation. Otherwise the enterprise collapses at the outset since a part of a minimal part of water would not be water, but via transitivity, it would be a part of that "whole" of exclusively watery parts (Bunt 1985).

In his second proposal, Moravcsik seems to follow the logic of this argument and explicitly proposes distinct part-of relations for each substance. The expression:

$$x \leq_{SP(m)} m$$

means that x is a part of the mass term m and is large enough to count as a bit of m.[54] Moravcsik does not elaborate on how the various orderings are related; no transitivity between the different orderings is defined, for example. As it stands, this account cannot deal with the wet puddle puzzle, which is typically solved by using the transitivity of a part-of relation (Bunt 1985).

Other theories of mass terms can be taken to be essentially set-theoretic. Bunt divides the proponents of these theories into two camps, those that take the mass nouns to denote sets (Cartwright 1965, Cartwright 1970, Clarke 1970, Grandy 1973), and those that take them to denote predicates (Burge 1972, Grandy 1975, Pelletier 1974). He puts ter Meulen (ter Meulen 1980) in both these camps (Bunt 1985). In an extensional framework, these notions are related. Burge would represent, for example, the word 'snow' with a predicate that holds of any bit of snow. He takes '*the* snow' in:

The snow in the garden is two metres high.

to refer to some entity (Burge 1972). Bunt criticises the theory for being

[54]Size is not all that matters: the ordering relationship should also prevent, as an example, some water and a hydrogen atom being taken as a part of water in the sense of $\leq_{SP(m)}$. Generally, if $x \leq_{SP(m)} m$ then x must not include a non-m part of m, y, which is not a part of something z large enough to be a part of m in x, that is: $(x \leq_{SP(m)} m \;\&\; y \leq x) \rightarrow \exists z(y \leq z \;\&\; z \leq_{SP(m)} x)$. We could strengthen this to a biconditional: $x \leq_{SP(m)} m \leftrightarrow \forall y(y \leq x \rightarrow \exists z(y \leq z \;\&\; z \leq_{SP(m)} x))$.

too weak, it does not, in itself, give a treatment of the 'water is water' puzzle, for example.

There are set-based approaches which reduce the meanings of mass terms to those of count terms, by using some means of individuation. Then 'furniture' can be interpreted as 'pieces of furniture'; 'water' as perhaps 'puddles of water' (Strawson 1959, Clarke 1970). The individuating term is context-dependent. However, any set-theoretic treatment of these individuated terms will be highly extensional, so 'the ice', if interpreted as 'the pieces of ice' will denote different objects if the actual make-up of the ice changes (Cartwright 1965, Pelletier 1974). Bunt suggests that any move to avoid this problem by resorting to an artificial individuating standard faces the problem of what that individuating standard might be, particularly with abstract mass terms, such as 'time'.

Cartwright and Grandy have proposed that we take a mass term m to denote the set of all objects, or "quantities," that are m (Cartwright 1965, Grandy 1973). This notion of "quantity" is perhaps the artificial individuating standard to which Bunt alludes.

Ter Meulen takes 'quantity' to be an homogeneous notion, it can refer to the sums and parts of other quantities, not just some minimal elements. Both her and Pelletier's intensional theories make a Quinean-like distinction between predicative and nominal uses of mass terms, except that, unlike Quine's account, the relationship between the two uses is given: the nominal use of a mass term is represented by the intension of the predicative use, in the possible worlds sense of intension (Montague 1973, ter Meulen 1980, ter Meulen 1981, Pelletier 1974). Bunt believes that this distinction is of general applicability (Bunt 1985). To take one of his examples, the sentences:

> Gold is a metallic element.
> My tooth is filled with gold.

show the nominal and predicative uses of the mass term 'gold', just as:

> Diamonds are hard carbonites.
> The ring is ornamented with diamonds.

show the same uses of the count term 'diamonds'. We might suspect that these intensional accounts of mass terms are really striving to capture the notions of generic nominals. It should then come as no surprise that they can be used for both mass and count generics.

Bunt offers some criticisms of these theories. Ter Meulen's notion of 'quantity' causes some problems with non-logical quantifiers such as 'much' or 'most'. With the quantifier 'most', for example, we might wish to elucidate its semantics by means of taking an appropriate bipartition of the denotation of the subject noun phrase, the largest partition having the property in question. In ter Meulen's theory, there is no means of measuring the largest partition: assuming that they are infinitely subdivisible, there would be ω^2 quantities in each partition.

The interpretation of the definite descriptor similarly has problems, as 'the gold' intuitively refers to one thing. The only things that can be referred to in these theories are quantities, yet on ter Meulen's construal, such a quantity of gold will contain other quantities (Grandy 1975). Further, such quantities can be quantified over in turn as in 'all the gold'. The most natural solution, to treat the definite descriptor as denoting some maximal quantity, is not available to these set-theoretic approaches, as they have no means of constructing such an object: they have no formal notion of mereological fusion, or part. For similar reasons, they are presented with problems when trying to model the behaviour of non-homogeneous properties, such as in the sentence 'the gold weighs seven ounces'. If we were to say that the sum of the weights of the quantities of gold is seven ounces, we would be in error, as there is no means of preventing overlapping quantities from counting more than once (Bunt 1985).

Bunt's representation is based around "Ensemble Theory" (Bunt 1979, Bunt 1985). It is intended to capture the concept of "part-of." He strives to avoid an essentially atomic theory—a theory that requires there to be individuals with no further parts. He distinguishes between "continuous" and "discrete" ensembles, where the former are atomless, and the latter have minimal parts. He proves that his discrete ensembles behave like sets: for every atomic ensemble, there is a term (itself an ensemble) which is its unique element. This is like the member-singleton relation in set theory. In the continuous ensembles there is an empty ensemble that is a part of all other ensembles. This is unlike mereology, where there is no such term (Leonard and Goodman 1940). The set-like, discrete ensembles can be used to model the count nouns and verb-phrases and the continuous ensembles can be used to model (continuous) substances.

Bunt seeks to avoid the problems of minimal-parts and the distribution of properties to inappropriate parts by adopting what he terms the "homogeneous reference hypothesis." This asserts that:

> "Mass nouns refer to entities as having part-whole structure without singling out any particular parts and without making any commitments concerning the existence of minimal parts."

This he takes to be a linguistic point: it does not matter what our theory of the world may be like, language behaves (according to Bunt) as if this hypothesis holds. This could be distinguished from Cheng's view of distributive reference:

> "Any part of the whole of the mass object w is w."

where this is not a condition on the way a mass term refers, but on the referent of such a term, that is, it is an ontological commitment (Cheng 1973). We might argue that an ontology which satisfies Cheng will also satisfy Bunt's hypothesis.

We may be tempted to interpret Bunt's hypothesis as asserting that, within the theory, substances are independent of physical matter. That is, unlike matter, they do not have any parts that do not have the relevant property. This could be achieved by adopting something similar to Moravcsik's proposal for a restricted notion of the part-of relation (Moravcsik 1973). For example, by taking all parts of "the wood" to be "wood," we never reach parts too small physically to count as "wood" (or else linguistic intuitions provide no insight into the limiting case). As mentioned above, Bunt rejects Moravcsik's proposal because, as expressed, it is not coherent.

The principle of homogeneous reference could also be interpreted as advocating an intensional, or Platonic view of substances, as adopted by Parsons (Parsons 1970, Parsons 1975) (see §3.2.1) which avoids Quine's objection to distributive inferences with mass terms. On this account, even if all the wood in the world were turned into sawdust, the denotations of 'the wood' and 'the sawdust' would be genuinely different. But, as we shall see, Bunt rejects Parsons' ontology as being too complex.

Link has a lattice-theoretic account of mass terms (Link 1983) which he tries to integrate with a theory of plurals. Essentially, any fusion of substance in the lattice D, used to represent mass terms, can appear as an atom in the lattice E, used to represent count terms. The elements of the lattice D are then a subset of the atoms of the lattice E. This is intended to correspond to the notion of being able to "quantise" substances, turning them into count terms, with phrases such as "a quantity of m." Link avoids some problems in the count domain by giving the representation extra structure: in his account, "windows" and "window parts" are not directly related, thus there is no equation of "the windows" with "the window parts." He defines a function h, a complete join-homomorphism,[55] which maps every count term onto a mass term, and is the identity function for mass terms. This corresponds to the notion of an object being composed of substances. Thus, count terms may

[55] If h is a complete join-homomorphism, then $h(\bigsqcup_E X) = \bigsqcup_D X$ where $\bigsqcup_E, \bigsqcup_D$ are the join operators for the lattices E, D respectively.

be distinguished, that is:

$$[\![\text{the windows}]\!] \neq [\![\text{the window parts}]\!]$$

even if they are composed of the same stuff:

$$h([\![\text{the windows}]\!]) = h([\![\text{the window parts}]\!])$$

This allows distribution to be blocked correctly in the count domain.[56] However, we may still question whether this is adequate for mass terms: are mass terms (substances) and count terms (individuals and collections of individuals) all that there are, or are these too realised by some other ontological category, such as physical matter? If substances are equated with physical matter then, in addition to mud being part of muddy water, atoms of hydrogen must also be part of water. Homogeneous properties predicated of muddy water (or water) must then also be predicated of the mud in the muddy water (or the hydrogen in the water). This leads to the familiar problem of how we are then to interpret the sentence (attributed to Emmon Bach):

> The snow making up the snowman is quite new but the H_2O making it up is very old.

The problem could be addressed by adopting a richer ontology, more like that proposed by Parsons (§3.2.1): rather than have count objects constituted by substance, both count objects and substances could be constituted by physical matter.

At first glance, Link's theory can account for the fact that mass terms can only be counted if they are first quantised. However, any arbitrary fusion of substance can be taken to be a "quantity." Thus 'the three quantities of water' can refer to any bit(s) of water: it is always possible to divide a quantity of water into three quantities. It seems that 'quantity of water' has more intensionality than it is attributed in Link's theory. We can refer to 'the quantity' itself, rather than 'the beer' in 'the quantity of beer that I drank'. The syntactic structures which quantise substances seem rather like collective noun-phrases (§3.1.7), which we take to have an intensional aspect (Link 1983, Landman 1989, Barker 1992).

Lønning seeks to account for the semantics of sentences involving mass terms, negation, and non-logical determiners such as 'most', 'much', 'little', 'less than two kilogrammes of' (Lønning 1987b). He notes that the semantics will be seriously in error if we adopt the set theoretic approach—as in the theories of Montague and ter Meulen (Montague 1973, ter Meulen 1980)—and take 'not p' to refer to the complement of p, and use the cardinality of sets to determine the truth of sentences in-

[56] We are ignoring Link's treatment of "group" readings here.

volving non-logical determiners. If "some water disappeared," modelling negation as complement can entail that "the water did not disappear." As discussed above in connection with ter Meulen's theory, if mass terms, modelled as sets of quantities, are potentially infinitely divisible, then the cardinality of quantities will be the same. We shall follow Lønning in making mass terms denote elements of a Boolean algebra, although our axiomatisation will be weaker than a Boolean algebra, as bottom will not be denotable. Lønning uses a Boolean algebra together with a generalised quantifier-like interpretations of determiners which allows him to address the representation of non-logical determiners and negation; additive measure functions on the algebraic structure can be used in place of the cardinalities of sets.[57]

Lønning adopts an "homogeneous constraint" as an heuristic principle, similar in motivation to Bunt's notion of homogeneous reference. He recognises that mass terms may not actually refer homogeneously, but that they behave as if they do. He expresses his heuristic as:

> Mass noun phrases combine only with *homogeneous expressions* to form sentences.

This can be viewed as a test for mass nouns. Lønning takes δ to be an homogeneous expression if the following distributive and cumulative inferences hold:

Cumulative:	The $\beta\alpha$ δ	Distributive:	The α δ
	The not-$\beta\alpha$ δ		There is some $\beta\alpha$
	$\therefore$ The α δ		$\therefore$ The $\beta\alpha$ δ

where β is a predicative or intersective adjective.[58] The adjective β must itself be an homogeneous expression for it to combine with a mass term. Note that the expression of distribution used by Lønning effectively restricts distribution into a noun phrase involving the term α to those sub-quantities that are also α. In order to control distribution into mass terms, we might like to use inference rules that enforce this restriction: if we have 'much water δ', then the sub-quantities of "much water" that are themselves water, have the property δ (Fox 1993, Fox 1998). However, it is simpler to take the denotation of mass terms to be homogeneous, so that all parts of water are water.

The sentence:

> Much water weighed two grammes.

[57]A measure function μ is additive if $\mu(a \sqcup b) = \mu(a) + \mu(b)$ when $a \sqcap b = 0$ (that is, when a, b are disjoint).

[58]Lønning assumes an extensional treatment of adjectives, where $\beta\alpha$ is to be taken to be the intersection of those things that are β and α.

is ill-formed, according to Lønning, because 'weighed two grammes' is inhomogeneous, yet:

The water that John drank weighed two grammes.

is a sentence, thus 'the water that John drank' should not be taken to be a mass noun phrase. As with plurals, it can be argued that the distributive behaviour is bestowed by the verb phrase, and does not reside in the noun phrase, as definite descriptors involving mass terms combine with homogeneous properties that license distributive (and cumulative) inference.[59]

Counter to Lønning's general principle, there are homogeneous properties, such as 'weighed less than three grams or more than two grams', that cannot combine with mass terms. In this case, the underlying reason for this uncharacteristic behaviour seems to be that the disjoint property is composed of inhomogeneous properties (Lønning 1987b).

Roeper also points to a problem with disjunctive properties that arises when they are given a naive analysis (Roeper 1983). If we represent 'all' conventionally, then 'all claret is wine' is represented by

$$\forall x(\mathit{claret}'(x) \rightarrow \mathit{wine}'(x))$$

where x ranges over denotables. This effectively says that claret is, in some sense, part of wine. The distributive nature of predications involving mass terms is obtained "for free" in such a representation. If we say that:

All dirty water is water.

then only those denotables of which we would predicate 'dirty water', are to be counted as "water." This apparently avoids any question as to the relevant parts of dirty water: we do not even contemplate how to avoid predicating 'water' of the dirt in dirty water. Dirty water is part-of, or a subclass of, water, yet the dirt itself is not.[60]

[59] In Lønning's theory, homogeneous expressions denote elements of a Boolean algebra: they will hold of a mass term if they dominate it in the algebra. Inhomogeneous expressions denote subsets of the Boolean algebra (Lønning 1987b).

[60] Hans Kamp (PC) has pointed out that this may not be adequate: taking the sentence 'all water is liquid', then this proposal would allow the inference that anything that is water is liquid. Yet whilst a single water molecule is conceivably "water," it would seem possible that 'being liquid' is a property of a body of water (or collections of bodies of water) not of individual molecules (or collections of discrete molecules). If these views of the meaning of 'water' and 'being liquid' are accepted, then such an approach to distributive inferences is too strong. We could defend this position by stating that 'water' does not apply to individual molecules of water, but to collections of molecules that can display the property of, for example, being liquid at room temperature and pressure (Fox 1993). Indeed, recent research in the science of materials has shown that we need collections of at least five molecules of water in

However, Roeper discredits this approach by using the example:

All phosphorus is red or white.

There are some quantities of phosphorus that will be both red and white, and so it would be erroneous to say the sentence entails:

$$\forall x(\mathit{phosphorus}'(x) \rightarrow (\mathit{white}'(x) \vee \mathit{red}'(x)))$$

as we would not usually say something is red (or that it is white) if it has both red and white parts. An adequate account of distributive behaviour is tied up in the reduction of 'red or white'. We could reinterpret this as:

> quantity such that it is red or it is white, or part of it is red, and the remainder is white

In the second part of this definition, there is a problem in restricting the parts that are considered: we want to take parts that avoid splitting any parts which count as phosphorus into parts that are not phosphorus. This is not does not arise if the extension of mass terms is taken to be homogeneous.

3.2.1 PARSONS' ONTOLOGY REVISITED

In Parsons' approach to the semantics of mass terms there is no ambiguity between substances before and after the copula, and unlike Moravcsik's proposal (Moravcsik 1973), there is only one ordering relation over the substances (Parsons 1970). His theory is presented with a particular ontology in mind, where there are objects, bits of matter, and substances. In this account, mass terms denote substances. There are two relations, one, C ("composed of") between objects and substances, and another, $\triangleright$ ("constitutes") between matter and substance. The expression:

$$\mathit{my} \cdot \mathit{ring}' C \mathit{gold}'$$

intuitively means "my ring is gold," and:

$$m \triangleright \mathit{gold}'$$

means that m is the matter that constitutes the gold. By distinguishing between substance and matter (and substance and object), the problem of considering inappropriate parts is avoided. The distinction between objects and matter avoids problems concerning the metaphysics of change. According to Parsons, no two of these three—objects, substances, and physical matter—should be equated.

Bunt argues that Parsons' notion of substance is not well-defined. He notes that substances defined in terms of a property such as small', for

certain configurations before we start to obtain the bulk behaviours attributed to water, such as acting as a solvent.

example, might not have that property when fused. Thus we may have m_1 and m_2 defined in terms of being small, yet m_1 fused with m_2 need not be small (Bunt 1985). We can take this as an argument in support of the view that substances should be homogeneous, or at least, that they may only be defined by way of cumulative properties.

In the rest of this section, we will briefly summarise the arguments concerning the relationships between objects, substances and matter. Let us initially consider whether two distinct objects can have the same physical manifestation. Carter suggests that different objects might have the same manifestation, provided that they are of different kinds (Carter 1990). Presumably, in the case of plurals, "a deck" may be of a different kind to "some cards" when talking about playing cards. One criterion for judging whether objects are of the same kind might be to see whether they have the same elements, or "nice" parts, where the nice parts of a mereological fusion of cats are cats, as opposed to bits of cats (Lewis 1991). Plural objects with different nice parts may then have the same physical manifestation. It does not necessarily follow that objects with the same elements, or nice parts, must be equated, as we shall see below, when discussing whether substance should be distinguished from physical matter.

Should objects and physical matter be equated? As objects can outlast a particular physical make-up, the answer is surely "no." If we consider the metaphysics of change, as it applies to the count terms, then we can see the problems in taking count terms to be the sums of their physical parts. A cat may lose a whisker, but it remains the same cat. A person, over the period of a lifetime, has few, if any, physical parts in common with the person they were at birth, yet they are the same person. These are the familiar arguments from Aristotle (Burge 1975).[61]

Should substances (denoted by mass terms) be distinguished from physical matter, as Parsons suggests? He cites the argument, for which he credits Quine, that:

> "[E]ven if all and only furniture was composed of wood, it would not follow that wood = furniture, since parts of the chairs might be wood without being furniture."

Bunt disputes this example, claiming that the problem lies in taking 'furniture' to be a mass term with minimal parts. He suggests that by replacing the individuating term 'furniture' in the example with the mass term 'sawdust'—so that all the wood in the world is made into sawdust—it can be seen that 'wood' and 'sawdust' can legitimately be

[61] As mentioned previously (footnote 52), Jubien presents a clear discussion of the different perspectives on this issue (Jubien 1993, Jubien 1997).

equated, in non-intensional contexts (Bunt 1985). However, this seems to be mistaken, as we might truthfully say "this *sawdust* was made yesterday," without commitment to "this *wood* was made yesterday." Presumably, Quine could argue that the sawdust and wood are still distinguishable because they have different nice parts: there are parts of the sawdust that are not sawdust, but are wood. However, it is conceivable that some sawdust might be sufficiently finely ground for its minimal nice parts to denote the same physical matter as the minimal nice parts of wood, but we might still dissent from the view that the sawdust is the very same thing as the wood.

It might be argued that the fusions can be distinguished because the properties are genuinely different—even on a possible worlds analysis—as the extensions of the properties vary differently with time: though they may now have the same extension, they are different properties because they had different extensions. Even so, we can still offer support for an intensional ontology: if we point at the wood/sawdust and say "this sawdust was made yesterday" then, with an extensional ontology, the stuff that "was made yesterday" is the extension of both 'the wood' *as it is now* and 'the sawdust' *as it is now*. No matter that the properties once had different extensions, the stuff being predicated of will be the same, unless we adopt the view that 'the wood' and 'the sawdust' denote different things *now*, which requires that we have an intensional ontology.[62]

Bunt interprets Parsons as saying that in the case of the wood-furniture example, it is not the role of a semantic theory to make such distinctions. One could then question what the role of a semantic theory is. We could instead take Parsons' point to be that it is not the role of a *semantic* theory to dictate essentially *philosophical* choices. This is an argument for the philosophical neutrality of a semantic theory, whenever possible, not for getting the semantics wrong.

Consideration of the metaphysics of change provides an additional argument in favour of the absence of identity between substance and physical matter. In an everyday setting, if we have some water and part of it evaporates, we might say it is the same water that we started with.

We can give a more elaborate example: it is possible to say 'this is the water I pumped from the well yesterday. I spilt some of it'. The continuation suggests that physically, 'this water' and 'the water I pumped from the well' must be different, as I spilt some of the latter. We can also say

[62]An intensional ontology creates a problem for the semantics of demonstratives: how do we know what is being indicated when different objects can have the same physical extension? Landman suggests that we never really indicate a thing in itself with a demonstrative (Landman 1986).

'I spilt some of this water'. So, 'this water' at some time previously had a greater physical extension than it does now, yet to be able to refer to it as 'this water' seems to imply there is some individual representing 'this water' which can survive physical mereological change—in this case, a spillage of part of it—just as objects in the count domain can. Thus, although these are perhaps not conclusive arguments, care should be taken in assuming that the semantics of natural language should take theories of physics into account. The mereology used for representing mass terms might not comply with the behaviour of the physical extension.

As a final example, some dirty water may be taken to be the same dirty water tomorrow, even if the dirt is in dynamic equilibrium with some sludge at the bottom, and even if some water evaporates. Thus we can have a part-whole structure which survives physical mereological changes.[63]

Finally, should substances be distinguished from objects? There are two relevant issues:

(i) Are substances of the same *order* as objects—both manifest by physical stuff, neither subsuming the other?

(ii) Are the fusions of substances to be equated with particular objects (at a certain time)—when we have a gold statue, is "the statue" (at a particular time) the same thing as "the gold" (Grandy 1975)?

Considering the first issue, Laycock seems to suggest that substances are of the same order as objects (Laycock 1972, Laycock 1975), as both substances and objects seem capable of surviving physical change (Cartwright 1965).

As to the second issue, if we take the view that stage level count nominals (Carlson 1977) are akin to mass terms (Chierchia 1982a, Chierchia 1982b) then it might be tempting to equate particular objects with fusions of substances. However, there are problems with equating stage level predication with predication of either substance, or physical manifestation. If it is agreed that stage level predication is akin to predication of (a representation of) some physical manifestation, and present progressives are taken to exemplify such readings, then we would loose the required intensionality. This is perhaps best exemplified by an example involving collective count nouns: if committee A has the same members as committee B, then 'committee A is meeting' would imply 'committee B is meeting'—as the physical manifestation of the committees is the same—and perhaps further, that all the members are in attendance. But

[63] A similar argument is presented by Cartwright (Cartwright 1965). In Jubien's terminology, we are attempting to characterise the behaviour of the "vague" referring terms of natural language (Jubien 1997, Chapter 9).

neither of these conclusions necessarily follow. Even if we exploit Landman's notion of individuals under roles (Landman 1989)—as explored in Chapter 4—and take the stage level committees as their physical manifestations *under the role of being a certain committee*, there are still problems: 'committee A is being disbanded at this moment' appears to be a stage level predication, yet it is surely the committee itself that is being disbanded, not the members under the role of being committee A members.

These arguments suggest we can take the extension of nouns to be homogeneous regardless of the inhomogeneous nature of physical matter.

3.2.2 $\mathrm{PT}^{\mathfrak{D}}$: MEREOLOGY IN PT

It seems that it is possible to defend Parsons' ontology, where we distinguish individuals, substances and physical matter. The denotation of mass terms should have a part-whole, or mereological structure, but if we adopt Parsons' ontology, and have mass terms denote substances, then this will be distinct from the part-whole structure of physical matter (although related to it). This is counter to the nominalistic motivation of earlier presentations of mereology (Leonard and Goodman 1940) which seeks to deny the need for abstractions that are not founded on the physical realm.

In effect, here we are just considering the part-whole structure of Parsons' substances. We do not consider Parsons' relations C (between individuals and substances) nor the relation $\rhd$ (between matter and substances) in the formal theory.

The theory presented here will be a weaker version of $\mathrm{PT}^{\mathfrak{P}}$ (§3.1.3). It seems that we might be able to use just the one part-whole structure to represent both plurals and mass terms (corresponding to Parsons' objects and substances, respectively), as sketched in §3.3.

To represent mass terms directly in this theory, and to allow distributive inferences, would require some means of stopping distribution of properties to inappropriate parts. This suggests a commitment to homogeneous extensions for mass terms, as adopted by Bunt (Bunt 1985).

Following the methodology of least commitment (§1.2), the structure of the domain of denotables should be the weakest required to capture the appropriate part-whole relationships in the extensions of nominal expressions. For example, a theory that did not require substances to be atomic would be weaker than one which did. If we distinguish the denotation of mass terms from physical matter, then we are not constrained by the ontology of physical matter. We can decide independently whether or not it is appropriate for substances to be atomic or homogeneous.

Although theories in modern physics suggest that the physical manifestations of substances are atomic (they have minimal parts), it need not be the case that the formal semantics of natural language has to embody this atomicity. In particular, it is clear that people can communicate, and use mass terms, without being aware of the theories of physical atoms, molecules and composites. What is at issue, is whether the everyday usage of natural language mass terms in itself requires, or presupposes some atomic level in their semantics. These atoms need not correspond to physical atoms.[64] We could be suspicious as to whether such an issue has any meaning to someone not versed in the ways of formal semantics. Should such atoms exist, we might question their countability, and ponder whether the part-whole ordering is dense. These questions may have no definitive answer. We can axiomatise the domain so that the issue of atomicity is undecided; there may be atoms, but their existence will not be provable in the formal system. The model for the theory may well be atomic, but those atoms are not accessible to the theory, just as natural language expressions denoting substances that are constituted by physically atomic matter are in themselves neutral as to the existence of atoms.

Regardless of whether substances are atomic or not, we have to decide whether they are homogeneous. That is, whether all parts of a substance are the same substance. It is perhaps simplest to assume that they are, as this results in the observed behaviour of mass terms with distributive inferences. According to this view, even "compound" substances such as 'muddy water' are homogeneous, so that there are no parts that are just mud or water—although of course the substance is related in some way to the pure mud and pure water, not least by way of their physical manifestation.

Given an homogeneous ontology, it may be appropriate to formalise a generalisation of Parsons' "composed of" relation C, which not only relates individuals with the substances of which they are composed, but also the substances that compose other substances, and the individuals that are parts of other complex individuals. Although we shall not explore this here, C would then effectively take on the role of an inhomogeneous part-of relation, rather like Link's function h above (page 83) and Barker's function f that maps the denotations of collective nominals with their members (Barker 1992) (§3.1.7).

[64] If we were to assume that the denotations of substances are homogeneous, and that the minimal parts of mass terms correspond to some notion of minimal part in the physical realm, then only elemental substances could have atoms that correspond to the atoms of physics. With aggregates, sols and other composites (and even with molecular and elemental substances), it may be very difficult to determine precisely what would constitute a salient minimal part.

As an alternative, we could adopt an inhomogeneous ontology, where muddy water has parts that are the substances mud and water. Recovering the notion of an homogeneous part in such a theory requires additional complications in the semantics of natural language expressions. Such a treatment is pursued elsewhere (Fox 1993, Fox 1998).[65]

In effect, deciding whether substances are homogeneous or inhomogeneous is a decision about the appropriate basic notion of "part-of" in the theory. In either case, it may be possible to obtain the alternative notion of "part-of" with suitable embellishments to the theory.

As in the theory of plurals, $\mathrm{PT}^{\mathfrak{P}}$ (§3.1.3), it is not clear that there is some denotable bottom element that is a part of all denotable terms. As before, it will be possible to define a bottom element, but the theory will be formulated so that it will not be possible to demonstrate that it is denotable.

The following theory axiomatises a mereology as a Boolean algebraic-like structure, which will not provably be atomic, and will not provably contain a bottom element. This theory is primarily concerned with the homogeneous structure of substances, which we take to be the denotations of mass terms. However, the same structure can also be used for the denotation of count nouns, as we shall see in §3.3, thus we should consider this to be a formalisation of the category of substantive denotables.

Language of mereological terms

To the basic vocabulary of terms is added:

Predicative constant:	$\eth$
Operative constants:	$+, \sigma$

[65]Unlike the theory developed here, if we were to allow inhomogeneous extensions, then we would need to be able to represent denotable terms with some indication of its appropriate nice parts for the purposes of distributive inferences. A standard PTQ-like interpretation would not be sufficient. One possibility would be to pair a denotable with the property used to conjure it up. Then all the relevant nice parts could be constructed. The phrase 'the furniture' could be represented as something like "the fusion of that which is furniture, as furniture" and 'the wood' as "the fusion of that which is wood, as wood." No matter whether the two fusions are equated, the appropriate nice parts could always be found. This would avoid the need to make the representations of substances homogeneous, so muddy water could have parts that are mud, for example.

Landman has considered the problem of representing individuals under different guises, or roles, within a theory of plurals (Landman 1989). This is examined in Chapter 4. Such "intensional" individuals can be used to control distribution in a theory of mass terms which allows inhomogeneous extensions (Fox 1993, Fox 1998), and so can be used to increase the ontological neutrality of the theory. We will not explore this variant of the theory here, although the formal theory to be presented is much like the basic mereological structure of the inhomogeneous theory.

It is intended that $\mathfrak{d}$ will hold of natural language denotable terms. It corresponds with a "small type" (§2.5). In the category of substances, it plays the same role that $\mathfrak{p}$ served in the theory of plurals (§3.1.3). As before, σ is the supremum operator, and $+$ is the summation operator.

The language of wff remains unchanged, and the theory is governed by the axioms of the λ-calculus as before, together with PT's axioms for propositions P and truth T given in Chapter 2 (§2.2).

Further Axioms For PT$^{\mathfrak{D}}$

The operator $+$ is used to indicate a fusion of terms. The order in which the terms are considered is irrelevant, and so the operator is both symmetric and associative:

Axiom 3.11 *Symmetry (cf. Axiom 3.1).*

$$a + b = b + a$$

Axiom 3.12 *Associativity (cf. Axiom 3.2).*

$$a + (b + c) = (a + b) + c$$

Combining a term with itself will result in nothing new:

Axiom 3.13 *Idempotence (cf. Axiom 3.3).*

$$a + a = a$$

As in PT$^{\mathfrak{P}}$, an ordering can be defined in terms of $+$, which simplifies the expression of some of the axioms:

Definition 3.19 *Definable ordering (cf. Definition 3.1).*

$$t \leq s =_{\text{def}} (t + s = s)$$

This is intended to capture the notion of "homogeneous part of."

An internal form of the ordering can be defined:

Definition 3.20 *Internal ordering (cf. Definition 3.2).*

$$t \ll s =_{\text{def}} (t + s \approx s)$$

The terms that are of interest are those which correspond to the extensions of referring descriptions. The predicative constant $\mathfrak{d}$ is a property which holds of any such natural language denotable term:

Axiom 3.14 *The term $\mathfrak{d}$ is a property (cf. Definition 3.4).*

$$\mathrm{P}(\mathfrak{d}t)$$

As syntactic sugar, the predicate $\mathfrak{D}$ can be defined in the language of wff which holds of natural language denotables:

Definition 3.21 *Predicate $\mathfrak{D}$ (cf. Definition 3.3).*

$$\mathfrak{D}t =_{\text{def}} \mathrm{T}(\mathfrak{d}t)$$

The fusion of two denotables will itself be denotable:

Axiom 3.15 *The sum of denotables is a denotable (cf. Axiom 3.5).*

$$(\mathfrak{D}a \;\&\; \mathfrak{D}b) \rightarrow \mathfrak{D}(a + b)$$

As with $\mathrm{PT}^{\mathfrak{P}}$, which adds plurals to PT (§3.1.3), we want to be able to form the supremum of classes of denotables. Again, the term σ is intended to do this.

The previous closure condition on denotables can be generalised so that the fusion (supremum) of a class of denotables is itself denotable. The axiom requires that the class be non-empty, in order to prevent a proof of the denotability of a bottom element (an element that is part of all denotables):

Axiom 3.16 *If some property has an extension, and it is contained in the domain of denotables, then its supremum is also in the domain of denotables (cf. Axiom 3.6).*

$$\forall p((\mathsf{Pty}(p) \;\&\; \forall x(\mathrm{T}(px) \rightarrow \mathfrak{D}(x)) \;\&\; \exists x(\mathrm{T}px)) \rightarrow \mathfrak{D}(\sigma x(px)))$$

Typically, the "properties" of interest in the representation of natural language need only form propositions with denotable terms:

Definition 3.22 *A property of denotables produces a proposition, given some denotable (cf. Definition 3.4).*

$$\mathsf{Pty}_{\mathfrak{D}}(p) =_{\text{def}} \forall x(\mathfrak{D}(x) \rightarrow \mathrm{P}(px))$$

This restricted class of properties is useful in weakening the theory so that "non-denoting" definite descriptors need not have natural language denotable extensions. By restricting natural language derived properties to this class, it is not possible to prove that applying such a "property" to a non-denotable (or rather, not provably denotable) term results in a proposition.

We can define forms of the quantifiers that are restricted to denotable terms:

Definition 3.23 *(cf. Definition 3.7).*

$$\forall x \varepsilon \mathfrak{D}.\varphi =_{\text{def}} \forall x(\mathfrak{D}x \to \varphi)$$

Definition 3.24 *(cf. Definition 3.8).*

$$\exists x \varepsilon \mathfrak{D}.\varphi =_{\text{def}} \exists x(\mathfrak{D}x \mathbin{\&} \varphi)$$

Restricting ourselves to these quantifiers, as in the plural domain, we again achieve the effect of a free logic, where free variables range over all terms, and quantified variables range over denoting terms. As before, these quantifiers can be given internal analogues, and a supremum operator which is restricted to denotables can be defined.

Definition 3.25 *(cf. Definition 3.9).*

$$\Theta x \epsilon \mathfrak{d}.t =_{\text{def}} \Theta x(\mathfrak{d}x \Rightarrow t)$$

Definition 3.26 *(cf. Definition 3.10).*

$$\Xi x \epsilon \mathfrak{d}.t =_{\text{def}} \Xi x(\mathfrak{d}x \mathbin{\vec{\wedge}} t)$$

Definition 3.27 *(cf. Definition 3.11).*

$$\sigma x \epsilon \mathfrak{d}.t =_{\text{def}} \sigma x(\mathfrak{d}x \mathbin{\vec{\wedge}} t)$$

As with Definitions 3.10 and 3.11, we need the stronger form of "conjunction" in these last two definitions—$\vec{\wedge}$ rather than just $\wedge$—so that we can show that $\Xi x \epsilon \mathfrak{d}.t$ forms a proposition for all x (as required for the axioms of truth to be applicable), and also that $\sigma x \epsilon \mathfrak{d}.t$ is a denotable, even if t only forms a proposition when x is a denotable.

If two denotables are not equal, then there is a denotable that is part of one, but not part of the other. The antecedent can be strengthened: if one denotable is not part of a second, then there must be a denotable that is part of the first but not part of the second:

Axiom 3.17 *Different denotables have different parts (cf. Axiom 3.7).*

$$\forall xy \varepsilon \mathfrak{D}.(x \not\leq y \to \exists u \varepsilon \mathfrak{D}.(u \leq x \mathbin{\&} u \not\leq y))$$

The term $\sigma x \epsilon \mathfrak{d}.px$ is intended to form the fusion of all denotables having the property p. Any denotable with the property p should be part of this term:

Axiom 3.18 *All denotables having a particular property must be a part of the supremum of denotables having that property (cf. Axiom 3.8).*

$$\forall p \forall y \varepsilon \mathfrak{D}.((\mathsf{Pty}_{\mathfrak{D}}(p) \mathbin{\&} \mathrm{T}(py)) \to y \leq \sigma x \epsilon \mathfrak{d}.px)$$

We can illustrate the need for the next axiom by way of example. If we consider the denotable substance "cold mud," any bit of cold mud will be part of the fusion of mud. If we take the fusion of bits of cold mud, it will also be part of the fusion of mud:

Axiom 3.19 *If all denotables having property p are part of some other denotable y, then the supremum of denotables having p must also be a part of y (cf. Axiom 3.9).*

$$\forall p \forall y \varepsilon \mathfrak{D}.((\mathsf{Pty}_{\mathfrak{D}}(p) \,\&\, \forall x \varepsilon \mathfrak{D}.(\mathrm{T}(px) \rightarrow x \leq y)) \rightarrow \sigma x \epsilon \mathfrak{d}.px \leq y)$$

The intuition behind the following axiom is akin to that of Axiom 3.10 ($\mathrm{PT}^{\mathfrak{P}}$, §3.1.3) where different collections of minimal parts have different suprema. There are some complications following from the fact that there is no reference to atoms in this theory: (i) we cannot consider a unique way of dividing a denotable into its minimal parts; (ii) different collections of denotables may have the same supremum if they "cover" the same denotables; further, (iii) we cannot guarantee to pick denotables that are part of a denotable with the required property. However, in this final case, the denotable will have a part with the required property.

Axiom 3.20 *Different portions of denotables have different supremums: something that is part of the supremum of a property must be part of something with that property, or have a part with that property (cf. Axiom 3.10).*

$$\begin{aligned}&\forall p \forall u \varepsilon \mathfrak{D}.((\mathsf{Pty}_{\mathfrak{D}}(p) \,\&\, u \leq \sigma x \epsilon \mathfrak{d}.px) \rightarrow \\ &\quad (\exists z \varepsilon \mathfrak{D}.(pz \,\&\, u \leq z) \vee \exists z \varepsilon \mathfrak{D}.(pz \,\&\, z \leq u)))\end{aligned}$$

Obviously, this is not much use if we have uncountable parts, but that would always cause problems.

With an homogeneous ontology, we can define what it is to be a distributive property:

Definition 3.28 *(cf. Definition 3.13)*

$$\mathsf{distributive}(p) =_{\mathrm{def}} \mathsf{Pty}_{\mathfrak{D}}(p) \,\&\, \forall t u \varepsilon \mathfrak{D}.(\mathrm{T}(pt) \,\&\, u \leq t \rightarrow \mathrm{T}(pu))$$

A class of collective predicates can also be defined:

Definition 3.29 *(cf. Definition 3.12)*

$$\begin{aligned}&\mathsf{collective}(p) =_{\mathrm{def}} \mathsf{Pty}_{\mathfrak{D}}(p) \,\&\, (\exists t \varepsilon \mathfrak{D}.\mathrm{T}(pt) \rightarrow \\ &\qquad (\forall t \varepsilon \mathfrak{D}.(t = \sigma x \epsilon \mathfrak{d}.(px \wedge x \ll t)) \rightarrow \mathrm{T}(pt)))\end{aligned}$$

The homogeneous predicates are those that are both collective and distributive:

Definition 3.30

$$\mathsf{homogeneous}(p) =_{\mathrm{def}} \mathsf{distributive}(p) \;\&\; \mathsf{collective}(p)$$

As with plurals (§3.1.3), the denotable of which all other denotables are a part (top) can be given as:

Definition 3.31 *The top element* $\top$ *of the denotables is the supremum of all denotable terms (cf. Definition 3.14).*

$$\top =_{\mathrm{def}} \sigma x\epsilon\mathfrak{d}.(x \approx x)$$

Complement can be defined as:

Definition 3.32 *The complement* $\overline{s}$ *of the supremum* s *of denotables having property* p *is the supremum of denotables not having property* p *(cf. Definition 3.15).*

$$\overline{\sigma x\epsilon\mathfrak{d}.t} =_{\mathrm{def}} \sigma x\epsilon\mathfrak{d}.\neg t$$

Again, a bottom element $\bot$ can be defined as $\overline{\top}$, but it cannot be proven that $\mathfrak{D}\bot$.

Note that, as with the plural domain, it is possible to make $+$ definitional by way of the following equality:

$$\sigma x\epsilon\mathfrak{d}.px + \sigma x\epsilon\mathfrak{d}.qx = \sigma x\epsilon\mathfrak{d}.(px \vee qx)$$

To implement the formal semantics of natural language in a Montague style using $\mathrm{PT}^{\mathfrak{D}}$ we can follow the account in Chapter 2 (§2.3.3) and define a restricted set of types, constrained to denotables, as in $\mathrm{PT}^{\mathfrak{P}}$ (§3.1.3):

Definition 3.33 *(cf. Definition 3.16)*

$$\mathsf{Det}_{\mathfrak{D}}(f) =_{\mathrm{def}} \forall x(\mathsf{Pty}_{\mathfrak{D}}(x) \rightarrow \mathsf{Quant}_{\mathfrak{D}}(fx))$$

Definition 3.34 *(cf. Definition 3.17)*

$$\mathsf{Quant}_{\mathfrak{D}}(f) =_{\mathrm{def}} \forall x(\mathsf{Pty}_{\mathfrak{D}}(x) \rightarrow \mathrm{P}(fx))$$

The function space predicates can also be defined as before:

Definition 3.35 *(cf. Definition 3.18)*

$$(P \Longrightarrow Q)_{\mathfrak{D}}(f) =_{\mathrm{def}} \forall x(P(x) \rightarrow Q(fx))$$

These axioms are no stronger than those given in $\mathrm{PT}^{\mathfrak{P}}$; the theory of plurals in PT. As this is the case, a model of PT extended with plural terms will also be a model of this theory of potentially atomless terms. Although the model may possess atoms, this has no effect on a proof of the consistency of this logic.

3.3 A UNIFICATION

The proposals given here for the domain of mass terms, $\mathrm{PT}^{\mathfrak{D}}$ (§3.2.2), and that of plurals, $\mathrm{PT}^{\mathfrak{P}}$ (§3.1.3), are very similar. The key difference is that the plural domain is atomic.[66] In principle, we should be able to manage with just one domain which is inherently not provably atomic, but which can be strengthened so that the extensions of count expressions are atomic. To this end, we can define the notion of *singular* (Sing) as follows:

Definition 3.36 *A singular is a property of denotables which, if it holds of a denotable, does not hold of any of its denotable parts.*[67]

$$\mathsf{Sing}(p) =_{\mathrm{def}} \mathsf{Pty}_{\mathfrak{D}}(p)\ \& \\ \forall x\varepsilon\mathfrak{D}.(\mathrm{T}(px) \rightarrow \sim\exists y\varepsilon\mathfrak{D}.(y \leq x\ \&\ \mathrm{T}(py)\ \&\ y \neq x))$$

For the next axiom we first require a notation that links a singular property with its plural form.

Definition 3.37 *If p is a singular property, ${}^{\mathsf{p}}p$ will denote its (improper) plural form.*[68]

The intention of the axiom is to state that any supremum of terms that have the singular property s will have the plural property ${}^{\mathsf{p}}s$:

Axiom 3.21 *If some denotables each have the singular property p, then the supremum of those denotables has the plural property ${}^{\mathsf{p}}p$.*

$$\forall p(\mathsf{Sing}(p) \rightarrow \\ \forall q(\mathsf{Pty}_{\mathfrak{D}}(q)\ \&\ \forall x\varepsilon\mathfrak{D}.(\mathrm{T}(qx) \rightarrow \mathrm{T}(px)) \rightarrow \mathrm{T}({}^{\mathsf{p}}p(\sigma x\epsilon\mathfrak{d}.qx)))))$$

[66] We will restrict the discussion to non-classifier languages. Note, however, that classifier languages could also be given a unified extension, where the relevant notion of "atomicity" is given by the classifiers, rather than by singular count nouns.

[67] It might be thought that there are singular properties which do hold of their denotable parts, counter to this axiom, namely the so-called "group denoting" singular nouns (§3.1.4). We follow Barker, and take the extensions of such properties to be singular terms that are systematically related to the appropriate plurality (Barker 1992). Thus the notion of 'part of' which allows us to deduce, for example, that part of a "group" can also be a "group" does not correspond directly to the formal notion $\leq$ in this axiom.

[68] The improper plural form subsumes the singular form: ${}^{\mathsf{p}}p$ will hold of one or more ps, as opposed to the two or more with English plurals.

This is a generalisation of the intuition that the sum of two terms with the singular property s have the plural property ${}^{\mathsf{p}}s$:

$$\forall p \forall a \varepsilon \mathfrak{D}.(\mathsf{Sing}(p) \,\&\, \mathrm{T}(pa) \,\&\, \mathrm{T}(pb) \rightarrow \mathrm{T}({}^{\mathsf{p}}p(a+b)))$$

There must also be a means of relating terms in the extension of a pluralised property with those in the extension of the singular property:

Axiom 3.22 *A term in the extension of a pluralised property must be founded on terms that are in the extension of the singular property.*

$$\forall p(\mathsf{Sing}(p) \rightarrow \forall u \varepsilon \mathfrak{D}.(\mathrm{T}({}^{\mathsf{p}}pu) \rightarrow \\ \exists q(\mathsf{Pty}_{\mathfrak{D}}(q) \,\&\, \forall x(\mathrm{T}(qx) \rightarrow \mathrm{T}(px)) \,\&\, u = \sigma x \epsilon \mathfrak{d}.qx)))$$

This is effectively the converse of the previous axiom. Taking these two axioms together, a plural property holds of a term if and only if that term is the fusion of terms having the singular property.

The equivalence:

$$\sigma x \epsilon \mathfrak{d}.px = \sigma x \epsilon \mathfrak{d}.{}^{\mathsf{p}}px$$

can be proven, where p is a singular property.

If a plural property holds of a term, but does not hold of any proper part of that term, then it must be the case that the underlying singular property also holds of the term:

Axiom 3.23 *If a denotable has the property ${}^{\mathsf{p}}p$, (where p is a singular property) and no proper part of it does, then it also has the property p.*

$$\forall p \forall x \varepsilon \mathfrak{D}.((\mathsf{Sing}(p) \,\&\, \mathrm{T}({}^{\mathsf{p}}px) \,\&\, \\ \sim \exists y \varepsilon \mathfrak{D}.(y \leq x \,\&\, y \neq x \,\&\, \mathrm{T}({}^{\mathsf{p}}py))) \rightarrow \mathrm{T}(px))$$

There have been other proposals that seek to give a unified account of mass terms and plurals (Chierchia 1998, Gillon 1992, Link 1983). We take it that plurals are mereological terms that are provably atomic, whereas mass terms may be atomic, but we cannot prove it. Chierchia takes mass terms to be atomic, but the nature of the atoms is vague or implicit. The difference between mass terms and plurals then lies in the fact that the extensions of mass terms are qualitatively homogeneous sublattices, whereas plurals are underpinned by singulars whose extensions are associated with atoms. On his account, mass terms have "plurality built in"; the distinction between the plural and singular of a mass noun is "neutralised." Any attempt to give a mass term a plural morphology then fails simply because mass terms are already pluralised. Semantically, Chierchia's pluralisation operator will yield the empty set when applied to mass terms (Chierchia 1998). In the unification sketched here, we could take the pluralisation operator $^{\mathfrak{p}}$ to correspond to morphological pluralisation. Its behaviour is then undefined for terms that are already plural.

More work is needed to see how well such a semantic unification can be made to fit the relevant empirical facts, such as those governing the combination of numerals with plurals and mass terms, and the nature of the quantifiers with which they can felicitously appear. We might also wish to amend this theory (and perhaps the formalisation of $\mathrm{PT}^{\mathfrak{P}}$) to capture the notion of a proper plural, in order to allow us to enforce semantic number agreement between properties and their arguments in felicitous propositions.[69]

3.4 A Model of PT with Boolean Terms

We can show that $\mathrm{PT}^{\mathfrak{D}}$ (§3.2.2) and $\mathrm{PT}^{\mathfrak{P}}$ (§3.1.3)—PT with mass terms and plurals, respectively—are consistent if we can provide a (non-trivial) model which verifies all their axioms. We require the model of PT (§2.6) to be strengthened in order to satisfy the axioms for plural or denotable terms. Link and Lønning have both effectively shown that their axioms, with atomicity, are satisfiable if the denotable domain is a (definably) complete atomic Boolean algebra (where a definably complete atomic Boolean algebra is an atomic Boolean algebra) (Link 1991a, Lønning 1989). As the axioms for plural terms ($\mathrm{PT}^{\mathfrak{P}}$) and denotables ($\mathrm{PT}^{\mathfrak{D}}$) are essentially weaker versions of Link's axioms, then a Boolean algebra should also satisfy them.

We thus need a model of PT in which the natural language denotable/plural terms belong to a (definably) complete (atomic) Boolean algebra. The model we present "naturally" satisfy full completeness, as opposed to definable completeness, but, as we are only interested in demonstrating that $\mathrm{PT}^{\mathfrak{D}}$ and $\mathrm{PT}^{\mathfrak{P}}$ are consistent, then the model can be stronger than these theories: even if we only need definable completeness for both theories, it does not matter if we actually have full completeness in the model, nor, in the case of $\mathrm{PT}^{\mathfrak{D}}$, does it matter that the Boolean algebra is atomic.

A wff φ of PT is valid in a model $\mathcal{M}$ iff $\mathcal{M} \models_g \varphi$ for all assignment functions g, where $\mathcal{M}$ is defined as in §2.6. For a model of $\mathrm{PT}^{\mathfrak{D}}$ (and $\mathrm{PT}^{\mathfrak{P}}$) we need a stronger base model than $\mathcal{M}$. We require those terms representing denotables to form a complete (atomic) Boolean algebra. Models of the λ-calculus, in general, do not possess these properties. This problem can be addressed by giving a substructure of $\mathcal{M}$ the desired

[69] This enhancement would be required by any practical implementation of the discourse representation theory PT^{dt} of Chapter 5.

properties, and letting the natural language denotable terms (or plural terms) denote appropriate objects in this structure. Thus, denotable objects will form a sub-domain.

A Complete Atomic Boolean Algebra

A Complete Atomic Boolean Algebra B is given by the following axioms:[70]

(i) B contains at least 2 elements.

(ii) If $a, b \in B$ then $a' \in B$ and $a \sqcup b \in B$.

(iii) If $a, b \in B$ then $a \sqcup b = b \sqcup a$.

(iv) If $a, b, c \in B$ then $a \sqcup (b \sqcup c) = (a \sqcup b) \sqcup c$.

(v) For all $a, b \in B$, if there is some $c \in B$ such that $a \sqcup b' = c \sqcup c'$ then $a \sqcup b = a$.

(vi) For all $a, b, c \in B$ if $a \sqcup b = a$ then $a \sqcup b' = c \sqcup c'$.

(vii) For all $a \neq (c \sqcup c') \in B$ there exists $u \in B$, such that $u \sqcup a = q$ and for all $i \in B$ such that $i \sqcup u = u$ either $i = (c \sqcup c')$ or $i = u$.

(viii) Any (non-empty) set $E \subseteq A$ has a least upper-bound, $\bigsqcup E \in A$.

The axioms (i)–(vi) characterise a Boolean algebra. Axiom (vii) makes the algebra atomic. Axiom (viii) makes it complete. The notions *bottom* $\mathbf{0}$; *top* $\mathbf{1}$; *meet* $a \sqcap b$; and *difference* $a - b$ can be defined:

$$\mathbf{0} =_{\text{def}} a \sqcup a'$$
$$\mathbf{1} =_{\text{def}} \mathbf{0}'$$
$$a \sqcap b =_{\text{def}} (a' \sqcup b')'$$
$$a - b =_{\text{def}} a \sqcap b'$$

There is one well-known theorem that will be of use later:

Lemma 3.1 *In an atomic Boolean algebra, every element is the supremum of the atoms it dominates (each element of B is* defined *by the atoms it dominates).*

Proof. From Halmos (Halmos 1963): each element $p \in B$ is an upper-bound of the set of atoms $E \subseteq B$ that it dominates. We must demonstrate that if r is an arbitrary bound of E, then $p \sqsubseteq r$. Assume otherwise, that $p - r \sqsubseteq \mathbf{0}$. From atomicity it follows there is a $q \in B$ where $q \sqsubseteq p - r$. As $p - r \sqsubseteq p$, the atom $q \in E$. But since $(q \sqcap r) \sqsubseteq ((p - r) \sqcap r)$ this contradicts that r is an upper-bound of E. □

We can draw two corollaries from this result:

[70] These axioms are adapted from those given by Hughes and Cresswell (Hughes and Cresswell 1973)

Corollary 3.1 *Different collections of atoms have different suprema.*

Corollary 3.2 *Different suprema dominate different atoms.*

Definition 3.38 *Let* $\mathcal{M}_{\mathfrak{D}} = \langle \mathcal{D}, T, P, B \rangle$ $(\mathcal{M}_{\mathfrak{P}} = \langle \mathcal{D}, T, P, B \rangle)$ *be a model of* $\mathrm{PT}^{\mathfrak{D}}$ $(\mathrm{PT}^{\mathfrak{P}})$*. Where* $B : D \longrightarrow \{0, 1\}$ *characterises those elements of* D *that are in a complete atomic Boolean sub-domain of* D*, with the same ordering and join operator.*

We can now express the conditions for $\mathfrak{D}(t), t \leq t'$:

$$\begin{array}{lll} \mathcal{M}_{\Delta} \models_g \mathfrak{D}(t) & \text{iff} & B(\mathcal{I}[t]_g) = 1 \\ \mathcal{M}_{\Delta} \models_g t \leq t' & \text{iff} & \mathcal{I}[t]_g \sqsubseteq \mathcal{I}[t']_g \end{array}$$

Thus, natural language denotable terms denote items in the complete atomic Boolean algebra. To give a model for the plural denotables, as opposed to the potentially atomless, mereological denotables, $\mathfrak{D}$ can be replaced by $\mathfrak{P}$ in the above.

As it does not matter what "non-denoting" definite descriptors denote, the definite descriptor $\sigma x \varphi$ can be given the following interpretation:

$$\mathcal{I}[\sigma x \varphi]_g = \bigsqcup \{a : T(\mathcal{I}[\varphi]_{g[a/x]}) = 1\}$$

We will demonstrate that the axioms given for plural denotables in $\mathrm{PT}^{\mathfrak{P}}$ are satisfied by the model. As the axioms for a potentially atomless mereology in $\mathrm{PT}^{\mathfrak{D}}$ are weaker, they too will be satisfied by the model.

Theorem 3.1 *The summation operator* $+$ *is symmetric, idempotent and associative (Axioms 3.1; 3.2; 3.3):*

Proof. Trivial: the summation operator is modelled by the lattice theoretic join $\sqcup$ which is also symmetric, idempotent and associative. □

Theorem 3.2 *The domain of plurals is closed (Axiom 3.5).*

$$(\mathfrak{P}a \;\&\; \mathfrak{P}b) \rightarrow \mathfrak{P}(a + b)$$

Proof. From the axioms of the Boolean algebra: if $a, b \in B$, then $a \sqcup b \in B$. □

Theorem 3.3 *The domain of plurals is (definably) complete (Axiom 3.6).*

$$\forall p((\mathsf{Pty}(p) \;\&\; \forall x(\mathrm{T}(px) \rightarrow \mathfrak{P}(x)) \;\&\; \exists x(\mathrm{T}(px))) \rightarrow \mathfrak{P}(\sigma x p x))$$

Proof. From the completeness of the Boolean algebra: $X \subseteq B$, then $\bigsqcup X \in B$. The axiom is weaker, as it requires that there is a plural denotable in the extension of the property. □

Theorem 3.4 *Different plural denotables have different atoms (Axiom 3.7).*

$$\forall xy\varepsilon\mathfrak{P}.(x \not\leq y \rightarrow \exists u\varepsilon\mathfrak{P}.(\mathfrak{A}u \;\&\; u \leq x \;\&\; u \not\leq y))$$

Proof. From Corollary 3.2. □

Theorem 3.5 *Plurals within the extension of a property (of plurals) must have an upper-bound (Axiom 3.8).*

$$\forall p\forall y\varepsilon\mathfrak{P}.((\mathsf{Pty}_{\mathfrak{P}}(p) \;\&\; \mathrm{T}(py)) \rightarrow y \leq \sigma x\epsilon\mathfrak{p}.px)$$

Proof. The axioms of the Boolean algebra define $\bigsqcup X$ as an upper-bound on the members of the set $X \subseteq B$. The supremum operator σ is modelled by $\bigsqcup$. Further, all PT definable properties of plurals will have an extension within B. □

Theorem 3.6 *The supremum of the extension of a property of plurals is the smallest plural, which dominates all the terms in the extension (Axiom 3.9).*

$$\forall p\forall y\varepsilon\mathfrak{P}.((\mathsf{Pty}_{\mathfrak{P}}(p) \;\&\; \forall x\varepsilon\mathfrak{P}.(\mathrm{T}(px) \rightarrow x \leq y)) \rightarrow \sigma x\epsilon\mathfrak{p}.px \leq y)$$

Proof. From the axioms of the Boolean algebra: $\bigsqcup X$ is the *least* upper-bound of X, where $X \subseteq B$. □

Theorem 3.7 *Different atoms in the plural domain have different suprema (Axiom 3.10).*

$$\forall p\forall u\varepsilon\mathfrak{P}.((\mathsf{Pty}_{\mathfrak{P}}(p) \;\&\; \mathfrak{A}u \;\&\; u \leq \sigma x\epsilon\mathfrak{p}.px) \rightarrow \exists z\varepsilon\mathfrak{P}.(\mathrm{T}(pz) \;\&\; u \leq z))$$

Proof. From Corollary 3.1. □

3.5 CONCLUSIONS

The issues addressed here may not seem to be central to the concerns of natural language semantics; they do not add significantly to the coverage of natural language phenomena. However, the major contribution of this theory of plurals and mass terms is intended to be a formalist one, concerning the appropriate approach to producing formal semantic theories; it presents an essentially *axiomatic* formal semantics of plurals and mass terms. In part, it is the axiomatic method that leads to some novelty in the coverage of non-denoting terms and atomicity, as it provides a fairly direct way of allowing the theory to be deliberately incomplete in a useful manner; an axiomatic system can remain silent on issues which are irrelevant for the purposes of the theory. This gives us the means to explore the weakest theory that produces the desired behaviour.

This methodology can be applied to other phenomena. Indeed, this is the approach taken by PT when confronted by "paradoxical" terms: the theory is too weak to show that they are propositions, and hence too weak to give them truth values. When the objective of an axiomatic system is to capture certain intuitions, if these become unclear on issues that are independent of the core points we wish to capture, then the axioms can be made to be incomplete with respect to these more debatable points. Our mereology, $PT^{\mathfrak{D}}$, is incomplete with respect to the proof of both the existence of atoms, and the nature of a bottom element. The inappropriate predication of non-denoting terms can be assigned to the same conceptual dustbin as other category mistakes, such as paradoxical assertions.

Broadly speaking, axiomatic semantics could be seen as being in contrast to a model-theoretic approach, which aims to look for some mathematical structure, or system which appears to display the appropriate behaviour.[71] This structure is then used as a model for the formal semantics of natural language. The representation is made to adopt the behaviour of this model by asserting that all the entailments of the model are legitimate inferences in the representation (completeness), and all inferences in the representation are supported by the model (soundness). By insisting that the entailments of the representation are precisely those of the model, there is a possibility that artifacts of the model may lead to too strong a logic. For example, if the model employs a type hierarchy to avoid self-application paradoxes, as in Montague semantics, then the constraints of the strongly typed regime are inherited by the semantic representation, even if not justified by (or even counter to) consider-

[71] To an extent, the dichotomy between axiomatic and model-theoretic semantics is an artificial one; for example, set-theoretic models can be presented axiomatically. The difference is perhaps more one of practice, where the axiomatic and model-theoretic methodologies both lie on a spectrum of possibilities. A "pure" model-theoretic approach would be to map natural language into some independently motivated mathematical structure. In practice, these structures might be strengthened or weakened by adding or deleting axioms. Also, an axiomatic system can adopt independently motivated structures. The axiomatic formalisation proposed here embodies the methodology of least commitment; we do not want to be committed to artifacts of such structures unless these artifacts correspond to behaviours of the system which we seek to formalise.

ations of natural language itself. Demanding completeness requires all issues to be decided one way or another, even when our intuitions provide no useful insight.

Although we could adopt a model-theoretic approach in which our models are incomplete in the way that mimics the incompleteness of our axioms,[72] it seems better first to establish the appropriate behaviour of the phenomena in question and then axiomatise this in a suitable framework. These axioms, together with inference rules such as *Modus Ponens* and Universal Generalisation, allow the representation to be used directly for performing proofs. A model that satisfies these axioms is only required in order to show that the theory is consistent. The framework chosen here, PT, has a fine-grained intensionality that is suitable for capturing the intensional aspects of natural language. The weakness of the theory means that no implicit, and possibly erroneous assumptions are made concerning valid natural language inferences. The theory can be strengthened with axioms that satisfy our intuitions, as required. Only those aspects of behaviour of which we are certain need be axiomatised. Any term whose status is in doubt can be left unanalysed, as here in the representation non-denoting terms, and predication of non-denoting terms.

What does not seem to be in any doubt is that the semantics of plurals and mass terms both require a genuine strengthening of the theory; it is not possible to account for the data in a classical, quantified logic with unstructured terms. This is in contrast to the phenomena addressed in the following two chapters.

[72]For example, if we model mass terms and plurals in a classical mereology, we remain neutral as to whether or not the structure is atomic.

4

Roles and Guises

In this chapter, we reappraise Landman's formal theory of "intensional individuals" (Landman 1989) within Property Theory (PT) (Chapter 2) (Turner 1990, Turner 1992). Landman's theory seeks to characterise the behaviour of individuals acting under some "role" or "guise." As some of his axioms are required merely because of the strong typing of his representation, casting his ideas in weakly typed PT produces a simpler theory.

However, there is the possibility of an even greater simplification: if roles, or guises, are represented by "property modifiers" then there is no need for Landman's intensional individuals. Landman's argument against the use of property modifiers is re-examined, and shown to be mistaken. This suggests that there is no need to complicate the ontology of individuals in order to account for Landman's examples of intensional individuals; the intensionality of his example can be seen to reside in the properties that we predicate of individuals, and not within the individuals themselves.

4.1 Intensional Individuals

Landman is concerned with the problem of representing sentences involving reference to individuals acting under different guises, and in particular, how to allow the predication of mutually exclusive properties of the same individual when referred to under different guises. The following example illustrates the problem:

> The judge is strict.
> John is liberal.
> John is the judge.

It seems that all three statements can be true, even if 'strict' and 'liberal' are taken to be contradictory (Landman 1989). However, in a standard analysis we would predicate *strict′* of 'The judge', and *liberal′* of 'John'. The third sentence would give rise to an assertion of equality between

'John' and 'the judge'. This would then allow us to infer that "John is strict" contradicting the statement that "John is liberal." Similarly, from the equality of 'The judge' and 'John', we can infer that "The judge is liberal." contrary to the original claim. Thus, with the standard analysis of individuals, predication and equality, if all three sentences are true together then we obtain a contradiction. This, according to Landman, is contrary to our intuitions; we may entertain circumstances in which all three sentences are true together without contradication.

Another of Landman's examples helps to clarify this issue; from the sentences:

> The judge earns exacty \$50,000.
> The janitor earns exactly \$10,000.
> John is the judge, in his spare time he is the janitor.

we should be able to conclude (3), and not (1) or (2):

(1) John earns exactly \$50,000.

(2) John earns exactly \$10,000.

(3) John earns exactly \$60,000.

However, on the standard interpretation of individuals and their equality criteria, we can infer both (1) and (2), leading to a contradiction.

Landman suggests that a contradiction can be avoided in the representation of these examples if the nominals are taken to refer to individuals acting under some role, or guise. According to this view, the sentences in the first example give rise to the following interpretation:[73]

> John-as-a-judge is strict.
> John-as-himself is liberal.

With the sentences:

> The janitors are on strike.
> The judges are not on strike.

it may be the case that a person, John, is both a judge and a janitor. Landman seeks to avoid any contradiction by taking the following to be the appropriate consequence:

> John-as-a-janitor is on strike.
> John-as-a-judge is not on strike.

Landman gives a formal theory in which these intensional (or "restricted") individuals can be represented. He takes these objects to be of the same type as generalised quantifiers.

[73]Note that these are taken to be paraphrases of the formalisation. It is not our intention to address the semantics of natural language '... as a ...' constructions.

The formal framework in which Landman presents his ideas is strongly typed. This creates complications for any theory of plural individuals, as it requires that we have two plural domains, one for ordinary individuals, and one for intensional individuals. For this reason, he suggests that it might be useful to examine these ideas in a more weakly typed framework. This is one goal of the chapter: we will see how Landman's ideas can be simplified by taking individuals under guises to be a new class of terms in PT.

It could be argued that PT is *too* weakly typed, as there is no constraint on term formation: we may formally keep iterating the construction of individuals under guises. It is not intuitively obvious what function, if any, such iterated constructions might have in natural language semantics. The absence of relevant intuitions could be reflected by adopting axioms that enforce no particular behaviour on such constructions.

There is an alternative analysis of these examples, where sentences involving apparently intensional individuals give rise to the modification of a property, rather than a modification of an individual. Landman agrees that this analysis could be used in many cases, but he presents examples involving comparatives which he claims can only be represented by way of individuals under guises. However, a re-examination of the truth conditions of these examples shows that they *can* be treated with property modifiers. As it is weakly typed, PT is a useful vehicle for a theory of property modifiers: a term can be taken to be both a property and a property modifier.

4.2 Landman's Formal Theory

Landman's formal theory is constructed within a strongly typed intensional logic, based upon Thomason's model of propositional attitudes (Thomason 1980). The intensional individuals form quantifiers rather than terms.

In Landman's formal theory, if t is a term and P is a predicate, then $t{\restriction}P$ is an expression denoting t restricted to its aspect of being a P. The expression $t{\restriction}P$ is not a new term. Landman cannot analyse it in this way as, the logic he adopts has an impoverished language of terms.

Properties are of type $\langle e, p\rangle$. The denotation of NPs are second-order properties of type $\langle\langle e, p\rangle, p\rangle$. John in all his aspects, $\lambda P(Pj)$, is such a second-order property. John, himself, is of type e. John-as-a-P is $j{\restriction}P$, where j is of type e, P of type $\langle e, p\rangle$ and $j{\restriction}P$ of type $\langle\langle e, p\rangle, p\rangle$. This is summarised in Table 3.

The expression:

$$(j{\restriction}\mathit{Judge}')(\mathit{Strike}')$$

represents the proposition that John, as a judge, is on strike.

Notion	Representation	Type
Properties	P	$\langle e, p\rangle$
Noun phrases	*Generalised quantifiers*	$\langle\langle e, p\rangle, p\rangle$
John, in all his aspects	$\lambda P(Pj)$	$\langle\langle e, p\rangle, p\rangle$
John (himself)	j	e
John-as-a-P	$j{\restriction}P$	$\langle\langle e, p\rangle, p\rangle$

TABLE 3 Landman's Representations

4.2.1 LANDMAN'S AXIOMS

The first three axioms concern the nature of individuals under roles:

(i) $(j{\restriction}J)\lambda x(x = j)$ (John-as-a-judge is John.)

(ii) $(j{\restriction}J)(J)$ (John-as-a-judge is a judge.)

(iii) $(j{\restriction}\lambda x(x = j)) = \lambda P(Pj)$ (John-as-John is John.)

The next four axioms give "predication" of restricted individuals the expected behaviour:

(iv) $(j{\restriction}J)(P)\ \&\ (j{\restriction}J)(Q) \rightarrow (j{\restriction}J)\lambda x(Px\ \&\ Qx)$

(v) $(j{\restriction}J)(P)\ \&\ P \vdash Q \rightarrow (j{\restriction}J)(Q)$

(vi) $\sim\exists P((j{\restriction}J)(\lambda x(Px\ \&\ \sim Px)))$

(vii) $\forall P((j{\restriction}J)(\lambda x(Px \vee \sim Px)))$

Essentially, Axioms (iv) and (v) make restricted terms act as filters of properties, Axiom (vi) additionally makes them proper filters, and Axiom (vii), ultra-filters.

The final axiom seeks to constrain the appearance of restricted individuals:

(viii) $(j{\restriction}J)(P) \rightarrow J(j)$

Presumably, this last axiom is intended to enforce the requirement that the restricted individual 'John-as-a-judge' can only appear as the argument of a predicate P if John is a judge. However, this is not what the axiom expresses. Furthermore, Landman's formal requirements are too strong: they result in a trivial or contradictory theory.

Theorem 4.1 *Landman's axioms allow all individuals to have all predicates hold of them.*

Proof. Consider any individual i and property P. Axiom (ii) $(i{\restriction}P)(P)$ provides the antecedent for Axiom (viii) $(i{\restriction}P)(Q) \rightarrow P(i)$. An application of *Modus Ponens* thus yields $P(i)$. □

This suggests that the axioms should only consider an individual under some guise if the individual has that guise as a property. That is, we should only consider the expression $(i \restriction p)$ as a restricted individual if p holds of i. Although not captured by Landman's axioms, this does seem to be his intention.

In effect, we require a semantic, rather than a syntactic constraint on the expressions that are considered to be meaningful. This cannot be achieved in the formalism adopted by Landman, but it is exactly how the class of propositions are formalised in PT.

Four of Landman's axioms are concerned with overcoming the strong typing of the representation, and just give "predication" of individuals under guises the expected behaviour. In his initial system, only singular individuals can be restricted. If plural individuals are considered, then both the theory of plurals, and the theory of intensional individuals need to be strengthened. For these reasons, he suggests that the theory may be more appropriately treated in a weakly typed theory such as PT. In addition, he notes that individuals under guises could be represented as terms, rather than generalised quantifiers. This is the approach adopted in the initial property-theoretic treatment, below.

4.3 ROLES IN PT

We can embody Landman's ideas in PT.[74] This results in a logic similar to Landman's but without the complications of types, where all individuals are terms. Those of Landman's axioms which are used to overcome strong typing correspond with theorems of this PT formalisation. Any structure imposed on the terms, such as a Boolean algebra-like structure used in the semantics of plurals, can be imposed uniformly on all terms without strengthening the theory.

4.3.1 ROLES IN PT, INFORMALLY

We must limit those objects considered to represent intensional individuals. Presumably, a term may only be considered under the guise of having a property if it has that property. It is not desirable to restrict the formation of terms themselves, as this would require a complete change to the character of the underlying Property Theory. The class of terms considered felicitously to represent intensional individuals must instead be restricted, just as those terms considered as propositions and properties are restricted, without restricting the language of terms. We can define a new predicate $\mathfrak{R}$ in the language of wff which characterises

[74]The axioms are weakened in a manner implicit in the text of his paper in order to avoid an inconsistent or trivial theory.

intensional individuals. A *restricted term* of the form $i{\restriction}p$ (i under the guise of being p), will only be in $\mathfrak{R}$ if p is a property which holds of i:

$$\mathfrak{R}(i{\restriction}p) \leftrightarrow (\mathsf{Pty}(p) \mathbin{\&} \mathrm{T}(pi))$$

Via the definition of Pty, this is provably equivalent to:

$$\mathfrak{R}(i{\restriction}p) \leftrightarrow \mathrm{T}(pi)$$

Additionally, we can add an operator $\Downarrow$ to the language of terms. Given an intensional individual, this will return the "naked" individual that underlies it. We can also give an "internal" form, $\mathfrak{r}$, of the predicate $\mathfrak{R}$, for use in intensional contexts.

4.3.2 Roles in PT, Formally

To the basic vocabulary of the language of terms in PT (§2.2) is added:

Predicative constant:	$\mathfrak{r}$
Operative constants:	${\restriction}, \Downarrow$

The theory is governed by the axioms of the λ-calculus as before. The language of wff is also as before.

We can define $\mathfrak{R}$ so that it satisfies $\mathfrak{R}(i{\restriction}p) \leftrightarrow \mathrm{T}(pi)$:

Definition 4.1 *Restricted terms.*

$$\mathfrak{R}(x) =_{\text{def}} \exists pi(\mathsf{Pty}(p) \mathbin{\&} (i{\restriction}p) = x \mathbin{\&} \mathrm{T}(pi))$$

The intuition behind Landman's Axiom (viii) is embodied in this definition: if we can consider the restricted term of 'John under the aspect of being a judge', then John is a judge.

The term $\mathfrak{r}$, the internal analogue of $\mathfrak{R}$, can be given the following truth conditions:

Axiom 4.1 *"Internalised" $\mathfrak{R}$.*

$$\mathsf{Pty}(p) \rightarrow (\mathrm{T}(\mathfrak{r}(t{\restriction}p)) \leftrightarrow \mathfrak{R}(t{\restriction}p))$$

Note that we could define $\mathfrak{r}$ by:

$$\Theta pi(\varpi(p) \wedge i{\restriction}p \approx x \wedge px)$$

where ϖ is the internal analogue of Pty such that:[75]

$$\mathsf{Pty}(p) \rightarrow \mathrm{P}(\varpi(p))$$
$$\mathsf{Pty}(p) \rightarrow (\mathrm{T}(\varpi(p)) \leftrightarrow \mathsf{Pty}(p))$$

In this case, Axiom 4.1 becomes a theorem.

[75] We cannot fully internalise ϖ by stating that $\mathsf{Pty}(\varpi)$ as this leads to inconsistency via the paradoxes, as with the internalisations of T and P (§2.5).

In Landman's theory, 'John-as-a-judge' has the property of being equal to 'John' (Axiom (i)). In PT this is of little use: to say that 'John-as-a-judge' is 'John' amounts to losing the distinction between terms and restricted terms. It is better, in this formalisation, to say that the *underlying individual* of 'John-as-a-judge' is 'John'. In PT we first must preface this with the restriction that 'John-as-a-judge' is a legitimate restricted term:

Axiom 4.2 *The "extension" of 'i-as-a-p' is i (cf. Axiom (i) of Landman's theory).*

$$\mathfrak{R}(i{\upharpoonright}p) \rightarrow (\Downarrow(i{\upharpoonright}p) = i)$$

Landman's Axiom (ii) says "John-as-a-judge is a judge." Again, the axiom must be weakened so that it only applies to the appropriate terms:

Axiom 4.3 *'i-as-a-p', is a p (cf. Axiom (ii) of Landman's theory).*

$$\mathfrak{R}(i{\upharpoonright}p) \rightarrow \mathrm{T}(p(i{\upharpoonright}p))$$

Axiom (iii) of Landman's theory says 'John-as-John' is the individual sublimation of John. This is motivated by the fact that he takes restricted individuals to be quantifiers (which are of the same type as individual sublimations). When restricted individuals are taken to be terms, it seems more intuitive to have 'John-as-John' being 'John' himself, rather than the individual sublimation of John.

Axiom 4.4 *'i-as-i' is i (cf. Axiom (iii) of Landman's theory).*

$$i{\upharpoonright}(\lambda x(x \approx i)) = i$$

We naturally have guises as proper filters of properties, as an intensional individual is just a term. Because of the strong typing of Landman's base theory, and because he does not take intensional individuals to be terms, additional axioms are required to obtain this behaviour. Further, when plurals are added to Landman's theory he requires two plural structures: one structure for ordinary individuals; and a second for intensional individuals. He also needs type shifting for predicates—to allow them to apply to individuals from both structures—and requires additions to his theory of restricted individuals to cope with plural intensional individuals. In the property-theoretic treatment, only one plural structure is required over the language of terms, and the theory can represent plural intensional individuals with no alterations.

4.3.3 A Problem

As PT is weakly typed, and this formalisation treats both ordinary individuals and intensional individuals as terms, we might question whether limits should be placed on the kinds of objects which can be restricted by roles or guises. For example, can a restricted term, representing an intensional individual, itself be further restricted? The term:

$$(j{\restriction}J){\restriction}H$$

exists, according to the weak syntax of the language of terms, but should it be in $\mathfrak{R}$? It cannot just be made equivalent to:

$$j{\restriction}\lambda x(Jx \wedge Hx)$$

because the existence of the former presupposes $\mathrm{T}(H(j{\restriction}J))$, whilst the latter would presuppose $\mathrm{T}(Hj)$.

Taken in combination with a theory of plural terms, such as $\mathrm{PT}^{\mathfrak{P}}$ (Chapter 3, §3.1.3), we may enquire whether sums of restricted terms themselves can be restricted:

$$((j{\restriction}J) + (b{\restriction}H)){\restriction}S$$

where $(j{\restriction}J) + (b{\restriction}H)$ is the plural sum of $(j{\restriction}J)$ and $(b{\restriction}H)$.

It is possible to have axioms that are too weak to decide these issues, or to assume that they never arise in the consideration of natural language semantics. However, rather than pursue the question of iterated constructions here, we shall turn to an alternative analysis of the examples using "property modifiers," where the appropriate behaviour can be obtained by considering theories of natural language modifiers, such as adjectives and adverbs. This will bring into question the need to take intensional individuals as a new basic category in the ontology of natural language semantics.

4.4 Property Modifiers

Landman notes that in many cases, such as when the proposition consists of just a simple property predicated of an individual, there is an equivalent analysis available where the appropriate role is taken to modify the property, rather than the individual (Landman 1987). Instead of representing the 'strict judge' example as before:

John-as-a-judge is strict.
John-as-himself is liberal.

a property-modifier approach would effectively represent this as:

John is a strict judge.
John is liberal. (or 'John is a liberal person.')

This has some advantages. Property modifiers are already required in the semantics of natural language to represent modifier expressions such as adjectives and adverbs. With this representation, roles can share the axioms and behaviours of such modifiers. A property-modifier analysis of Landman's examples would thus use existing notions, rather than requiring a new category of terms. Also, demonstratives of the same kind do not have to denote different individuals depending upon the relevant role: it is the act of predication that gives rise to intensionality. Thus the demonstratives in the following sentences:

> That is the Morning Star.
> That is the Evening Star.

may denote the same individual, although subsequent predication of the individual will be modified as appropriate.

Landman argues against using a property-modifier analysis in general, because of comparatives such as:

> The judge and the janitor have different incomes.

where the same individual may be both judge and janitor. As the nominals give rise to the roles, there are the same number of roles as there are nominals. If each nominal gives rise to a mention of an individual in the representation, then there will be the same number of roles as mentions of individuals. Thus the representation of this sentence is straightforward if the roles modify individuals. In contrast, according to Landman, the roles cannot give rise to property, or predicate modifiers, as there are two roles but only one modifiable act of predication in this example.[76]

This argument assumes that the application of the verb phrase 'have different incomes' to the subject noun phrase can only be considered to give rise to a single irreducible act of predication. However, against this, and against Landman's counter example, there is nothing to prevent the appropriate truth conditions giving rise to several acts of predication. In particular, there is nothing to prevent there being an equal number of predications as roles, or constituent nominals.[77] This can be seen if the comparative is paraphrased as:

> The income earned *from being a janitor* by the person who is the janitor is different from the income earned *from judging* by the person who is the judge.

If John is both janitor and judge, this becomes:

[76]Note that a role may either modify the main predicate in the verb phrase, or, equivalently, it may be the main predicate, modified by the verb phrase. The latter is assumed in the following representations.

[77]The argument given here has also been presented elsewhere (Fox 1998).

John's income as a judge is different from his income as a janitor.

Assuming that we allow conjoined individuals, as in $\mathrm{PT}^{\mathfrak{P}}$, the truth conditions of the original sentence can be represented by:

$$\begin{aligned}\mathrm{T}(\Xi ab(\ & \mathit{income}'a \wedge \mathit{income}'b \wedge \\ & ((\mathit{earn}'a)\mathit{judge}')(\mathit{The}\cdot\mathit{judge}') \wedge \\ & ((\mathit{earn}'b)\mathit{janitor}')(\mathit{The}\cdot\mathit{janitor}') \wedge \\ & \mathit{different}'(a+b)))\end{aligned}$$

and if John is both judge and janitor, this is equivalent to:

$$\begin{aligned}\mathrm{T}(\Xi ab(\ & \mathit{income}'a \wedge \mathit{income}'b \wedge \\ & ((\mathit{earn}'a)\mathit{judge}')\mathit{John}' \wedge \\ & ((\mathit{earn}'b)\mathit{janitor}')\mathit{John}' \wedge \\ & \mathit{different}'(a+b)))\end{aligned}$$

The property *different*$'$ takes a sum as its argument to ensure a consistent interpretation of conjunction, and to allow arbitrary numbers of terms to be "different." In this particular case, some meaning postulate such as:

$$\mathrm{T}(\mathit{different}'(a+b)) \leftrightarrow a \neq b$$

would have the desired outcome. This could be generalised to arbitrary nominal conjunctions.[78] However, even in the absence of a comprehensive treatment of 'different', we can see that all of Landman's examples can be analysed without recourse to a new category of intensional individuals.

Note that it is possible to define restricted equivalences between a property modifier representation of the examples, and a representation which uses individuals under guises. If we restrict ourselves to truth conditions which give at least one predication relation for each role, and we do not iterate roles, then the following provides an indication of the equivalences between the representations.

Translation 4.1 (Property Modifiers to Restricted Terms) *If we rewrite strict$'$, when acting as a property modifier, as $\lambda p.p(\mathit{strict}')$, and*

---

[78]It is not immediately clear what the appropriate decomposition of 'different' is. A weak reduction would be that one pair of constituent terms in the sum are not equal. A strong one would require that all atomic parts differ from each other. But it is far from obvious that the notion of two individuals differing can be reduced to simple inequality between the corresponding terms; the salient aspect under which individuals is context dependent. Under some circumstances, we might say that two spanners are different (or are the same) because they are of different (or the same) sizes, in other circumstances it might be because they are made of different (or the same) alloys. We can see that there might be a connection between a comprehensive treatment of 'different' and Schwarzschild's proposal for analysing intermediate distribution and reciprocals (Schwarzschild 1992).

judge′, when acting as a property, as $\lambda q \lambda x.q(x \lceil judge')$ *then property modifier expressions are effectively rewritten as expressions involving individuals under guises. That is,* $strict' judge'(x)$ *becomes* $strict'(x \lceil judge')$.

Translation 4.2 (Restricted Terms to Property Modifiers) *Assuming that postfix* $\lceil p$ *is rewritten as a prefix, and we rewrite the property* $strict'$ *as* $\lambda p.p(strict')$, *and the term* $\lceil$ *is defined to be* $\lambda q \lambda x \lambda p(pqx)$ *then propositions given in terms of individuals under guises are equivalent to propositions involving property modifiers. That is,* $strict'(x \lceil judge')$ *becomes* $strict' judge'(x)$.

Thus, at least in the simple cases, Landman's intensional individuals can be taken to be definable in terms of more familiar notions. Of course these translations are incomplete; by themselves they do not account for transitive verbs, for example. However, they give an idea of the relationship between the two different approaches.

An alternative way of illustrating the connection between property modifiers and intensional individuals is to define a function as that maps properties into property modifiers.[79] The expression:

$$\mathsf{as}(p)(q)(i)$$

is intended to assert that i has property q as a p. The notion of 'as-a-judge' can be represented by:

$$\lambda x \lambda p(\mathsf{as}(judge')px)$$

Then 'John-as-a-judge' is expressed by:

$$\lambda q(q(John'))(\lambda x \lambda p(\mathsf{as}(judge')px)) =_\beta \lambda p(\mathsf{as}(judge')p(John'))$$

We can now apply predicates to these "intensional individuals" in the same manner adopted by Landman's formalisation, so that the proposition:

'John-as-a-judge is strict'

is expressed by something like:

$$\lambda p(\mathsf{as}(judge')p(John'))(strict') =_\beta \mathsf{as}(judge')(strict')(John')$$

This indicates quite clearly how Landman's notation for intensional individuals can be taken to be syntactic sugar for a property modifier analysis. Additional axioms would be required to give the term as all the appropriate behaviours. It should be a fairly straight-forward matter to re-express the axioms governing the behaviour of property modifiers (§4.7) in terms of as.

[79] This was suggested by Chierchia (PC), and an anonymous reviewer.

4.5 Appropriate Guises

So far we have just presented the principles of a theory that addresses Landman's examples of apparently intensional individuals. If we are to use such a theory, then we need to consider how to ascertain the appropriate guises, and the nature of anaphoric reference to "intensional individuals" when represented with property modifiers.

When a term is introduced with a common noun, then it seems appropriate, at least in some cases, to take the term to be introduced under the guise of that common noun.[80] This is the approach taken in the next section. With proper nouns, however, we do not have this option. If we have the two sentences:

> John is tall.
> Everest is tall.

we probably mean:

> John is a tall *person.*
> Everest is a tall *mountain.*

yet the appropriate roles are not contained within the sentence. It might be possible for the appropriate guise to be obtained from some sortal hierarchy.

With anaphoric reference, we must decide whether pronouns refer to an individual, the individual under some guise, or whether it is ambiguous. From the sentences:

> Sue is a judge.
> She is strict.

we might wish to conclude:

> Sue is strict.

or:

> Sue is a strict judge.

If pronouns can refer to an individual under a guise, then we need appropriate mechanisms to keep the individual associated with its guise. It may not be immediately apparent how we can do this if we stick rigidly to a property modifier representation. However, it should be pointed out that the argument in favour of property modifiers presented here is intended to show that we do not require a new basic category of terms. That is, all sentences apparently involving individuals under a guise can

[80]There is a parallel here with the default case of Schwarzschild's proposal for intermediate distribution and reciprocals (§3.1.5), when there is no other relevant contextual information (Schwarzschild 1992).

be treated by alternative means. This should not be taken as an argument against using syntactic sugar—where the guise is syntactically associated with the individual—when appropriate.

4.6 SEMANTICS WITH PROPERTY MODIFIERS

In a simple, PTQ-like interpretation (Montague 1973) of natural language semantics, the representations of 'every' and 'some' can be defined by:

$$\begin{aligned} every' &=_{\mathrm{def}} \lambda p \lambda q(\Theta x(px \Rightarrow qx)) \\ some' &=_{\mathrm{def}} \lambda p \lambda q(\Xi x(px \wedge qx)) \end{aligned}$$

We can then derive the following:

$$\begin{aligned} \mathsf{Pty}(p) \;\&\; \mathsf{Pty}(q) \quad &\rightarrow \quad (\mathrm{T}(every'(p)(q)) \leftrightarrow \mathrm{T}(\Theta x(px \Rightarrow qx))) \\ \mathsf{Pty}(p) \;\&\; \mathsf{Pty}(q) \quad &\rightarrow \quad (\mathrm{T}(some'(p)(q)) \leftrightarrow \mathrm{T}(\Xi x(px \wedge qx))) \end{aligned}$$

The axioms of truth (§2.2.2) allow us to go further:

$$\begin{aligned} \mathsf{Pty}(p) \;\&\; \mathsf{Pty}(q) \quad &\rightarrow \quad (\mathrm{T}(every'(p)(q)) \leftrightarrow \forall x(\mathrm{T}(px) \rightarrow \mathrm{T}(qx))) \\ \mathsf{Pty}(p) \;\&\; \mathsf{Pty}(q) \quad &\rightarrow \quad (\mathrm{T}(some'(p)(q)) \leftrightarrow \exists x(\mathrm{T}(px) \;\&\; \mathrm{T}(qx))) \end{aligned}$$

As we are using property modifiers, the truth conditions must be complicated somewhat. Just keeping with the determiners 'every' and 'some', and assuming that $\mathsf{Pty}(p)$ and $(\mathsf{Pty} \Longrightarrow \mathsf{Pty})(q)$, the required truth conditions can be stated as follows:

$$\begin{aligned} \mathrm{T}(every'(p)(q)) &\leftrightarrow \mathrm{T}(\Theta x(px \Rightarrow qpx)) \leftrightarrow \forall x(\mathrm{T}(px) \rightarrow \mathrm{T}(qpx)) \\ \mathrm{T}(some'(p)(q)) &\leftrightarrow \mathrm{T}(\Xi x(px \wedge qpx)) \;\; \leftrightarrow \exists x(\mathrm{T}(px) \;\&\; \mathrm{T}(qpx)) \end{aligned}$$

Notice that the verb phrase and noun combine to form a modified property qp. As mentioned above, this is rather an inadequate treatment; there will be cases when we want other properties appearing in place of p in qpx.

We can incorporate the notion of natural language "denotables" from the previous chapter, so that if $\mathsf{Pty}_{\mathfrak{D}}(p)$ and $(\mathsf{Pty}_{\mathfrak{D}} \Longrightarrow \mathsf{Pty}_{\mathfrak{D}})(q)$, then the truth conditions would be:

$$\begin{aligned} \mathrm{T}(every'(p)(q)) &\leftrightarrow \mathrm{T}(\Theta x \epsilon \mathfrak{d}(px \Rightarrow qpx) \leftrightarrow \forall x \varepsilon \mathfrak{D}.(\mathrm{T}(px) \rightarrow \mathrm{T}(qpx)) \\ \mathrm{T}(some'(p)(q)) &\leftrightarrow \mathrm{T}(\Xi x \epsilon \mathfrak{d}(px \wedge qpx)) \leftrightarrow \exists x \varepsilon \mathfrak{D}.(\mathrm{T}(px) \;\&\; \mathrm{T}(qpx)) \end{aligned}$$

Transitive verbs require some thought. We will consider verbs that are read "transparently"; where the object of the sentence is given an extensional, or *de re* reading. In the PTQ-style analysis, a transitive verb such as 'convicts' would have the semantics:

$$\lambda r x(r(\lambda y(convicts' yx)))$$

We need to amend this so that the sentence:

A judge convicts a criminal.

has something like the following representation:

$$\Xi j(judge' j \wedge \Xi c(criminal' c \wedge (convicts' criminal' c) judge' j))$$

The term $(convicts' criminal' c) judge' j$ is intended to denote the proposition that what j does as a judge is convict c as a criminal. In Landman's notation, this would be:

$$convicts'(c \restriction criminal', j \restriction judge')$$

To obtain the property-modifier interpretation of the sentence, 'convicts' should have the following representation:

$$\lambda rwx(r(\lambda yz(convicts' yzwx)))$$

Basically, wherever a PTQ-style analysis requires a single abstraction for each of the argument of the main relation, there now needs to be two abstractions. The typing of transitive verbs has to be changed to accommodate this difference.

Of course, obtaining such representations does not tell us how, or even whether, the truth conditions of propositions involving property modifiers are related to those of less intensional, PTQ-like representations. In the next section, we look at some of the behaviours that property modifiers might have.

4.7 THE BEHAVIOUR OF PROPERTY MODIFIERS

The sentence 'John is a strict judge' will have the representation:

$$strict' judge' j$$

The word 'strict' is a subsective adjective. Indeed, many of the motivating examples for intensional individuals involve the attribution of an adjective using the copula. Their interpretation as property modifiers then corresponds with them being taken to be subsective, by default. We can take this as motivation for treating all verbs to be the semantic equivalent of a subsective adjective. To avoid undue combinatorial complexity, here we will restrict our attention to intransitive verbs and copula expressions.

Representing non-adjectival syntactic categories as if they were a form of adjective is not a new idea. For example, Hoepelman has suggested that, in the semantics, nouns may be treated as a special case of adjective (Hoepelman 1983).

It is fruitful to look at the kinds of behaviours defined in the literature on the semantics of adjectives, as it transpires that these behaviours are also useful in explaining how to obtain intuitively useful inferences in a semantic theory which uses property modifiers to represent Landman's intensional individuals.

As PT is weakly typed, to some extent we can avoid deciding whether adjectives should be exclusively property modifiers, or properties;[81] there is no need for formal devices, such as operators or dummy predicates, to change the type of a subsective adjective (and property modifiers in general).

We will take property modifiers to be terms that not only modify other properties to produce new properties, but also act as properties in their own right. An example of a property modifier is the term corresponding to 'red'; it produces a proposition when applied to a term—the proposition will be true if that term represents a red object—and when applied to some other property, like 'book', a new property is created, that of being a red book. Unless extra conditions are added, a red book need not be red, but it is a book. Note that we can assume that properties introduced in the representation of natural language are typically properties of denotables (§3.2.2).

Definition 4.2 *A term r is a* property modifier *($\mathfrak{M}_{\mathsf{Pty}}(r)$) if it is a property of denotables which, when given a property of denotables p, forms a new property of denotables rp whose extension is a subset of p's.*

$$\mathfrak{M}_{\mathsf{Pty}}(r) =_{\text{def}} \mathsf{Pty}_{\mathfrak{D}}(r) \mathbin{\&} \forall p(\mathsf{Pty}_{\mathfrak{D}}(p) \rightarrow (\mathsf{Pty}_{\mathfrak{D}}(rp) \mathbin{\&} \forall x \varepsilon \mathfrak{D}.(\mathrm{T}(rpx) \rightarrow \mathrm{T}(px))))$$

It is possible to define notions corresponding to transparent, or predicative adjectives, like those presented by Bunt and Roeper (Bunt 1985, Roeper 1983). For example, if we say that 'a judge died', then from the truth of $died'judge'x$ we should be able to infer that $died'x$. We would then say that $judge'$ is transparent with respect to $died'$. The definition below is intended to give the general principle. If we are interested in producing an empirically adequate semantic theory, then we should explore whether there are any patterns or generalisations in the transparency of properties with respect to property modifiers.

Definition 4.3 *A property (of denotables) p is* transparent *with respect to a property modifier r ($\mathfrak{T}_r(p)$), iff r is a property modifier, and when restricting p, if it holds of denotables x, it also holds of x by itself. Further, if r and p hold of x, by themselves, then rp holds of x.*

$$\mathfrak{T}_r(p) =_{\text{def}} \mathfrak{M}_{\mathsf{Pty}}(r) \mathbin{\&} \mathsf{Pty}_{\mathfrak{D}}(p) \mathbin{\&} \forall x \varepsilon \mathfrak{D}.(\mathrm{T}(rpx) \leftrightarrow (\mathrm{T}(rx) \mathbin{\&} \mathrm{T}(px)))$$

[81] Kamp has compared these two approaches (considering "predicates" rather than "properties") (Kamp 1975).

This is rather like Hoepelman's notion of "strongly predicative adjectives" (Hoepelman 1983), except that here transparency is indexed to *particular* properties of denotables, whereas strongly predicative adjectives are transparent with respect to *all* properties (of denotables). Hoepelman also proposes a notion of "weakly predicative adjectives." As an example, 'red' could be taken to be weakly predicative: a red tomato may be red compared to the existent tomatoes, but we might not wish to class it as unadorned 'red'. It is weakly predicative as a red tomato is definitely not 'unred', the polar opposite of 'red', and a tomato that is truly red is a red tomato. This notion cannot be expressed in this theory as it stands, as there is no formal notion of polar opposites (tall v. short, for example).

We may wish to maintain that all property modifiers are transparent with respect to themselves, echoing one of Landman's axioms, which can be paraphrased as 'John as a judge is a judge' (Landman 1989):

$$\forall p(\mathfrak{M}_{\mathsf{Pty}}(p) \to \mathfrak{T}_p(p))$$

This does not cause the collapse of compound property modifiers, which might be useful in a theory of adjectives: Hoepelman, for example, would use $\mathit{tall}'\mathit{tall}'\mathit{man}'x$ to indicate a man who is tall for a tall man. However, it would cause the collapse of $\mathit{chessplayer}'\mathit{chessplayer}'x$ to just $\mathit{chessplayer}'x$. Hoepelman would prefer to use this to indicate chessplayers who are relatively good at chess, in a body of other chessplayers (Hoepelman 1983).

Landman makes some comments concerning the guise under which an individual is restricted and its relationship to the properties predicated of the restricted individual. For example, 'being well paid' and 'being a judge' both relate to jobs. Landman contends that this gives rise to greater intensionality in the subject of propositions like 'John-as-a-judge is well paid'. He believes that some aspects, or guises, are naturally more intentional than others. An aspect of an individual is more intensional when properties attributed to the individual under that guise are less likely to hold of the individual in itself. According to Landman, 'judge' is more intensional than 'drunk', which is in turn more intensional than 'man with a big nose', for example. If this is accepted, then the notion of transparency proposed here would need some further elaboration to capture these intuitions.

4.8 Conclusions

We have shown that Property Theory allows us to consistently formalise Landman's ideas concerning intensional, or restricted, individuals. This results in a theory that is simpler than Landman's, where some of his axioms become theorems. As all individuals are taken to be terms, the theory is compatible with treatments of plurals without additional complications for either the theory of plurals or that of intensional individuals. All that is required is to add some Boolean algebra-like structure—such as the one in §3.1.3 or §3.2.2—to a class of terms which includes such individuals.

Further, we have seen how all of Landman's examples can be treated using property modifiers. This shows that there is no need to take these individuals under guises as some new category of terms. A property modifier treatment of the examples uses existing notions; property modifiers are already required for the semantics of modifiers such as adjectives and adverbs. The weak typing and the intensionality of PT provides a suitable framework for their representation.

This does not mean that the concept of an individual acting under a guise should not be represented. Indeed, as has been shown, it is possible to define an intensional individual in terms of property modifiers, and *vice versa*. But it does mean that such a notation can be regarded as syntactic sugar, rather than an argument for re-appraising the ontology of individuals required for the semantics of natural language.

Here, we have looked at property modifiers in isolation. In a more comprehensive semantic theory, we would have to see how they can be integrated with theories concerning more conventional modifiers, such as adjectives and adverbs. We would also need to ensure that they behave appropriately with a treatment of plural phenomena, and discourse.[82]

[82]Some of the interactions between property modifiers, plurals, and mass terms have been explored elsewhere. Property modifiers can be exploited to reduce the ontological commitments of a semantic theory, so that the extensions of nominal expressions need not be homogeneous (Fox 1993, Fox 1998).

5

Discourse Representation

The goal of this chapter is to demonstrate that we can systematically translate natural language (NL) discourse into appropriate classical truth conditions within one theory, just using existing notions, such as the classical logical quantifiers, dependent types, and λ-calculus, all with their "natural" interpretations. This shows that we do not need a new ontological category of "Discourse Representation Structures" (DRSs) (Kamp 1981, Kamp and Reyle 1993). Nor do we have to abandon a classical logic, for either a dynamic theory (Groenendijk and Stokhof 1990, Groenendijk and Stokhof 1991) with a non-classical re-interpretation of quantification and a new "improper" form of abstraction-application (Chierchia 1991) (see Appendix A), or for a constructive type theory (Sundholm 1989, Ranta 1991, Ranta 1994, Ahn and Kolb 1990, Dávila-Pérez 1995) with a non-classical notion of "proposition" (Appendix B). All we need is to find appropriate representations that only use basic functional notions, and demonstrate that any terms used to simplify the exposition of the theory do not actually extend its power or lead to any additional ontological commitments.

Here, we give the formal details of a treatment of singular anaphora in Property Theory (PT, Chapter 2), together with a preliminary analysis of plural anaphora, and a proof that the system does not extend the logical power of PT (and, hence, is also consistent). The application of this theory is demonstrated in Appendix C. A way of representing appropriate truth conditions for discourse with negation and disjunction is proposed in Appendix D.

In a sense, the basic treatment of singular pronouns is a classical revision of the treatment of NL discourse afforded by constructive theories but where a classical, non-constructive view of propositions is adopted. This seems an appropriate approach as PT can embody constructive type theories such as Martin-Löf's Type Theory (MLTT) without any alteration of the basic the theory (Aczel 1980, Smith 1984, Turner 1992).

We are concerned with some of the familiar examples from the literature on the representation of discourse, such as:

> A man walked in. He whistled.
> If a farmer owns a donkey, he beats it.
> Every farmer who owns a donkey beats it.

as well as explaining why singular anaphoric reference is blocked in examples such as:

> Every man walked in. He sat down.
> No man walked in. He sat down.

where 'he' cannot refer to the subject of the preceding sentence.

It is not our intention to find a treatment of some of the more recalcitrant linguistic phenomena, such as dependent anaphora, and non-logical quantification. Nor is it the intention to provide a theory that *selects* the most intuitively acceptable antecedent for a pronoun from amongst the plausible candidates. Rather, the objective is to show how at least these more basic cases of anaphora in discourse can be dealt with entirely within an intensional, classically quantified theory, without any additional ontological commitments.

We are more concerned with a foundational issue in semantics—namely, determining the weakest formal system in which we can analyse NL semantics—rather than with obtaining a wide coverage of linguistic phenomena. Here, representations of discourse are to be obtained by increasing the *expressiveness* of a first-order theory, without increasing its formal power.

Following the approach in Chapter 3, the theory characterises as a category mistake infelicitous discourse that arises when an anaphoric expression is "co-indexed" with an inappropriate antecedent. This is achieved by way of first-order typing rules. In the case of discourse, the typing rules have to be generalised to take account of the more complex representations. As with the treatment of non-denoting definite descriptors, these typing rules are used to avoid considering the truth conditions of discourse when the anaphora are not resolved appropriately.[83]

5.1 Discourse in Classical Logic

In general, first-order classical logic seems expressive enough for us to be able to state within it the truth conditions of discourse involving pronouns, including some of the proposed readings of the so-called donkey

[83] As mentioned in Chapter 3, page 49, the underlying cause of any category mistake may be found at the meta-level by seeing how the axioms fail to prove that a discourse is felicitous.

sentences. For example, the truth conditions of the following sentences:

A man walked in. He whistled.
If a farmer owns a donkey, he beats it.

can be represented by the following first-order expressions in classical logic:

$$\exists x(man'x \ \& \ walked{\cdot}in'x \ \& \ whistled'x)$$
$$\forall x \forall y((farmer'x \ \& \ donkey'y \ \& \ owns'yx) \rightarrow (beats'yx))$$

What is not clear is how we can obtain such representations directly from natural language in some systematic fashion. As has often been observed, if we adopt the PTQ-like interpretations of the determiners and conditionals (Montague 1973), we will produce the following representations:

$$\exists x(man'x \ \& \ walked{\cdot}in'x) \ \& \ whistled'x$$
$$\exists x(farmer'x \ \& \ \exists y(donkey'y \ \& \ owns'yx) \rightarrow (beats'yx))$$

These are erroneous. In the first example, the final x is not bound correctly. In the second example, not only are x and y not bound correctly in the final predication, but also they should really be universally quantified.[84]

We take these examples as indicating a need to reconsider how the constituent categories of discourse are to be expressed within classical logic. However, they are usually taken as motivation for abandoning the representation of NL discourse directly within classical logic, in favour of non-classical theories either with discourse markers—such as Discourse Representation Theory (DRT) (Kamp 1981), or File Change Semantics (Heim 1982)—or with non-standard semantics for the logical quantifiers and connectives—as in Dynamic Predicate Logic (DPL) (Groenendijk and Stokhof 1991)—so that the "erroneous" representations are given the same truth conditions as the desired representations. This is achieved by revising the semantics of the logical connectives, so that, for example, existential quantifiers can bind variables that lie outside their scope.[85]

---

[84]It is debatable whether this is the only appropriate reading. Another plausible reading would have the y existentially quantified, so that the sentence is true if all farmers who own one or more donkeys beat at least one of them. We shall ignore such complications here.

[85]In a sense, existential quantifiers then correspond with `let` statements in procedural programming languages, which assign values to variables. Procedural programming languages can be given a semantics using states consisting of assignment functions that map variables to their values. Dynamic logics can be given this same style of semantics. Chierchia achieves this effect with a generalisation of λ-abstraction-application (Chierchia 1991) (see Appendix A).

In DRT, a "construction algorithm" translates a discourse into a Discourse Representation Structure (DRS). A DRS consists of discourse referents and conditions, usually expressed in the form:

$$\begin{array}{|c|}\hline \langle \textit{referents} \rangle \\ \hline \langle \textit{conditions} \rangle \\ \hline \end{array}$$

DRSs can be recursive; sub-DRSs can appear in the condition part of a DRS.

Ignoring some of the finer detail and the various extensions and refinements that have been made to DRT, we can summarise the salient aspects of the construction algorithm as follows. We start off by creating an DRS to represent the entire discourse. When an indefinite ('a') is encountered, a discourse referent is added to the current DRS. The noun and the verb phrase are interpreted as conditions on that referent. If a sentential conditional "if A then B" is encountered, then a structure of the form:

$$A' \Rightarrow B'$$

is added to the condition part of the current DRS, where A', B' are DRSs that represent A and B respectively. A similar structure is added when a universal quantifier ('every') is encountered. In this case, A contains a discourse referent that satisfies the property denoted by the noun.

Pronouns are resolved by equating them with discourse referents. Accessibility constraints limit the referents to which a particular pronoun can refer in a way that is intended to accord with our intuitions.

These DRSs can be given a classical semantics. Except when appearing as A' in a structure of the form $A' \Rightarrow B'$, the DRS:

$$\begin{array}{|l|}\hline r_1, \ldots, r_n \\ \hline c_1 \\ \vdots \\ c_m \\ \hline \end{array}$$

can be given the same interpretation as $\exists r_1 \ldots r_n(c_1, \ldots, c_m)$. The conditional structure:

$$\begin{array}{|l|}\hline r_1, \ldots, r_n \\ \hline c_1 \\ \vdots \\ c_m \\ \hline \end{array} \Rightarrow B'$$

can be given the same interpretation as $\forall r_1 \ldots r_n((c_1, \ldots, c_m) \rightarrow B')$

In the case of DPL, the essence of the approach is to give discourse a PTQ-like analysis except that there is a dynamic existential quantifier $\exists_\Delta$ which arises in the representation of indefinites. This quantifier can bind outside its scope, and has the semantics of a universal quantifier when appearing as the antecedent of a conditional. So, except when appearing as the antecedent of a conditional, the expression

$$\exists_\Delta x(\varphi) \;\&\; \psi$$

has a semantics equivalent to $\exists x(\varphi \;\&\; \psi)$, and the expression:

$$\exists_\Delta x(\varphi) \rightarrow \psi$$

has an interpretation that is equivalent to $\forall x(\varphi \rightarrow \psi)$.

In DRT, DRSs are intended to form an essential part of the representation; they are not merely syntactic sugar. In the strong view of DRT, these objects have a psychological reality. If we adopt the DRT analysis, then DRSs have to be accepted as a new ontological category.

In the DPL-style approach to representing discourse, we have to change the underlying model of the formal theory. Not only do we need to change the interpretation of the logical quantifiers, we also need to reconsider the nature of abstraction and application in order to obtain the appropriate compositional semantics.

Following the methodology of least commitment, if we can find a way of representing discourse that require neither a new ontological category of DRSs, nor a change in the interpretation of the underlying theory, then we should favour it over either of the two approaches sketched here.

Note that the classical interpretations of both the DRT and DPL representations embody an element of "non-compositional" context dependency; the contribution that indefinites make to the classical truth conditions is not fixed, it depends upon the context of the indefinite. A similar context dependency will be evident in the theory that we develop here.

Both DRT and DPL, and related theories, do not seek to produce the classical representations directly in the semantic theory. However, as we have seen, the representations obtained in these semantic theories *can* be translated into classically quantified representations. If one of the objectives of formal semantics is to provide translations between NL and classical, quantified logic, then these theories effectively provide an intermediate representation between NL discourse and standard quantified logic.

Such theories can be seen to model two aspects of NL semantics: (i) a truth conditional component; and (ii) a contextual component. However, both of these components are already present in classical logic. If we take the logical quantifiers, we can see that in the proposition:

$$\exists x \varepsilon t . \varphi$$

the sub-expression "$\exists x \varepsilon t$" provides a context for the interpretation of φ, and, of course, the whole expression has truth conditions. Using this classical notation, we can represent the problematic examples on page 127 by:

$$\exists x \varepsilon \{ y \varepsilon man' . walked{\cdot}in' y \} . whistled' x$$
$$\forall x \varepsilon farmer' . (\forall y \varepsilon \{ z \varepsilon donkey' . own' x z \} . beats' x y)$$

We could produce these semantics by allowing indefinites (and other expressions) to give rise to types. The dynamics in the semantics is then provided by quantification ranging over these types. This would reproduce some elements of a DRT-style treatment. In producing classical truth conditions, the problem we must solve is allowing the determiners to have appropriate contributions to the semantics in all possible contexts.

The perceived problem that classical logic has with these examples is not that it is incapable of representing them, rather it is the apparent absence of any systematic means of generating these representations directly. Here we pursue this naive classical semantics for discourse phenomena by defining the formal means by which we can express appropriate representations of the constituent categories of NL discourse.

There is some complexity in producing a classical representation of discourse. We could try using DPL or DRT as an intermediate representation, and then use aspects of their Tarski definition to obtain the classical representations. However, it is hard to see how such an approach would be any simpler than our proposal; as we are trying to use the weakest theory that accounts for the data, additional work would be required to show that the semantics never makes use of anything more powerful than the first-order logic we shall use.

To understand some of the details and motivations behind this theory, we will turn our attention to an alternative to DPL and DRT-style approaches, where discourse is represented compositionally in a constructive type theory such as MLTT (Sundholm 1989, Ranta 1991, Ranta 1994, Dávila-Pérez 1995, Martin-Löf 1982, Martin-Löf 1984). In such theories, propositions are taken to be just another type. Indeed, there is no distinction between propositions and types in MLTT. A proposition is true if it is an inhabited type. The elements, or "witnesses," of a propositional type can be considered to be its proofs. Such theories have their roots in the intuitionistic, rather than the classical view of propositions. In this approach, NL discourse is represented directly within a "quantified" logic, although of a constructive rather than of a classical nature. The dynamic effects are captured using dependent types.[86] These can be thought of as constructive versions of the quantifiers. Details of one theory for representing NL discourse in MLTT are given in Appendix B.

In axiomatically obtaining the classical truth conditions of discourse, we will use a representation that is akin to constructive type theory to mediate between natural language and the final, classical truth conditions. This demonstrates a certain uniformity; along with DRT and DPL, MLTT-like representations of discourse can be taken to be an intermediate step towards obtaining classical truth conditions. It also circumvents any dissatisfaction with the non-classical, intuitionistic nature of such representations, and provides classical truth conditions for discourse within one axiomatic framework. We will show that this intermediate representation of discourse in PT does not effectively strengthen the theory.

In representing discourse, it may be formally convenient to have DRT-like representations, but—as with Landman's intensional individuals (Chapter 4)—they can be taken to be a form of syntactic sugar that has no ontological significance. The theory to be presented here allows us to abandon any ontological commitment to Discourse Representation Structures without being forced into making fundamental changes to the underlying model, as would be required if we adopted a DPL-like treatment.

5.2 Discourse in Property Theory

The fine-grained intensionality and weak typing of the property theory PT (§2.2) make it an appropriate vehicle for expressing natural language semantics. In addition, PT is a classical theory that is expressive enough to capture the operators of MLTT (Turner 1992, Aczel 1980, Smith 1984). Thus it constitutes a suitable framework for exploring an axiomatic analysis of discourse using MLTT-like dependent types within a classical setting.

As we have seen, both DRT and DPL can be considered to be an intermediate level of representation between natural language and its classical truth conditions. However, PT already provides an intermediate representation between natural language and its classical truth conditions, namely the language of terms.

---

[86]Ahn and Kolb have shown how the Discourse Representation Structure of DRT can be translated into dependent types in the Calculus of Constructions (Ahn and Kolb 1990).

We can achieve the goal of producing an axiomatic treatment of discourse in a classical logic by mapping natural language into appropriate terms in PT, and providing relevant truth conditions in the language of wff. In effect, we can go from natural language to its classical truth conditions within the one semantic theory.

By following the approach to non-denoting definite descriptors in Chapter 3, we can also capture the notion of infelicitous discourse as it occurs with non-denoting pronouns: just as paradoxes can be represented in PT but cannot be proven to have propositional content (Chapter 2), we will arrange the theory so that infelicitous discourse can be represented, but it has no truth conditions.

Let us consider the desired classical representations of some sentences and discourses that contain indefinites. A sentence on its own, such as:

A man walked in.

has truth conditions that we might express as:

$$\exists x \varepsilon man'.walked{\cdot}in'x$$

However, in the context of a discourse, such as:

A man walked in. He whistled.

the sentence can be seen to contribute an individual to which we can refer in subsequent sentences. In this case we can think of the first sentence as specifying the type $\{x\varepsilon man'.walked{\cdot}in'x\}$. If the sentence is true, then the type is inhabited (there is a man who walked in). When the pronoun is resolved, the discourse could then be represented by:

$$\exists y \varepsilon \{x\varepsilon man'.walked{\cdot}in'x\}.whistled'y$$

We can see that components of the discourse can sometimes be considered to give rise to a type specification which is inhabited if the sentence is true, whereas the entire discourse is represented by a classical proposition.

The solution that will be proposed effectively questions the usual assumptions concerning which natural language constructs give rise to the appropriate quantifiers in the final classical representation. We will take it that, in this particular case, $\exists$ arises from the concatenation of two sentences, and $\{\cdot\}$ arises from the indefinite 'a'.

In the truth conditions of the sentence "If a farmer is rich, he is happy":

$$\forall y \varepsilon \{x\varepsilon farmer'.rich'x\}.happy'\mathrm{he}_0$$

the universal quantifier arises not from the indefinite, but from the representation of the "if... then..." construction. In this case, the pronoun 'he_0' can be resolved to the farmer in question by replacing it by y.

In general, the types that will arise in the truth conditions of discourse will be more complicated because the discourse might contain several nominals, as well as constructions such as conditionals, universal quantification and relative clauses.

If we can give a systematic interpretation which allows the representation of a sentence to act as either a type or a proposition, as appropriate, then we have a solution to the problem of obtaining classical truth conditions for discourse in PT, without introducing an ontology of "discourse structures" and without changing the classical interpretation of the logical quantifiers.

There are two components to the problem of obtaining such representations: (i) we need to obtain a semantics where the representations of sentences are sometimes classical propositions, and sometimes types; (ii) we must obtain the appropriate quantifiers and logical connectives in the representation systematically.[87]

As already mentioned, there are semantic theories that cope with discourse phenomena, such as intersentential anaphora and donkey sentences, by allowing sentences to be represented as types; following Ranta and Dávila-Pérez , we can analyse such examples compositionally within MLTT. In such treatments, indefinites, sentence concatenation, conjunction and relative clauses are interpreted by the dependent-sum operator Σ. Implication and universal quantification are represented by the dependent-function type operator Π (Ranta 1991, Dávila-Pérez 1995). These dependent type operators can be defined in PT (§2.3.4).

The expression Σfg specifies a pair of objects $\langle a, b\rangle$ such that $a\varepsilon f$ and $b\varepsilon ga$. In the semantics of natural language this can be used to create nested pairs of discourse references. Selector functions operating on the specified pairs can then be used to extract appropriate individuals wherever a singular pronoun appears. The expression Πfg specifies functions h which take elements $a\varepsilon f$ to elements of ga. In the setting of natural language semantics, these Π types effectively block singular anaphoric reference into the scope of a universal quantifier or a conditional: selector functions can only operate on nested pairs of individual, and not functions.

After first giving a little more detail of the analysis of discourse in MLTT[88] (and some criticisms), we shall see how we can make use of a dependent type analysis of anaphora without abandoning the classical notion of proposition.

[87] One could say "compositionally" in place of "systematically." This temptation will be avoided for reasons that should become clear.

[88] A more comprehensive account is given in Appendix B.

In MLTT, the discourse:

A man walked in. He whistled.

can be represented by the constructive proposition, or type:[89]

$$\Sigma(\Sigma man' \lambda y(walked\cdot in' y))\lambda x(whistled' \mathrm{he}_0)$$

Here, Σ can be considered to be the MLTT equivalent of classical existential quantification $\exists$ expressed in something resembling a generalised quantifier style notation. These are expressions of the form:

$$\langle quantifier\rangle\langle range\rangle\langle body\rangle$$

where $\langle body\rangle$ typically contains some abstract. The notation adopted here uses an explicit λ-abstract. As with the logical generalised quantifiers, it is possible to re-express $\langle quantifier\rangle(r)\lambda x(b)$ as $\langle quantifier\rangle x \varepsilon r.b$.[90]

The constructive proposition (or type) that represents the discourse is true if there is a term of the form $\langle\langle m, t'\rangle, t''\rangle$ of that type. That is:

$$\langle\langle m, t'\rangle, t''\rangle \,\varepsilon\, \Sigma(\Sigma(man')(\lambda y(walked\cdot in' y)))\lambda x(whistled' \mathrm{he}_0)$$

where m will be a man and t' a proof of the proposition that he walked in and t'' a proof of the proposition that he whistled. In effect, the variable x ranges over pairs $\langle m, t'\rangle$. The pronoun in the second sentence can be resolved to 'the man who walked in' if it is replaced by a selector function that picks the first element of x, $\mathsf{fst}(x)$, namely m.

MLTT can be shown to be effectively first-order. For example, it can be incorporated into PT (Aczel 1980, Turner 1992, Smith 1984). Sentences are then represented with non-classical propositions, where propositions are properties which hold of their proofs.

Here we have a hint as to how we might systematically obtain appropriate quantifiers in the representation. It is the operations that combine sentences, such as concatenation and conditional constructions, that provide the appropriate quantifiers, not just the determiners. Thus, pronouns here are not outside the scope of the appropriate quantifiers, unlike in the naive PTQ-like analysis. They are still problematic, but only in the sense that we have to decide to what part of the complex, quantified term they refer.

In the case of NL semantics in MLTT, (constructive) existential quantification in the representation of the first example ("A man walked in. He whistled.") arises from the concatenation of sentences, not from the indefinite. And (constructive) universal quantification in the representation of the second example ("If a farmer owns a donkey he beats it.")

[89] Modulo differences in the representation of abstraction.

[90] In Appendix B, this is written $\langle quantifier\rangle(r).(x)b$ to conform with a common notation for MLTT.

arises from the interpretation of implication in the sentence, and not, as in DPL, from a reinterpretation of the indefinite in the scope of the conditional.

The use of constructive type theories, such as MLTT, seems to give an elegant solution to the problem of anaphoric reference in discourse. They are independently motivated theories that achieve the required results. However, such theories, and MLTT in particular, have attributes that might be considered undesirable. We can summarise some of the objections to a constructive treatment of NL semantics in MLTT as follows:

(i) The notions of proposition and property are conflated. In MLTT, 'some bikes' is just as much a proposition as 'there are some bikes'. Similarly, the natural numbers are to be thought of as propositions indistinguishable in kind from '2+2=4'.

(ii) There is no means of distinguishing between false propositions.

(iii) There is no extensional-intensional contrast in the basic theory.

These last two points do not fit the requirements of natural language semantics.[91] A further source of dissatisfaction is that, arguably, there is no natural, non-circular notion of proof for atomic natural language sentences. A proof of 'snow is white' is presumably that "snow is white," but it is not obvious how to express the latter naturally, within the representation language.

We might seek to counter some of these problems by adopting a more sophisticated constructive type theory that does not equate types with propositions. Of course, this does not by itself satisfy the goal of representing dynamic effects in a classical theory that is sympathetic to an Aristotelean ontology, such as Property Theory: even if they were distinguishable from them, propositions would still be of the same fundamental kind as types.

As MLTT can be encoded within PT, (Aczel 1980, Turner 1992, Smith 1984) (Appendix B) we can implement an MLTT-like approach to natural language semantics in PT. This counters some of the criticisms and also gives additional flexibility as it provides a meta-language in which operations can be defined without explicitly encoding them as λ-terms.[92] Also, a classical notion of proposition and the standard classical connectives become available. However, MLTT is essentially constructive in

[91]This drawback might be overcome if we add a Universe of propositions to the terms of MLTT, but such an approach seems to admit to the primitive nature of propositions, and so produce a realist theory, counter to the intended spirit of MLTT.

[92]For example, we can give a relatively simple axiomatisation of Dávila-Pérez' app (Appendix B), as used in his treatment of relative clauses (Dávila-Pérez 1995).

nature, even when implemented in Property Theory. A different line can be followed, where we use the dependent types of MLTT, but in combination with an essentially classical view of NL semantics.

We could maintain a classical view of NL semantics by giving MLTT type expressions a classical interpretation. This effect can be achieved by suppressing the witnesses of constructive propositions (Fox 1994a).[93] However, here we shall not follow this route. Instead, we shall take a more conservative path where NL expressions will be represented by terms that, in themselves, are neutral as to whether they are types or classical propositions. It is only when we come to evaluate the truth conditions of the representation of a discourse that these terms are given an appropriate interpretation, depending upon their context. The sentence:

A man walked in.

will be given the same representation regardless of whether it appears as an isolated sentence, or as part of a discourse. However, the representation can play different roles in the truth conditions. The role it plays depends on whether it is the truth conditions of this sentence that are in question (perhaps in the context of some preceding discourse), or whether this sentence occurs in a non-final position of the discourse whose truth conditions are in question. In the former case, the representation will be the proposition that there is a man who walked in. In the latter case, the representation of the sentence will be used to specify a type. If the sentence is true, then that type will have as a member a man who walked in. In the truth conditions of a discourse ds ending with the sentence s, s will be interpreted as a proposition within the scope of a quantifier ranging over terms that satisfy d, where d is interpreted as a type.

This proposal seems to break the constraints of compositionality: the appropriate interpretation for the representation of a term depends upon its semantic context. In any theory that copes with discourse phenomena, there must be some element of context sensitivity when we consider the classical truth conditions, as we have seen in the case of DRT and DPL, where the impact of an indefinite on the classical truth conditions depends upon its context. In this theory, the representation will be obtained compositionally, but its evaluation will be systematic, although not strictly compositional.

[93] It is possible to give outermost uses of Σ and Π the classical interpretations of $\exists$ and $\forall$. We can take a representation in MLTT, within PT, and then map this representation into a classical proposition by way of various translations functions (Fox 1994a). Here, we give an alternative characterisation where we seek to embody the effect of such functions directly in the axioms of truth for the theory.

It is desirable for terms representing the discourse to be combined in a uniform manner, so that we can compose the semantics without regard to the number of "accessible" discourse referents over which we have to quantify. We can do so by arranging the theory so that referents that are made available by one part of the discourse are passed on to a subsequent part by way of a single, structured argument. This leads to the desired simplicity, although some complications arise in the typing of the quantified variables in the truth conditions.

Theories that adopt a constructivist perspective are simpler, as every natural language category is represented by a type; this allows them to be combined uniformly. In the theory presented here, the way we combine the representations in the truth conditions will depend upon where they occur and whether they contain embedded nominals.

5.3 A Sketch of the Basic Theory

Although we will make use of the dependent types that appear in constructive type theories, we do not adopt the constructive semantics programme; instead, we make use of dependent types within an essentially classical theory. To do so requires that compositionality is weakened so that the interpretation of a determiner, for example, is context sensitive.

In MLTT, propositions and types (or properties) are seen to belong to the same category: in some sense propositions are properties that are satisfied by objects corresponding with proofs of the appropriate proposition. It is this uniformity of the categories of semantic primitives in MLTT which allows so many constructs in NL semantics to be interpreted by just two type operators (Appendix B). To have a classical analysis, we can follow the constructive approach in so far as it uses one operator to represent indefinites, concatenated sentences, conjunction and relative clauses, and another for universals and implication, but then we give different interpretations to those operators in the truth conditions, depending upon their context.

In PT^{dt}, the theory to be developed here, we shall use the two "discourse operators" ς and π where we would use Σ and Π in an MLTT semantics of NL. Both of these operators can have three different interpretations in the truth conditions. The appropriate interpretation systematically depends upon the context in which they occur.

Note that ς and π do not have to be taken to be primitive. For example, we could represent both of these operators by triples consisting of the operators' three possible interpretations, to be given below. Then when evaluating the truth conditions of a discourse we just "project" the appropriate interpretation.

These operators appear in "discourse terms" of the form $\langle \varsigma, s, t \rangle$ and $\langle \pi, s, t \rangle$. Such expressions can be thought of as a kind of generalised quantifier representation, with ς or π as the quantifier, s as the domain and t as the body.

A simplified characterisation of the three interpretations of ς and π in the truth conditions is as follows:[94]

(1) When ς and π occur as the main discourse operator with wide scope over the representation of the complete discourse, or when they have widest scope within the body t, then they behave like the classical quantifiers $\exists$ and $\forall$ (respectively).

(2) When they occur in the domain s of another discourse term, but have no further discourse terms in their body, then they behave like a separation type (§2.3.1) and a "pluralisation" of it (respectively).

(3) When they occur in the domain s of another discourse term, and, in turn, have a further discourse term in their body, then they behave like Σ and a "pluralisation" of it (respectively).

The pluralisations of the types are intended to allow a uniform account of the inaccessibility of singular antecedents and the existence of plural antecedents.

In case (1) we are interpreting a discourse term t as a classically quantified proposition. We indicate this by writing ${}^{\kappa}t$. In both cases (2) and (3) we are interpreting a discourse term t as a type, either a dependent type if there are additional discourse terms within t, or a non-dependent type otherwise. In either of the latter cases, we indicate the interpretation of t as a type by writing ${}^{\tau}t$.

The full formalisation of this theory is given later, in §5.4, where the axioms of the theory are presented. A PTQ-like grammar that uses this theory is given in Appendix C. Before presenting the axiomatisation, we shall exemplify the different interpretations of the discourse terms, starting with ς.

5.3.1 ς Discourse Terms

The sentence:

A man laughed.

is represented by:

$$\langle \varsigma, man', \lambda x(laughed'x) \rangle$$

[94] In fact it is not *quite* as described: except in the simplest examples, we need to keep track of whether an expression is being interpreted as a "type" or as a classical "proposition." These classifications do not correspond exactly to the notions "domain" and "body," but the behaviour as described is sufficiently accurate to cope with the examples that follow.

Here, the ς term has widest scope over the representation of the discourse, so case (1), above, applies. When it is intended that this discourse is to be interpreted as a classical proposition, we write:

$$^{\kappa}\langle\varsigma, man', \lambda x(laughed'x)\rangle$$

We can think of $^{\kappa}$ as an operator that maps a discourse term into a proposition. When applied to a ς discourse term, the truth conditions of the resultant proposition will be some existentially quantified statement. In this example, the truth conditions are equivalent to:[95]

$$\exists x \dot{\varepsilon} man'.laughed'x$$

Note that here we use the notation $\dot{\varepsilon}$ (rather than just ε) to indicate that additional constraints are required on the terms over which quantified variables can range. In this case, we want x only to range over those terms that can be denoted by natural language nominals. This will allow us to capture a notion of felicitous discourse, whereby a discourse with inappropriately resolved pronouns cannot be shown to form a proposition. More complex discourse requires correspondingly more complex constraints to achieve the same effect.

The sentence:

A man owns a donkey.

is represented by:

$$\langle\varsigma, man', \lambda x\langle\varsigma, donkey', \lambda y(own'xy)\rangle\rangle$$

and when it is interpreted as a proposition it has the truth conditions:

$$\exists x \dot{\varepsilon} man'.\exists y \dot{\varepsilon} donkey'.own'xy$$

Note that as in (1) above, the outer-most ς has wide scope, and the inner ς has wide scope within the body of the main discourse term.

As an illustration of the interpretation of the ς expression as a type, the sentence:

---

[95] For clarity, we have elided some of the property-theoretic detail in the examples. Here we just have $laughed'x$, where, in full-dress, this should really be $\mathrm{T}(laughed'x)$, so as to distinguish between the extensional and intensional levels of the theory.

In general, the interpretation is a little richer than that given here. The expression:

$$^{\kappa}\langle\varsigma, f, g\rangle$$

is interpreted as:

$$\exists x \dot{\varepsilon}\, ^{\tau}f.^{\kappa}(gx)$$

We can assume that if f is a simple type then $^{\tau}f$ has the same extension as f, and if g is a simple proposition, then $^{\kappa}g$ has the same truth conditions as g. During the rest of this section, the details of how $^{\kappa}$ and $^{\tau}$ are used to obtain the classical truth conditions will be glossed over. The full theory in §5.4, and the grammar in Appendix C, give the correct typing constraints and maintain the extensional-intensional distinctions.

A man walked in. He whistled.

is represented by:

$$\langle \varsigma, \langle \varsigma, man', \lambda y(walked \cdot in'y)\rangle, \lambda x(whistled'he')\rangle$$

where the first ς term represents sentence concatenation. In the truth conditions it will be interpreted as $\exists$. Following case (2) above, the second ς term will be interpreted as a separation type of the form $\{x \varepsilon s.t\}$. This gives the discourse the following truth conditions:

$$\exists x \dot{\varepsilon} \{y \varepsilon man'.walked \cdot in'y\}.whistled'he'$$

In effect, the proposition $walked \cdot in'y$ is like a "test" in Dynamic Logic: it does not add any referents to the context (Groenendijk and Stokhof 1990, Groenendijk and Stokhof 1991).

The pronoun is resolved to 'the man who walked in' by replacing it with x. These truth conditions are then equivalent to:

$$\exists x \dot{\varepsilon} man'.(walked \cdot in'y \;\&\; whistled'x)$$

The discourse:

A farmer owns a donkey. He beats it.

can be used to illustrate case (3) for ς discourse terms. It has the representation:

$$\langle \varsigma, \langle \varsigma, farmer', \lambda f \langle \varsigma, donkey', \lambda d(own'(f)(d))\rangle\rangle, \lambda x(beats'(he')(it'))\rangle$$

The second ς (used in the representation of 'a farmer...') has another ς expression in its body (used to represent 'a donkey'). This means that it has to be interpreted as a Σ operator, so as to form a type that specifies pairs of objects, namely farmers and the individual donkeys they own:

$$\exists x \dot{\varepsilon} (\Sigma farmer'(\lambda f\{d \varepsilon donkey'.own'(f)(d)\}).beats'(he')(it')$$

So the existentially quantified variable x will range over farmer-donkey pairs, where the first element of each pair is a farmer, and the second element is a donkey owned by that farmer. The pronouns he', it' can be resolved by replacing them with the functions $\mathsf{fst}(x)$, $\mathsf{snd}(x)$ respectively, where fst picks the first element of the pair, and snd picks the second element (§2.3.2).

The truth conditions for this discourse are then equivalent to:

$$\exists \langle f, d\rangle . f \dot{\varepsilon} farmer' \;\&\; d \dot{\varepsilon} donkey' \;\&\; own'(f)(d) \;\&\; beats'(f)(d)$$

That is:

$$\exists f \dot{\varepsilon} farmer'.\exists d \dot{\varepsilon} donkey'.own'(f)(d) \;\&\; beats'(f)(d)$$

At the top level of analysis, we use classical quantifiers to give a non-constructive interpretation of NL semantics. We use the Σ type when we need to form nested pairs of discourse referents, which can then be passed on to subsequent discourse. The separation type $\{x\varepsilon t.\varphi\}$ allows us to keep a classical notion of proposition for the propositional body φ when it contains no further discourse terms.

In the truth conditions, the appropriate interpretation of a discourse term may change as the discourse progresses. Thus the truth conditions of a discourse must be re-evaluated if the discourse is extended. The distinct interpretation of the top-level of discourse is perhaps rather like the application of "existential closure" in Discourse Representation Theory (Kamp 1981, Kamp and Reyle 1993), and the closing off of the "discourse continuation" in some forms of dynamic semantics (Groenendijk and Stokhof 1990).

Singular pronouns are resolved by replacing them by some selector function. These are inductively defined as follows:

(i) The identity function is a selector function.

(ii) If s is a selector function, then the functional composition of fst and s is a selector function.

(iii) If s is a selector function, then the functional composition of snd and s is a selector function.

In effect, the truth conditions of a discourse give rise to quantification over a binary tree that contains all of the referents specified by the discourse. Singular pronouns select a referent by specifying the path to it from the root of the tree. A ς discourse term containing another discourse term in its body will give rise to a node with two branches with side conditions on the nature of those nodes. A ς discourse term without such an embedded discourse term will just add a terminal node with a side condition. So, the sentence:

A farmer who owns a donkey that has a long tail φs.

can be thought of as giving rise to quantification over binary trees of the form:

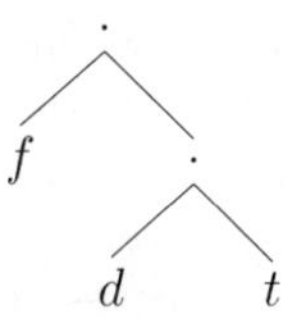

where

$$
\begin{array}{l}
f \varepsilon farmer' \\
d \varepsilon \{a \varepsilon donkey'.own' f a\} \\
t \varepsilon \{b \varepsilon long \cdot tail'.has' d b\}
\end{array}
$$

This binary tree can be represented within PT by a term of the form $\langle f, \langle d, t \rangle \rangle$.

Within the scope of quantification over terms of this form, the selector functions fst, $\lambda x(\mathsf{fst}(\mathsf{snd}(x))$ and $\lambda x(\mathsf{snd}(\mathsf{snd}(x))$ will select terms corresponding to "a farmer" (f), "a donkey owned by the farmer" (d) and "the tail of the donkey owned by the farmer" (t), respectively.

The notion of a fragment of discourse being interpreted within a context created by some preceding discourse is then equated with the interpretation of an expression within the scope of a classical quantifier that ranges over appropriate binary trees of discourse referents. It is, in part, the nature of objects over which the quantifiers can range that motivates the form of first-order "typing" rules in §5.4; the rules effectively have to guarantee that the terminal nodes of the discourse referent "trees" are all natural language denotables, and that all singular pronouns are resolved to paths which select denotables.

5.3.2 π Discourse Terms

Just as with ς, when π appears with widest scope over the discourse, or widest scope within the body of a ς or π term (as in case (1) on page 138), then in the truth conditions we seek to interpret it as a quantifier—a universal quantifier in this case. The sentence:

Every man walked.

is represented by:

$$\langle \pi, man', \lambda x(walked' x) \rangle$$

which, when interpreted as a proposition, will have the truth conditions:

$$\forall x \dot{\varepsilon} man'. walked' x$$

Of course, at this top most level, there are no subsequent plural pronouns, so we do not need to worry about providing appropriate referents.

Matters become more complicated when it comes to the interpretation of π discourse terms as types. In order to analyse the basic motivating examples for DRT and DPL, all we really require is that π discourse terms block singular anaphoric reference. However, we shall take this opportunity to present two alternatives, both of which license plural anaphoric reference. The second alternative is more generous than the first with regard to the number of plural antecedents which it makes available. The "correct" analysis probably lies somewhere between the two extremes that these analyses present.

A Simple Analysis

When a π expression appears in the domain of a ς or π expression, and it has a discourse term within its body (as in case (3) on page 138), then we could interpret it as a Π type (§2.3.4), (Fox 1994a). The discourse:

Every farmer owns a donkey. They have long ears.

is represented by:

$$\langle \varsigma, \langle \pi, \mathit{farmer}', \lambda f \langle \varsigma, \mathit{donkey}', \lambda d(\mathit{own}' f d)\rangle\rangle, \lambda x(\mathit{long}\cdot \mathit{ears}' \mathit{they}')\rangle$$

As before, the outer-most ς represents sentence concatenation. In the truth conditions, it will be interpreted as existential quantification. The inner-most ς is interpreted as a separation type. Interpreting the π operator as a dependent-function type operator Π would give:

$$\exists x \dot{\varepsilon}(\Pi(\mathit{farmer}')(\lambda f\{d \varepsilon \mathit{donkey}'.\mathit{own}' f d\})).(\mathit{long}\cdot \mathit{ears}' \mathit{they}')$$

To re-iterate, the meaning of the expression $\Pi f g$ is a type which holds of a term h if it is a function that takes elements a of type f to elements of type ga. In this case, the Π expression specifies a function from farmers to donkeys that are owned by the farmer in question.[96]

It might now be apparent how we could resolve the plural pronoun 'they' in this example. The domain of the function x specified by the Π expression will be the set of farmers, and its range will be the set of owned donkeys. If we adopt a lattice-theoretic approach to the semantics of plural terms (Link 1983), as in $\mathrm{PT}^{\mathfrak{P}}$ (§3.1), then the pronoun can be resolved by replacing it by either the supremum of the domain of x, in order to refer to the farmers, or by the supremum of the range of x, to refer to the owned donkeys.

We must consider the case where a π expression occurs within the scope of another discourse term, but contains no further discourse terms in its body (case (2), page 138). These circumstances arise in the representation of the following, rather contrived example:

Every farmer walked in. A donkey slept.

This is represented by:

$$\langle \varsigma, \langle \pi, \mathit{farmer}', \lambda f(\mathit{walked}\cdot \mathit{in}' f)\rangle, \lambda g\langle \varsigma, \mathit{donkey}', \lambda d(\mathit{slept}' d)\rangle\rangle$$

We cannot interpret the π discourse term as a giving rise to the set of farmers who walked in—as in the ς case—because this would license the subsequent use of a singular pronoun to refer to the farmers. In

[96]This function can be thought of as providing a skolemised representation of the existential quantification in the PTQ-like representation of the phrase "a donkey." For the discourse to be true, there must be an appropriate skolem function in the language of terms.

the previous case, we proposed interpreting the π term as a dependent function type. We could do the same here. This would have the advantage of producing some uniformity in the theory; when interpreted as types, all π discourse terms block anaphoric reference to singulars, and can be interpreted as giving rise to antecedents for plural anaphora, because they have a similar interpretation, regardless of the context in which they appear.

For the current example, one way of achieving this uniformity is to interpret the π term as specifying functions from farmers to farmers that walked in. To be more precise, it can specify an identity function over the farmers, with a side condition that each farmer walked in. An appropriate type operator, Id, can be defined by the following:

$$\mathsf{Id}ab =_{\text{def}} \Pi(a)(\lambda x\{y\epsilon a.y \approx x \wedge by\})$$

that is:

$$\mathsf{Id} =_{\text{def}} \lambda ab(\Pi(a)(\lambda x\{y\epsilon a.y \approx x \wedge by\}))$$

The truth conditions of this example would then be:

$$\exists x\dot{\varepsilon}(\mathsf{Id}(farmer')(\lambda f(walked{\cdot}in'f))).\exists y\dot{\varepsilon}donkey'.slept'y$$

As there is an identity function over all terms in the untyped λ-calculus ($\lambda x(x)$), the truth conditional effect of the first sentence is to verify the side condition, namely that $\lambda f(walked{\cdot}in'f)$ holds of all farmers. Given the definition of Id, the truth conditions of the discourse would be equivalent to:

$$\forall f\dot{\varepsilon}farmer'.walked{\cdot}in'f \ \& \ \exists y\dot{\varepsilon}donkey'.slept'y$$

There are two objections to this simple analysis of plural anaphoric reference. First, the use of the supremum of just the domain or range of a function to resolve plural pronouns might not be sufficient in all cases. In the representations of some discourses, we might have functions whose domains and ranges are nested pairs. This situation would arise in the discourse:

> If a farmer owns a donkey he beats it. They are really cruel.

and:

> Every director who had a son gave him a present. They were really happy.

In these cases we would have to select appropriate antecedent individuals from within the domain or range. They may not be particularly convincing examples, but we probably do not want to rule out such possibilities just for the sake of formal simplicity.

Second, the domain and range of a function is not worn "on its sleeve": just given an appropriate function alone we cannot deduce the relevant domain and range. The function may belong to more than one type. We could try to get around this second criticism by using a revised Π operator, Π', where if $w\varepsilon(\Pi' fg)$ then $w = \langle h, \langle f, g\rangle\rangle$ where $h\varepsilon(\Pi fg)$. Then we can obtain the domain f and derive the range $\{z : \lceil \exists w\dot{\varepsilon} f.(z\varepsilon(gw))\rceil\}$ of h by using selector functions.[97] Subsequent plural anaphora can refer to the supremum of these expressions. However, this proposal does not address the first problem, where plural antecedents may have to be abstracted from within more complex witness structures.

A Complex Analysis

There is another possibility where we abandon the Π interpretation of π. Instead, when interpreting a π expression as a type we make it behave a bit like a ς expression. However, the ς expression, when interpreted as a type, is potentially inhabited by a number of witnesses, each of which contains discourse referents, whereas the π discourse term will be inhabited by at most one witness. Each individual discourse referent within that witness will be the supremum of all the discourse terms occurring in that referent's position in the witnesses to the corresponding ς expression. Further, if the type is inhabited, then the relevant universal condition must be satisfied.

As an informal example, the representation of 'every farmer owns a donkey' will specify a set, when interpreted as a type. The set will be inhabited iff every farmer owns a donkey, and the sole member of the set will then be a pair consisting of the supremum of farmers, and the supremum of donkeys that are owned by farmers. If we take the example on page 141:

A farmer who owns a donkey that has a long tail φs.

and the binary tree notation for witnesses that was presented there, then, in the truth conditions, this leads to quantification over the set given in Figure 1.

The truth conditions of the pluralised form that arises with:

Every farmer who owns a donkey that has a long tail φs.

will be satisfied if there is a term of the form given in Figure 2.

With the more complex analysis, when $\langle \pi, f, g\rangle$ is interpreted as a

[97]Here, and elsewhere, we have written $\lceil p\rceil$ when we mean to have a property-theoretic *intension* which, when a proposition, has the same truth conditions as p. This notation is used here for clarity. In the full theory (§5.4), PT's language of terms is used to express such intensions.

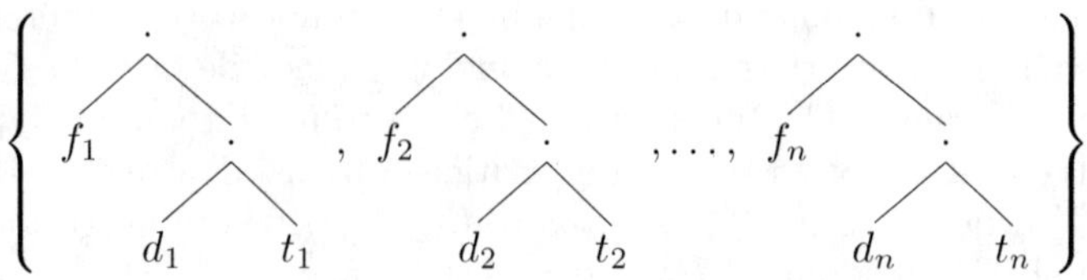

where

$$
\begin{array}{l}
f_m \varepsilon farmer' \\
d_m \varepsilon \{a \varepsilon donkey'.own' f_m a\} \\
t_m \varepsilon \{b \varepsilon longtail'.has' d_m b\}
\end{array}
$$

for all m such that $1 \leq m \leq n$.

FIGURE 1 Singular Discourse Referents

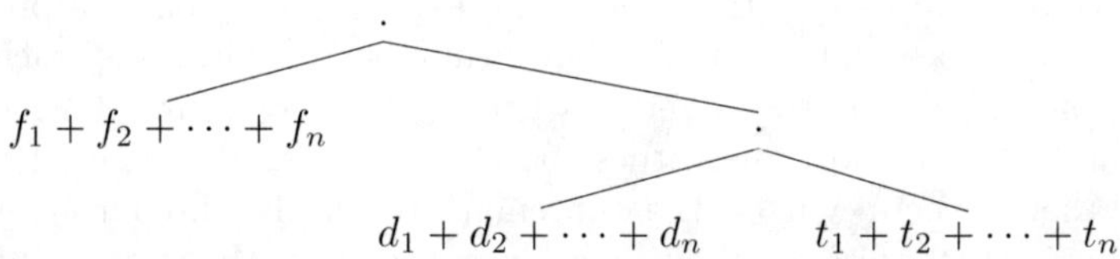

where

$$
\begin{array}{l}
f_m \varepsilon farmer' \\
d_m \varepsilon \{a \varepsilon donkey'.own' f_m a\} \\
t_m \varepsilon \{b \varepsilon longtail'.has' d_m b\}
\end{array}
$$

for all m such that $1 \leq m \leq n$.

FIGURE 2 Plural Discourse Referents

type it is, in brief, equivalent to the expression:

$$\{x : \lceil x = \biguplus \langle \varsigma, f, g \rangle \;\&\; \forall x \dot{\varepsilon}^{\tau} f.^{\kappa}(gx) \rceil\}$$

where $\biguplus\langle \varsigma, f, g \rangle$ is a "pluralised" witness to $^{\tau}\langle \varsigma, f, g \rangle$. There will be only one such witness, which allows us to use equality here. The operator $\biguplus$ will recurse through the expression $\langle \varsigma, f, g \rangle$ to produce the required term. To obtain this result formally is a little involved, as these are dependent type expressions: in order to find the full range of witnesses that can occur at any particular position in the witness, all the possible witnesses to the entire expression need to be considered. We cannot consider any one part of the expression in isolation. This means that as we recurse through the ς discourse term, we have to have access to a copy of the complete ς expression, and keep track of the selector function that would pick out the witnesses to the part of the ς expression under consideration.

For this reason, we need a richer notation. The expression:

$$\biguplus_{s}^{t} a$$

is intended to denote the pluralised form of the constituent a of the ς expression t, where s is the selector function that picks out witnesses to a from within the witnesses to t. When pluralising a ς expression, we require the initial selector function s to be an identity function, such as $\lambda x(x)$. So $\biguplus\langle\varsigma, f, g\rangle$ can now be defined in this richer notation by:

$$\biguplus\langle\varsigma, f, g\rangle = \biguplus_{\lambda x.x}^{\langle\varsigma, f, g\rangle} \langle\varsigma, f, g\rangle$$

In the recursive case, where g contains the representation of further nominals, we want to form pairs of the "pluralised" members, corresponding to the singular pairs that witness ${}^{\tau}\langle\varsigma, f, g\rangle$. So, in this case, we have the following:

$$\biguplus_{s}^{t} \langle\varsigma, f, g\rangle = \langle \biguplus_{\mathsf{fst}(s)}^{t} f, \biguplus_{\mathsf{snd}(s)}^{t} g\rangle$$

There are two base cases. The first is where the argument is of the form $\langle\varsigma, f, g\rangle$, and g does not include the representation of a nominal, that is, it is a "test." In this case we want just to return the suprema of the witnesses to ${}^{\tau}\langle\varsigma, f, g\rangle$ in the context provided by t. We will use the notation $\sigma x(\varphi)$ to mean the supremum of terms for which φ holds (§3.1.3, §3.2.2). The relevant witnesses can be picked out from the witness to t with the selector s. So, here we have:

$$\biguplus_{s}^{t} \langle\varsigma, f, g\rangle = \sigma x(\lceil \exists y \dot{\varepsilon}^{\tau} t.sy = x\rceil)$$

where g does not contain a further discourse term.

The second base case is where the argument is another "pluralised" context $\langle\pi, f, g\rangle$. Here, we just return the witness to ${}^{\tau}\langle\pi, f, g\rangle$, in the context provided by t, so we have the following:

$$\biguplus_{s}^{t} \langle\pi, f, g\rangle = \sigma x(\lceil \exists y \dot{\varepsilon}^{\tau} t.sy = x\rceil)$$

Now, assuming that various constraints are met (elaborated in §5.4), the truth conditions of:

$$s\varepsilon^{\tau}\langle\pi, f, g\rangle$$

will be those of:

$$s\varepsilon\{y : \lceil y = \biguplus \langle \varsigma, f, g \rangle \ \& \ \forall z \dot{\varepsilon}^{\tau} f.^{\kappa}(gz) \rceil \}$$

Plural anaphora can be replaced by selector functions, as in the singular case. Felicity of anaphoric reference can be ensured by formally requiring that pronouns select the appropriate kind of object (singular or plural in this case) for the discourse to be "meaningful." This accounts for cases of plural anaphora where the antecedents arise from the occurrence of some form of universal quantification, including conditional expressions.

It is debatable whether we really need the full generality of this more complex analysis, or whether it is too permissive in some cases; we might need to impose additional restrictions on the complexity of the form of permitted selector functions.

Even with the more complex analysis, some phenomena are not addressed. For example, we have no account of where the plural antecedent for 'they' arises in the discourse:

> Every lawyer hired a secretary who they liked.
> (Kamp and Reyle 1993)

This suggests that we need to consider extending the circumstances under which plural antecedents are produced.

We do not intend to address these deficiencies here; the relatively crude analysis of plural anaphora is presented not so much to account for any significant fragment of natural language, but rather to give an indication that the approach to representing singular anaphora in classical logic is not a formal dead-end.

After considering combined plural and singular antecedents, below, we give a detailed formalisation of the more complex of the two proposals presented here. Some additional complexity arises from the fact that we wish to ensure that the types of the terms which satisfy the singular and pluralised types are such that the "terminal nodes" of nominal witnesses are denotable.

5.3.3 COMBINED ANTECEDENTS

We can generalise the use of selector functions to account for plural anaphoric reference to the denotations of combinations of plural and singular nominals, as in:[98]

> If [a man]$_i$ and [a woman]$_j$ marry [they]$_{i+j}$ must be mad.

[98]There is not sufficient space here to describe the semantics of conjunction in discourse. Essentially it makes use of the ς operator. A proposal for the semantics of disjunction is given in Appendix D.

[One student]$_i$ went to Paris. [Every lecturer]$_j$ went to Lyons. [They]$_{i+j}$ (all) had a good time.

If plural anaphora are always plural, then there are the following possible kinds of reference:

1. reference to two or more singulars;
2. reference to one or more plural and one or more singular;
3. reference to one or more plural antecedents.

We can cover these cases by allowing joins of selectors to be substituted for plural anaphora. So, singular pronouns are resolved by simple selectors (as defined in §5.3.1, page 141), and plural pronouns are resolved by plural selectors that are inductively defined as follows:

(i) Singular selectors functions are plural selectors.

(ii) If p, p' are plural selectors, then $\lambda x(p(x)+p'(x))$ is a plural selector.

It can be seen that "coindexing" of a singular pronoun with an antecedent that lies within the scope of a universal will be infelicitous, on both the simple and complex analyses, because no singular antecedents are made available by universals. In the property-theoretic implementation, we can equate "felicity" with the notion of "proposition"; only expressions that can be shown to be propositions can have their truth conditions evaluated.

This is much like the treatment of the logical paradoxes in PT, as described in Chapter 2. The theory is axiomatised so that such statements cannot be shown to be propositions, and so they cannot have truth conditions. In Chapter 3 we saw how $\mathrm{PT}^{\mathfrak{D}}$ (and $\mathrm{PT}^{\mathfrak{P}}$) extends this idea to cover infelicitous definite descriptors. To reiterate, the class of terms $\mathfrak{d}$ can be referred to by natural language nominals, and the class of properties $\mathsf{Pty}_{\mathfrak{D}}$ form propositions with terms in $\mathfrak{d}$. That is:

$$(\mathsf{Pty}_{\mathfrak{D}}(p)\ \&\ t\varepsilon\mathfrak{d}) \rightarrow \mathrm{P}(pt)$$

The axioms of the theory do not allow non-denoting definite descriptors to be shown to be in $\mathfrak{d}$. Thus, predication of non-denoting (infelicitous) definite descriptors cannot be shown to give rise to a proposition, so the truth conditions of sentences like:

The present queen of France is bald.

cannot be considered. Questioning the truth conditions of this example, or the logical paradoxes, is to make a category mistake: their representation is not of the appropriate category to have truth conditions.

With pronouns, we can use this same approach, so that infelicitous resolution gives rise to a representation that cannot be shown to be a proposition. The problem is that we do not just have simple properties ($\mathsf{Pty}_{\mathfrak{D}}$) and denotable individuals ($\mathfrak{d}$). Instead we have complex types and structured witnesses. We need to ensure that in the truth conditions of a felicitous discourse, we only quantify over terms that have the appropriate structure and that all the individual terms within that structure are denotable. These complications will be addressed in the next section.[99]

5.4 PT^{dt}: PT WITH DISCOURSE TERMS

If we are prepared to accept the constructive interpretation of propositions in the representation of natural language, then we can simply use the types Σ and Π to cope with discourse phenomena, following the form of the theories of Ranta and Dávila-Pérez (Ranta 1991, Ranta 1994, Dávila-Pérez 1995). However, our intention is to keep a classical interpretation of propositions in the truth conditional semantics of natural language. As described in §5.3, PT^{dt} has two new operators ς and π.[100] They are used to represent the same natural language constructs as Σ and Π in constructive semantics.

The theory presented builds upon either $\mathrm{PT}^{\mathfrak{P}}$ or $\mathrm{PT}^{\mathfrak{D}}$, rather than basic PT. Either of these two theories will give us access to the notions that we require for infelicitous discourse and plural terms. The axioms presented below use the notation of $\mathrm{PT}^{\mathfrak{D}}$.

In the language of well formed formulae we can use ${}^{\kappa}t$ to mean that we are interpreting t as a classical proposition, and ${}^{\tau}t$ to mean that we are interpreting t as a type.[101] So, in the truth conditions, terms of the form $\langle\varsigma, f, g\rangle$ and $\langle\pi, f, g\rangle$ can be viewed as classical propositions (${}^{\kappa}\langle\varsigma, f, g\rangle$ and ${}^{\kappa}\langle\pi, f, g\rangle$) where the operators have the behaviour of $\exists$ and $\forall$. To allow structures of anaphoric antecedents to be built up, they can also be viewed as dependent types (${}^{\tau}\langle\varsigma, f, g\rangle$ and ${}^{\tau}\langle\pi, f, g\rangle$) where the operators have the behaviour associated with Σ and the pluralisation of it (§5.3.2).

At the top level, the truth conditions of a discourse will be given by a classically (non-constructive) quantified expression $qx\dot{\varepsilon}d.b$, where q is either $\forall$ or $\exists$, the domain of quantification d is given by a term interpreted as a type, and the body b is a term interpreted as a classical

[99] Note that the underlying theory, $\mathrm{PT}^{\mathfrak{D}}$ or $\mathrm{PT}^{\mathfrak{P}}$, requires some elaboration so that appropriate number agreement between properties and their arguments is a precondition of the felicity of the representation of the discourse in which they appear.

[100] Although, as mentioned above (§5.3), they do not have to be taken to be primitive. We could formalise ς and π as triples, then we would replace occurrences of ${}^{\kappa}$ and ${}^{\tau}$ by appropriate selector functions.

[101] In the formalisation given, the behaviour of ${}^{\kappa}$ and ${}^{\tau}$ are only defined for appropriately typed discourse terms.

proposition. The notation $x\dot{\varepsilon}d$ means that the quantified variable x will range over structured terms that correspond to discourse referent structures that are appropriate for the type d. For the treatment of infelicity used in $\mathrm{PT}^{\mathfrak{P}}$ and $\mathrm{PT}^{\mathfrak{D}}$ to be extended to discourse, we need to be able to characterise the structure cat_d (the "category" of d, defined below) of the discourse referents specified by d, assuming that d is felicitous. The body of the quantified expression b should then constitute a proposition when x ranges over terms of the form given by cat_d, if b is felicitous.

In a static PTQ-like theory, all quantifiers would range over simple denotable individuals, and all the bodies of quantifiers would have to form propositions when x is instantiated by a term in $\mathfrak{d}$ (using the notation of $\mathrm{PT}^{\mathfrak{D}}$). In PT^{dt}, this has to be generalised to take account of the fact that we will be quantifying over binary trees whose leaves are in $\mathfrak{d}$. That is, the quantification in $q\dot{\varepsilon}d.b$ is restricted so that x ranges over terms of cat_d.

In effect, for the discourse corresponding to the proposition $q\dot{\varepsilon}d.b$ to be felicitous, then the domain d of the quantifier should form a proposition with terms of cat_d, and the body b should form a proposition when x is instantiated by terms of cat_d. Typically, this will not be the case if either d or b contain non-denoting definite descriptors, or pronouns that do not refer to a term that is provably denotable.[102]

5.4.1 Axioms for cat

The expression $\mathsf{cat}_t(s)$ asserts that s viewed as a type, ${}^{\tau}s$, can form propositions with elements of t. In the case of terms of the form $\langle d, f, g\rangle$ where g contains no further nominals (like a "test" in dynamic logics) and d is one of ς or π, the expressions will have the same category as f. In the recursive cases, the cat of the expression will be the disjoint union of the cats of the constituents. The predicate dep holds of those terms that are represented by dependent types when they are interpreted as a type. The axioms also allow us to prove that dep just holds of those terms that contain further nominals.

Axiom 5.1 (cat) *Base Case.*

$$\mathsf{Pty}_{\mathfrak{D}}(f) \rightarrow \mathsf{cat}_{\mathfrak{d}}(f)$$

[102]Here, we gloss over the details of enforcing number agreement between a properties, relations and their arguments, which would be required in an effective implementation of this theory. There is also the possibility that b, d are paradoxical, or that their constituent terms are not appropriately typed, but these cases are not of central concern at this point.

Axiom 5.2 (cat) *When g is a "test," containing no further nominals.*

$$(\mathsf{cat}_a(f) \mathbin{\&} \forall x \varepsilon a.\mathrm{P}(gx)) \rightarrow (\mathsf{cat}_a\langle d, f, g\rangle \mathbin{\&} {\sim}\mathsf{dep}\langle d, f, g\rangle)$$

Axiom 5.3 (cat) *Fully recursive case.*

$$(\mathsf{cat}_a(f) \mathbin{\&} \forall x \varepsilon a.\mathsf{cat}_b(gx)) \rightarrow (\mathsf{cat}_{a\otimes b}\langle d, f, g\rangle \mathbin{\&} \mathsf{dep}\langle d, f, g\rangle)$$

The term $\otimes$ is to be defined as in §2.3.2.

5.4.2 Axioms for Propositions with $^\tau$ and $^\kappa$

We need axioms that allow us to prove the propositionhood of expressions of the form $^\kappa t$ when appropriate. Some economy can be made here by stating that if t is an atomic proposition then so is $^\kappa t$ and, in the complex cases, observing that $^\kappa t$ should only be a proposition if t can be assigned a cat.

Axiom 5.4 (Propositionhood of $^\kappa\cdot$) *Base case.*

$$\mathrm{P}(t) \rightarrow \mathrm{P}(^\kappa t)$$

Axiom 5.5 (Propositionhood of $^\kappa\cdot$) *Recursive case with ς.*

$$\exists t(\mathsf{cat}_t\langle \varsigma, f, g\rangle) \rightarrow \mathrm{P}^\kappa\langle \varsigma, f, g\rangle$$

Axiom 5.6 (Propositionhood of $^\kappa\cdot$) *Recursive case with π.*

$$\exists t(\mathsf{cat}_t\langle \pi, f, g\rangle) \rightarrow \mathrm{P}^\kappa\langle \pi, f, g\rangle$$

We must also add axioms that enable us to show when $^\tau tx$ (or equivalently, $x\varepsilon{}^\tau t$) is a proposition:

Axiom 5.7 (Propositionhood of $^\tau\cdot$) *Base case.*

$$(\mathsf{Pty}_{\mathfrak{D}}(p) \mathbin{\&} x \varepsilon \mathfrak{d}) \rightarrow \mathrm{P}(^\tau px)$$

That is:

$$\mathsf{cat}_{\mathfrak{d}}(p) \rightarrow \forall x \varepsilon \mathfrak{d}.\mathrm{P}(^\tau px)$$

Axiom 5.8 (Propositionhood of $^\tau\cdot$) *Recursive case with ς.*

$$\mathsf{cat}_t\langle \varsigma, f, g\rangle \rightarrow \forall x \varepsilon t.\mathrm{P}(^\tau\langle \varsigma, f, g\rangle x)$$

Axiom 5.9 (Propositionhood of $^\tau\cdot$) *Recursive case with π.*

$$\mathsf{cat}_t\langle \pi, f, g\rangle \rightarrow \forall x \varepsilon t.\mathrm{P}(^\tau\langle \pi, f, g\rangle x)$$

So, when interpreted as a type, these terms form propositions if their argument is of the appropriate cat.

5.4.3 Axioms of Truth with $^{\tau}$ and $^{\kappa}$

Now we are in a position to axiomatise the truth conditions for expressions of the form $^{\kappa}t$:

Axiom 5.10 (Truth of $^{\kappa}\cdot$) *Base case.*

$$\mathrm{P}(t) \rightarrow (\mathrm{T}^{\kappa}(p) \leftrightarrow \mathrm{T}(p))$$

Axiom 5.11 (Truth of $^{\kappa}\cdot$) *Recursive case with ς.*

$$(\exists t(\mathsf{cat}_t\langle\varsigma, f, g\rangle) \;\&\; \mathsf{cat}_a(f)) \rightarrow$$
$$(\mathrm{T}^{\kappa}\langle\varsigma, f, g\rangle \leftrightarrow \exists x\varepsilon a.(\mathrm{T}(^{\tau}fx) \;\&\; \mathrm{T}^{\kappa}(gx)))$$

Axiom 5.12 (Truth of $^{\kappa}\cdot$) *Recursive case with π.*

$$(\exists t(\mathsf{cat}_t\langle\pi, f, g\rangle) \;\&\; \mathsf{cat}_a(f)) \rightarrow$$
$$(\mathrm{T}^{\kappa}\langle\pi, f, g\rangle \leftrightarrow \forall x\varepsilon a.(\mathrm{T}(^{\tau}fx) \rightarrow \mathrm{T}^{\kappa}(gx)))$$

Axiom 5.10 provides the base case. The preconditions on Axioms 5.11 and 5.12 guarantee: (i) that the truth conditions can only be considered for those representations that are felicitous (there are no non-denoting definites and inappropriately resolved anaphora); and (ii) that the quantifier in the truth conditions ranges over terms of the appropriate cat.[103]

Note that in these cases we can write $\exists x\dot{\varepsilon}^{\tau}f.\varphi$ and $\forall x\dot{\varepsilon}^{\tau}f.\varphi$ in place of $\exists x\dot{\varepsilon}a(\mathrm{T}(^{\tau}fx) \;\&\; \varphi)$ and $\forall x\varepsilon a(\mathrm{T}(^{\tau}fx) \rightarrow \varphi)$. As before, $x\dot{\varepsilon}f$ is intended to mean that x is further restricted to be of cat_f.

We also need truth conditions for expressions of the form $^{\tau}px$ (or "membership" conditions for $^{\tau}p$):

Axiom 5.13 (Truth of $^{\tau}\cdot$) *Base case.*

$$(\mathsf{Pty}_{\mathfrak{D}}(p) \;\&\; s\varepsilon\mathfrak{d}) \rightarrow (\mathrm{T}(^{\tau}ps) \leftrightarrow \mathrm{T}(ps))$$

Axiom 5.14 (Truth of $^{\tau}\cdot$ with ς) *Where g is a "test" that does not introduce more discourse referents.*

$$(\sim\mathsf{dep}\langle\varsigma, f, g\rangle \;\&\; \exists t(\mathsf{cat}_t\langle\varsigma, f, g\rangle \;\&\; s\varepsilon t)) \rightarrow$$
$$(\mathrm{T}(^{\tau}\langle\varsigma, f, g\rangle s) \leftrightarrow s\varepsilon\{y : {}^{\tau}fy \wedge {}^{\kappa}(gy)\})$$

[103] These axioms give rise to the universal reading of the donkey sentences, where the truth conditions of 'if a farmer owns a donkey, he beats it' requires that all farmers beat all donkeys that they own. There are other readings, including the existential reading that corresponds to: 'if a farmer owns a donkey then there is a donkey he owns that he beats'. The axioms of truth for the theory would have to be changed to allow us to obtain the following truth conditions: $\forall f\dot{\varepsilon}\mathit{farmer}'.(\exists d\dot{\varepsilon}\mathit{donkey}'.\mathit{own}'fd \rightarrow \exists d\dot{\varepsilon}\mathit{donkey}'.(\mathit{own}'fd \;\&\; \mathit{beat}'fd))$. Determining how such ambiguities arise, and how they can be formalised, is beyond the scope of this work.

Axiom 5.15 (Truth of $^{\tau}\cdot$ with ς) *The fully recursive case, where g introduces more discourse referents.*

$$\begin{gathered}(\mathsf{dep}\langle\varsigma, f, g\rangle \ \& \ \exists t(\mathsf{cat}_t\langle\varsigma, f, g\rangle \ \& \ s\varepsilon t)) \rightarrow \\ (\mathrm{T}({}^{\tau}\langle\varsigma, f, g\rangle s) \leftrightarrow s\varepsilon\Sigma^{\tau} f(\lambda x^{\tau}(gx)))\end{gathered}$$

Axiom 5.16 (Truth of $^{\tau}\cdot$ with π)

$$\begin{gathered}(\exists t(\mathsf{cat}_t\langle\pi, f, g\rangle) \ \& \ \mathsf{cat}_a(f) \ \& \ s\varepsilon t) \rightarrow \\ (\mathrm{T}({}^{\tau}\langle\pi, f, g\rangle s) \leftrightarrow s\varepsilon\{y : y \approx \biguplus\langle\varsigma, f, g\rangle \wedge \Theta z\varepsilon a({}^{\tau} fz \Rightarrow {}^{\kappa}(gz))\})\end{gathered}$$

The meaning of $\biguplus\langle\varsigma, f, g\rangle$ is elaborated as follows:

Definition 5.1 ($\biguplus\cdot$) *Expansion of abbreviated form, to give an appropriate initial expression for the subsequent recursive axioms.*

$$\biguplus\langle\varsigma, f, g\rangle =_{\mathrm{def}} \biguplus_{\lambda x.x}^{\langle\varsigma, f, g\rangle} \langle\varsigma, f, g\rangle$$

Axiom 5.17 ($\biguplus_{\cdot}^{\cdot}\cdot$) *Recursive case, with ς.*

$$\begin{gathered}(\exists u(\mathsf{cat}_u\langle\varsigma, f, g\rangle) \ \& \ \mathsf{dep}\langle\varsigma, f, g\rangle) \rightarrow \\ (\biguplus_s^t \langle\varsigma, f, g\rangle = \langle\biguplus_{\mathsf{fst}(s)}^t f, \biguplus_{\mathsf{snd}(s)}^t g\rangle)\end{gathered}$$

Axiom 5.18 ($\biguplus_{\cdot}^{\cdot}\cdot$) *Base case; with non-dependent expressions.*

$$\begin{gathered}(\exists u(\mathsf{cat}_u(t')) \ \& \sim\mathsf{dep}(t')) \rightarrow \\ (\biguplus_s^t t' = \sigma x(\Xi y\varepsilon u.({}^{\tau} ty \wedge sy \approx x)))\end{gathered}$$

Axiom 5.19 ($\biguplus_{\cdot}^{\cdot}\cdot$) *Recursive case, with π.*

$$\begin{gathered}(\exists u(\mathsf{cat}_u\langle\pi, f, g\rangle) \ \& \ \mathsf{cat}_a(f)) \rightarrow \\ (\biguplus_s^t \langle\pi, f, g\rangle = \sigma x(\Xi y\varepsilon a.({}^{\tau} ty \wedge sy \approx x)))\end{gathered}$$

This is just a more pedantic formalisation of the treatment described in §5.3.2. In essence, $\biguplus\langle\varsigma, f, g\rangle$ is intended to have the same form as a term that satisfies the type ${}^{\tau}\langle\varsigma, f, g\rangle$, but where each atomic denotable in $\biguplus\langle\varsigma, f, g\rangle$ is replaced by the supremum of the denotables that can appear in its position in the witnesses to ${}^{\tau}\langle\varsigma, f, g\rangle$.

5.5 Relative Clauses

To represent relative clauses, it is necessary to modify the application of terms in the semantics in order to recover the witness to the head noun that is modified by the relative clause. Dávila-Pérez defines a function app for this purpose in MLTT (Dávila-Pérez 1995). We could adapt this to the theory here more or less directly (Fox 1994a). However, here we will give a slightly different formalisation.

The term H, when given suitable arguments, can be given the behaviour of a function that is equated with a selector that picks the referent corresponding to the head of the relative clause. In our notation, $H_f(t)$ is intended to recurse through the the discourse f to find the head of its witness t:

Axiom 5.20 ($H.(\cdot)$) *Base case (where* $\sim\exists gh(f = \langle\varsigma, g, h\rangle)$*).*

$$\mathsf{Pty}_{\mathfrak{D}}(f) \rightarrow (H_f(t) = t)$$

Axiom 5.21 ($H.(\cdot)$) *With* $\langle\varsigma, f, g\rangle$*, where* g *is a "test" containing no further nominals (i.e.* $\sim\mathsf{dep}\langle\varsigma, f, g\rangle$*).*

$$\begin{aligned}&(\sim\mathsf{dep}\langle\varsigma, f, g\rangle \,\&\, \mathsf{cat}_a(f) \,\&\, \forall x\varepsilon a.\mathrm{P}(gx)) \rightarrow\\ &\quad(H_{\langle\varsigma,f,g\rangle}(t) = \mathsf{fst}(t))\end{aligned}$$

Axiom 5.22 ($H.(\cdot)$) *With* $\langle\varsigma, f, g\rangle$*, where* g *contains further nominals (i.e.* $\mathsf{dep}\langle\varsigma, f, g\rangle$*).*

$$\begin{aligned}&(\mathsf{dep}\langle\varsigma, f, g\rangle \,\&\, \mathsf{cat}_a(f) \,\&\, \forall x\varepsilon a.\mathsf{cat}_b(gx)) \rightarrow\\ &\quad(H_{\langle\varsigma,f,g\rangle}(t) = \mathsf{fst}(H_f(t)))\end{aligned}$$

We might try to achieve this effect by strengthening the axioms for $^\tau$ and $^\kappa$. However, this would result in much duplication. By just strengthening the equality of terms involving H, we do not need to re-write the existing axioms for $^\tau$ and $^\kappa$.

To account for relative clauses in the representation of natural language, determiners like 'every' and 'a', rather than being represented by:

$$\lambda pq\langle\varsigma, p, q\rangle$$
$$\lambda pq\langle\pi, p, q\rangle$$

are instead represented by:

$$\lambda pq\langle\varsigma, p, \lambda x(q(H_p x))\rangle$$
$$\lambda pq\langle\pi, p, \lambda x(q(H_p x))\rangle$$

In the truth conditions, x will be bound to the term containing the discourse referents of p. Then H_p picks out the referent of the head noun represented by p.

The use of function H is illustrated in the example of §C.1.1.

5.6 SUMMARY

We have sketched how we can treat some simple examples of anaphora just using selector functions, dependent types, and pairs—all of which can be implemented in the λ-calculus—together with classical quantifiers, and a Link-style treatment of plurals. In this sense, we can see that existing classical machinery is adequate for obtaining the classical truth conditions of discourse.

In this theory, rather than stipulating that singular discourse referents are inaccessible when they occur within the scope of a universal or conditional, their inaccessibility is a consequence of the "plural context" which is created by such expressions. It is the very act of creating appropriate antecedents for plural pronouns that leads to the loss of singular referents from such contexts: the singular referents are inaccessible because they have been "transformed" into plurals.

It could be argued that the ς and π expressions used in the initial representation of discourse fall outside the domain of classical logic. Further, as they have perhaps a rather complex case analysis, they do not really satisfy the requirements of new logical constants. However, these operators do not need to be primitives; they can be implemented as triples in the λ-calculus, in which case their interpretation as propositions and as types, produced by $^{\kappa}$ and $^{\tau}$, can be obtained by using projection functions, all of which can be implemented in λ-calculus.

Even given the systematic nature in which the theory obtains the classical truth conditions, there is a sense in which the theory is not strictly compositional: despite the fact that they can be implemented as triples in the λ-calculus, the contribution that π and ς make in the final truth conditions still depends upon their context.

Due to the nature of the phenomena, all theories that deal with anaphora must bend the rule of compositionality to some extent, especially when we consider going all the way from discourse to truth conditions expressed in classically quantified logic. In DRT, a top-level DRS effectively gives rise to existential quantification. However, there is no corresponding existential quantification in the truth conditions when a DRS occurs as an antecedent to a condition (Kamp 1981, Kamp and Reyle 1993). Similarly in DPL, an "existential" quantifier is sometimes interpreted as classically existential, but in the antecedent to a conditional it is interpreted as classically universal (Groenendijk and Stokhof 1990, Groenendijk and Stokhof 1991) (see §5.1). However, in these theories the variations in behaviour are not encoded directly in the representation language, instead, these patterns of behaviour follow from their models.

The apparent complexity of PT^{dt} can be justified as follows. The goal is to produce a classically quantified representation of discourse mechanically. That is, we are interested in computational semantics. We could take any of the theories of discourse mentioned and implement them. However, the representations produced are not classically quantified, even though they have models which can be used to give them a classically quantified interpretation. The relevant aspects of their models can be encoded in the computational machinery to produce the classical interpretation. However, in doing so, the case-wise analysis used to obtain the classical interpretations of the representations is effectively encoded in the corresponding theories. This results in the same degree of complexity in the semantics as in PT^{dt}.

If uniformity of analysis is seen to be important, perhaps for aesthetic reasons, it is always possible to achieve this by keeping a representation that is constructive in character, and then providing a model of that theory which can be used to obtain classical truth conditions, if required.

This work shows that we can obtain classically quantified, first-order representations of some examples of discourse without at any stage resorting to more powerful systems. Additional work is needed to explore more fully the behaviour of plural anaphora and examples involving non-logical quantifiers, and also to see whether this approach can be extended to other, more recalcitrant discourse phenomena.

5.7 Consistency of PT^{dt}

We can show the theory PT^{dt} is consistent by showing that whenever an expression of PT^{dt} (such as ${}^{\kappa}\langle d, f, g\rangle$) forms a proposition, then it has truth conditions that can be expressed in $\mathrm{PT}^{\mathfrak{D}}$, which we already know is consistent. In effect, the additional axioms only allow us to consider the truth conditions of terms that are already known to be propositions in $\mathrm{PT}^{\mathfrak{D}}$.

This might seem strange: there is a sense in which PT^{dt} is no stronger than $\mathrm{PT}^{\mathfrak{D}}$. The difference is one of *expressivity* rather than formal *power*. In particular, PT^{dt} allows us to express propositions in a manner that is easy to produce compositionally from NL discourse. The terms used in the theory do not then constitute a new ontology of discourse, they are merely a sugar that sweetens the process of obtaining appropriate truth conditions.

We proceed by sketching the proofs of the consistency of PT and $\mathrm{PT}^{\mathfrak{D}}$, and then show that PT^{dt} is an "innocent" strengthening of $\mathrm{PT}^{\mathfrak{D}}$, and hence is also consistent.

An alternative approach would be to show how all the relevant terms in the PT^{dt} can be defined as λ-terms in PT, such that they have the appropriate behaviour as a consequence of the axioms of λ-calculus and PT. As mentioned before, ς and π can be implemented with triples (or pairings), and ${}^{\tau}, {}^{\kappa}$ would then merely act as projection functions.

Theorem 5.1 PT *is consistent.*

Proof. By presenting a model. Summary: Take a model of the λ-calculus, for example a *domain* of *complete lattices* (Scott 1973). Then, following Aczel, build a *Frege Structure* based on this *domain* which has sets P and T whose structural requirements satisfy the axioms for P and T (Aczel 1980) (§2.6). □

Theorem 5.2 $\mathrm{PT}^{\mathfrak{D}}$ *is consistent.*

Proof. By presenting a model. Summary: Take the model for PT, and strengthen the lattice-theoretic model of the λ-calculus so that a part of it corresponds to a *Boolean algebra.* Plurals and mass terms in $\mathrm{PT}^{\mathfrak{D}}$ can then be modelled by elements of this *Boolean algebra* in a way that satisfies the relevant axioms (Fox 1993) (§3.4). □

Definition 5.2 *(innocent terms): A term p in* PT *(or* $\mathrm{PT}^{\mathfrak{D}}$*) strengthened by E (i.e.* PT+E *or* $\mathrm{PT}^{\mathfrak{D}}$+$E$ *resp.) is* innocent *iff, for any consistent property-theoretic theory* Γ*, if p is a proposition in* $\Gamma + E$ *then it is truth conditionally equivalent to a proposition in* Γ.

Definition 5.3 *(innocent strengthening): A strengthening of* PT *(or* $\mathrm{PT}^{\mathfrak{D}}$*) by E is an* innocent strengthening *iff all terms in* PT+E *(*$\mathrm{PT}^{\mathfrak{D}}$+$E$ *resp.) are* innocent.

Theorem 5.3 PT^{dt} *is an* innocent strengthening *of* $\mathrm{PT}^{\mathfrak{D}}$.

Proof. From Lemmas 5.1–5.9 below, all terms whose behaviour are governed by the new axioms of PT^{dt} are innocent. □

Theorem 5.4 PT^{dt} *is consistent.*

Proof. (By contradiction.) Assume that PT^{dt} is inconsistent, then for some p in PT^{dt} such that $\mathrm{P}(p)$ and $\mathrm{T}(p) \leftrightarrow \sim \mathrm{T}(p)$. But from innocence of PT^{dt}, there must be some p' in $\mathrm{PT}^{\mathfrak{D}}$ such that $\mathrm{P}(p')$ and $\mathrm{T}(p') \leftrightarrow \sim \mathrm{T}(p')$. Therefore, $\mathrm{PT}^{\mathfrak{D}}$ would be inconsistent. However, we know that $\mathrm{PT}^{\mathfrak{D}}$ is consistent, therefore the assumption is false: PT^{dt} is consistent. □

Lemmas 5.1–5.9 contribute to the proof of the innocence of PT^{dt}. They proceed by examining all cases of the axioms governing ${}^{\tau}s$ and ${}^{\kappa}s$ for terms s. In outline, if the PT^{dt} axioms for cat (§5.4.1) together with some consistent assertions Γ allow us to show $\mathsf{cat}_t(s)$ for some t, then the additional rules for propositions in PT^{dt} (§5.4.2) assert the propositionhood of expressions involving ${}^{\tau}s$ and ${}^{\kappa}s$. However, we can show, via the additional PT^{dt} axioms of truth (§5.4.3), that these "new" propositions are truth conditionally equivalent with expressions involving terms that we can already show to be propositions from Γ.

If we look at the axioms in governing cat (§5.4.1) we see that we must show that the theory is well behaved in the following cases:

1. for ${}^{\tau}f$ and ${}^{\kappa}f$ when $\mathsf{Pty}_{\mathfrak{D}}(f)$;
2. for (a) ${}^{\tau}\langle\varsigma, f, g\rangle$; (b) ${}^{\kappa}\langle\varsigma, f, g\rangle$; (a)′ ${}^{\tau}\langle\pi, f, g\rangle$; and (b)′ ${}^{\kappa}\langle\pi, f, g\rangle$ when
   (i) $\mathsf{cat}_a(f)$ and $\mathrm{P}(gt)$ for all $t\varepsilon a$;
   (ii) $\mathsf{cat}_a(f)$ and $\mathsf{cat}_b(gt)$ for all $t\varepsilon a$;

First we must show that some of our type restrictions a on quantified variables obtained from expressions of the form $\mathsf{cat}_a(f)$ are innocent, by showing that a is a property.

Lemma 5.1 *If we can prove* $\mathsf{cat}_a(f)$*, then a is a property.*

Proof. By cases, one for each of the axioms 5.1–5.3 (trivial):

1. $\mathsf{Pty}_{\mathfrak{D}}(f) \to \mathsf{cat}_{\mathfrak{d}}(f)$, but we know that $\mathsf{Pty}(\mathfrak{d})$ (axioms of $\mathrm{PT}^{\mathfrak{D}}$).
2. (First inductive case with $d = \varsigma$ or π.) Assume $\mathsf{Pty}(a)$. If $\forall x\varepsilon a.\mathrm{P}(gx)$ then $\mathsf{cat}_a\langle d, f, g\rangle$ and $\mathsf{Pty}(a)$ (assumption).
3. (Second inductive case with $d = \varsigma$ or π.) Assume $\mathsf{Pty}(a)$ and $\mathsf{Pty}(b)$. If $\forall x\varepsilon a.\mathsf{cat}_b(gx)$, then $\mathsf{cat}_{a\otimes b}\langle d, f, g\rangle$. But if $\mathsf{Pty}(a)$ and $\mathsf{Pty}(b)$, then $\mathsf{Pty}(a \otimes b)$ (from the definition of $\otimes$, §2.3.2).

□

Now we can examine the innocence of terms ${}^{\tau}t$ and ${}^{\kappa}t$.

Lemma 5.2 ${}^{\tau}t$ *is* innocent*, where t is not a discourse term.*

Proof. When $\mathsf{Pty}_{\mathfrak{D}}(f)$ then $\mathsf{cat}_{\mathfrak{d}}(f)$ (PT^{dt} axioms for cat, §5.4.1) and $\mathrm{P}({}^{\tau}ft)$ when $t\varepsilon\mathfrak{d}$ (PT^{dt} axioms for P, §5.4.2). The truth conditions of $\mathrm{T}({}^{\tau}ft)$ are equivalent to $\mathrm{T}(ft)$ (PT^{dt} axioms for T, §5.4.3). We already know that $\mathrm{P}(ft)$ (from the assumptions and definition of $\mathsf{Pty}_{\mathfrak{D}}$). Therefore, this case is *innocent.* □

Lemma 5.3 ${}^{\tau}\langle\varsigma, f, g\rangle$ *is* innocent*, where g is a basic term.*

Proof. (By induction) Assume that for f such that $\mathsf{cat}_a(f)$, ${}^{\tau}f$ is *innocent.* When $\mathsf{cat}_a(f)$ and $\mathrm{P}(gt)$ for all $t\varepsilon a$, then $\mathsf{cat}_a\langle d, f, g\rangle$ and $\sim\mathsf{dep}\langle d, f, g\rangle$ (PT^{dt} axioms for cat, §5.4.1). Hence $\mathrm{P}({}^{\tau}\langle\varsigma, f, g\rangle t)$ (PT^{dt} axioms for P, §5.4.2), and $\mathrm{T}({}^{\tau}\langle\varsigma, f, g\rangle t)$ is equivalent to $t\varepsilon\{y : {}^{\tau}fy \wedge {}^{\kappa}(gy)\}$ for all $t\varepsilon a$

(PT^{dt} axioms for T, §5.4.3). This, in turn, is equivalent to $\mathrm{T}({}^{\tau}ft)$ & $\mathrm{T}^{\kappa}(gt)$ (Definition of $\{\cdot\}$, §2.3.1). Considering the second conjunct, we already know that $\mathrm{P}(gt)$ for all $t\varepsilon a$ (initial assumption), hence we have $\mathrm{P}^{\kappa}(gt)$ (PT^{dt} axioms for P, §5.4.2). The truth conditions of ${}^{\kappa}(gt)$ are exactly those of gt (PT^{dt} axioms for T, §5.4.3) and so it is *innocent.* Considering the first conjunct, we have $\mathrm{P}({}^{\tau}ft)$ (PT^{dt} axioms for P, §5.4.2, two cases), and from the inductive hypothesis we know this is *innocent.* Therefore, this case is *innocent.* □

Lemma 5.4 ${}^{\tau}\langle\varsigma, f, g\rangle$ *is* innocent, *for any* f, g.

Proof. (By induction) Assume that if $\mathsf{cat}_a(f)$ and $\mathsf{cat}_b(gt)$ then ${}^{\tau}(fs)$ and ${}^{\tau}(gs)t$ are *innocent* for all $s\varepsilon a$ and $t\varepsilon b$. When $\mathsf{cat}_a(f)$ and $\mathsf{cat}_b(gt)$ for all $t\varepsilon a$, then $\mathsf{cat}_{a\otimes b}\langle d, f, g\rangle$ and $\mathsf{dep}\langle d, f, g\rangle$ (PT^{dt} axioms for cat, §5.4.1). Hence, for all $u\varepsilon a\otimes b$, it is the case that $\mathrm{P}({}^{\tau}\langle\varsigma, f, g\rangle u)$ holds (PT^{dt} axioms for P, §5.4.2), and $\mathrm{T}({}^{\tau}\langle\varsigma, f, g\rangle u)$ is equivalent to $u\varepsilon\Sigma^{\tau}f(\lambda y^{\tau}(gy))$ (PT^{dt} axioms for T, §5.4.3). Now, this in turn is equivalent to $\mathrm{T}({}^{\tau}f(\mathsf{fst}(u)))$ & $\mathrm{T}^{\tau}(g(\mathsf{fst}(u)))(\mathsf{snd}(u))$ (Definition of Σ). Considering the first conjunct, $\mathsf{fst}(u)\varepsilon a$ (PT^{dt} axioms for T, §5.4.3, and definition of Σ), it follows that $\mathrm{P}({}^{\tau}f(\mathsf{fst}(u)))$. In the second conjunct, $\mathsf{snd}(u)\varepsilon b$ (PT^{dt} axioms for T, §5.4.3 and definition of Σ), and $\mathsf{cat}_b(g(\mathsf{fst}(u)))$ (initial assumption), hence it follows that $\mathrm{P}({}^{\tau}(g(\mathsf{fst}(u)))(\mathsf{snd}(u)))$ (PT^{dt} axioms for P, §5.4.2). From the inductive hypothesis, these conjuncts are *innocent.* Therefore, this case is *innocent.* □

Lemma 5.5 ${}^{\kappa}\langle\varsigma, f, g\rangle$ *is* innocent, *when* f, g *are basic terms.*

Proof. When $\mathsf{Pty}_{\mathfrak{D}}(f)$ then $\mathsf{cat}_{\mathfrak{d}}(f)$ (PT^{dt} axioms for cat, §5.4.1) and $\mathrm{P}^{\kappa}(fs)$ for all $s\varepsilon\mathfrak{d}$ (PT^{dt} axioms for P, §5.4.2 and definition of $\mathsf{Pty}_{\mathfrak{D}}$). Also $\mathrm{T}^{\kappa}(fs)$ is equivalent to $\mathrm{T}(fs)$ (PT^{dt} axioms for T, §5.4.3). However, we already know that $\mathrm{P}(fs)$ (from the assumptions and definition of $\mathsf{Pty}_{\mathfrak{D}}$). Therefore, this case is *innocent.* □

Lemma 5.6 ${}^{\kappa}\langle\varsigma, f, g\rangle$ *is* innocent *where* g *is a basic term.*

Proof. When $\mathsf{cat}_a(f)$ and $\mathrm{P}(gt)$ for all $t\varepsilon a$, then we can show $\mathsf{cat}_a\langle d, f, g\rangle$ and $\sim\mathsf{dep}\langle d, f, g\rangle$ (PT^{dt} axioms for cat, §5.4.1). Hence $\mathrm{P}^{\kappa}\langle\varsigma, f, g\rangle$ (PT^{dt} axioms for P, §5.4.2), and $\mathrm{T}^{\kappa}\langle\varsigma, f, g\rangle$ is equivalent to $\exists x\varepsilon a(\mathrm{T}({}^{\tau}fx)$ & $\mathrm{T}^{\kappa}(gx))$ (PT^{dt} axioms for T, §5.4.3). Now, first, we know that $\mathrm{P}^{\kappa}(gt)$ for all $t\varepsilon a$ (PT^{dt} axioms for P, §5.4.2 and initial assumption). The truth conditions of $\mathrm{T}^{\kappa}(gt)$ are exactly those of $\mathrm{T}(gt)$ (PT^{dt} axioms for T, §5.4.3), which we already know to be a proposition (initial assumption), so this is *innocent.* Second, for all $t\varepsilon a$, $\mathrm{P}({}^{\tau}ft)$ (PT^{dt} axioms for P, §5.4.2, two cases), and we know from previous proof, that P is not strengthened when we consider $\mathrm{T}({}^{\tau}ft)$, where $\mathsf{cat}_a(f)$ and $t\varepsilon a$. Therefore this case is *innocent.* □

Notice that, using these two cases (Lemma 5.5 and Lemma 5.6), if $\mathsf{cat}_{\eth}(gt)$ for $t\varepsilon a$, (where a is a property), we can show that ${}^{\kappa}(gt)$ is *innocent* (the proof is trivial). This provides a base case for the final inductive lemma concerning ς.

Lemma 5.7 ${}^{\kappa}\langle\varsigma, f, g\rangle$ *is* innocent *for any* f, g.

Proof. (By induction.) Assume that if $\mathsf{cat}_b(gt)$ for all $t\varepsilon a$, then ${}^{\kappa}(gt)$ is *innocent.* If $\mathsf{cat}_a(f)$ and $\mathsf{cat}_b(gt)$, then $\mathsf{cat}_{a\otimes b}\langle d, f, g\rangle$ and $\mathsf{dep}\langle d, f, g\rangle$ (PT^{dt} axioms for cat, §5.4.1). Hence $\mathrm{P}^{\kappa}\langle\varsigma, f, g\rangle$ (PT^{dt} axioms for P, §5.4.2), and $\mathrm{T}^{\kappa}\langle\varsigma, f, g\rangle$ is equivalent to $\exists x\varepsilon a(\mathrm{T}({}^{\tau}fx)\ \&\ \mathrm{T}^{\kappa}(gx))$ (PT^{dt} axioms for T, §5.4.3). Again, ${}^{\tau}fx$ is *innocent* (as in the previous case) as is ${}^{\kappa}(gx)$ (from the inductive hypothesis). Therefore, this case is *innocent.* □

Lemma 5.8 ${}^{\kappa}\langle\pi, f, g\rangle$ *is* innocent.

Proof. If $\exists t(\mathsf{cat}_t\langle\pi, f, g\rangle)$ then $\mathrm{P}^{\kappa}\langle\pi, g, f\rangle$ (PT^{dt} axioms for P, §5.4.2), and $\mathrm{T}^{\kappa}\langle\pi, g, f\rangle$ is equivalent to $\forall x\varepsilon a.(\mathrm{T}({}^{\tau}fx) \rightarrow \mathrm{T}^{\kappa}(gx))$ where $\mathsf{cat}_a f$ (PT^{dt} axioms for T, §5.4.3). This is innocent (trivial variant of proof of innocence of ${}^{\kappa}t$ with ς). □

Lemma 5.9 ${}^{\tau}\langle\pi, f, g\rangle$ *is* innocent.

Proof. If $\exists t(\mathsf{cat}_t\langle\pi, f, g\rangle)$ then $\mathrm{P}({}^{\tau}\langle\pi, f, g\rangle s)$ (PT^{dt} axioms for P, §5.4.2) and $\mathrm{T}({}^{\tau}\langle\pi, f, g\rangle s)$ is equivalent to $s\varepsilon\{y : y \approx \biguplus\langle\varsigma, f, g\rangle \wedge \Theta z\varepsilon a({}^{\tau}fz \Rightarrow {}^{\kappa}(gz))\}$ where $\mathsf{cat}_a(f)$ (PT^{dt} axioms for T, §5.4.3). This is equivalent to $s = \biguplus\langle\varsigma, f, g\rangle\ \&\ \forall z\varepsilon a(\mathrm{T}({}^{\tau}fz) \rightarrow \mathrm{T}^{\kappa}(gz))$ (definition of $\{\cdot\}$ and axioms of truth). The equality is innocent (axioms for T), and the second conjunct is innocent (from innocence of ${}^{\kappa}\langle\pi, f, g\rangle$). □

Concerning the terms H, $\biguplus$ and the axioms that govern them: again, we can show that any representation of felicitous discourse that involves these terms is equivalent to one in which they do not appear. We will illustrate with H. There are three axioms that give the equality conditions of expressions involving H. In all cases, H will be eliminated (two bases case, one recursive case). In the semantics of natural language, all the cases of felicitous discourse in which H arises are such that the axioms governing the equality of H allow it to be eliminated (provided that H is not itself a natural language denotable). The details of this, and the similar case of $\biguplus$, are left as an exercise for the interested reader.

Hence, in all cases, when the additional axioms of PT^{dt} apply to a term, the resultant truth conditions are equivalent to the truth conditions of a term in PT extended with a notion of denotables (such as $\mathrm{PT}^{\mathfrak{D}}$ or $\mathrm{PT}^{\mathfrak{P}}$). So, as stated in Theorem 5.3, PT^{dt} is an innocent strengthening of $\mathrm{PT}^{\mathfrak{D}}$.

5.8 Conclusions

We have seen how appropriate truth conditions for simple discourse can be found within a classical theory, without changing the interpretation of the logical quantifiers, and without proposing a new ontology of discourse structures.

We have shown that all of the formal devices used do not strengthen the basic theory (at least, not when used for their intended purpose), they merely increase the expressiveness of the notation.

The requirement of compositionality, in its strict sense, are broken here, perhaps to be replaced by a more general notion of computational tractability. All else being equal, a theory in which the representations can be obtained with functions of low computational complexity is to be favoured.

The theory does not offer any treatment of the more awkward anaphoric phenomena, and its analysis of plural anaphora is poor and requires considerable work to account for any significant fragment of plural phenomena. However, this is not the objective of the theory: it is not the intention that the theoretical approach advocated here stands or falls because of the existence or absence of a proposal to address any particular phenomena. Rather, the aim is to show that a first-order classical logic with a rich range of types can be used to obtain classical truth conditions of at least those examples of discourse that have been taken to motivate a move away from a classical logic with a basic Aristotelean ontology.

In this context, it is up to the advocates of essentially non-classical proposals to demonstrate that a non-classical interpretation of the logical quantifiers, or an ontology of discourse structures, is essential for an adequate account of discourse phenomena.

There are similarities between DRT and PT in that both take seriously the idea of a level of representation between natural language and the model-theoretic semantics. If the goal is to produce classically quantified truth conditions, it could be argued that dynamic logics also provide a representational level. However, in the case of PT, the representational level is independently motivated by consideration of the intensionality of propositions and properties.

6

Conclusions

This work could be viewed as providing examples of how semantic issues can be addressed in a property-theoretic setting, where properties and propositions are taken seriously as primitive notions, rather than notions that are derived from set theory. More generally, it provides examples of how various ontological questions can be answered by making the weakest commitments that can explain the data.

6.1 Properties

Although set theory is perhaps indispensable in mathematics, and although we may find it a familiar and "natural" way of expressing our semantic intuitions, it is perhaps mistaken to assume that the intrinsically extensional notions of "set" and "member" are appropriate when the objective is to capture the intensional nature of properties and propositions.

We should ask ourselves what the most natural model is for our intuitions on the subject of properties, propositions and individuals. We can adopt the mathematicians approach to formalising a notion: take it to be primitive, and present axioms that produce the desired behaviour.

Care has been taken about equating everyday terms, such as "member," "collection" and "group," with theoretical notions that seem to express similar ideas. It could be argued that a theory that does equate these notions has more explanatory power, in that everyday notions are then shown to parallel the behaviour of theoretical entities that have an independently motivated existence. However, it is perhaps rather optimistic to assume that everyday notions correspond with apparently similar but more sophisticated mathematical concepts, just as it would be remarkable if our everyday understanding of how physical objects behave corresponded exactly with the sophisticated theories of physical science.

A key objective is to avoid an inconsistent theory. One way in which inconsistency can arise is via the logical paradoxes. Type-theoretic semantics, such as Montague's Intensional Logic, provide a way of avoiding the paradoxes. However, they also provide a rod for our backs when it comes to explaining apparently straightforward, and unproblematic predications whose natural analyses are ruled inadmissible by the type system. If we adopt an axiomatic approach to truth and felicitous propositions, such as PT, we can obtain a finer appreciation of the nature of paradox without the unnecessarily rigid discipline of a strongly typed theory and with greater intensionality.

Just because we use an axiomatic approach to reflect semantic intuitions does not mean that the resultant theory lacks predictive power.

One possible inadequacy of the theory adopted here is that it does not allow the internalisation of the key predicates which characterise properties, propositions and truth. There might be analyses of some phenomena for which this presents a drawback, such as a formalisation of the propositional attitudes, although it is by no means an insurmountable problem.

6.2 Individuals

In addition to particulars, natural language seems to allow us to predicate properties of both properties and propositions. This suggests that they be taken seriously as individuals. The weak typing of PT means that we can accept this view without the encumbrance of heavy-weight type-lifting machinery that would, inevitably, force us to bend our intuitions to fit the requirements of the formal theory.

Natural language does require us to extend the notion of individual beyond this, to account for the semantics of sentences involving plurals and mass terms. These lead to a genuine extension of the theory, which allows us to express propositions that cannot otherwise be represented.

By adopting an essentially axiomatic, rather than model-theoretic approach, the theory can remain silent on those ontological issues that do not seem appropriate for the semantics of natural language, such as the existence of atoms for mass terms. We can also extend the notion of a category mistake, as used in the treatment of the paradoxes, to the case of infelicitous predication of non-denoting descriptors.

Just because we need to add additional structure to the semantic theory to account for certain phenomena does not mean that we should become cavalier about adding even more structure. This applies in the case of "group" readings, which initially might seem to require another level of structure in the representations of collections, but which, as Schwarzschild argues convincingly, can be accounted for by considering the dynamic nature of language.

Similarly, with Landman's proposals for intensional individuals, the data that they seek to explain can be accounted for by other means that are already available (and required), namely, property modifiers.

There is some tension here. We might argue that as we can refer to these intensional individuals with anaphoric expressions, the most natural interpretation is to accept the view that there are intensional individuals, rather than the more complex view that anaphora then refer back to combinations of individuals and properties. However, it should still be accepted that these new individuals can be eliminated from the ontology of the theory without affecting our ability to express the appropriate inferences.

6.3 DISCOURSE

In the case of representing discourse, the problem can be cast as one of finding an appropriate mapping from natural language discourse into a classical logic. This is, perhaps, to be contrasted both with Discourse Representation Theory, where new ontological structures are devised, and with the approach adopted by dynamic logics, where the results of a standard PTQ-like compositional translation are re-interpreted.

Of course, it can be shown that representations in dynamic logics, or Discourse Representation Theory can be mapped into classical, first-order logic. Such representations can then be thought of as providing a computational device for constructing the appropriate semantics in classical logic.

In the discourse theory PT^{dt}, natural language is translated into a language of terms which provides an intermediate level of representation between natural language and classical logic. The terms used in this representation are definable, and need not be taken to be primitive. They can be thought of as "programs" which are used to build terms that, if felicitous, can be given truth conditions in a classical logic. In the presentation of the theory given here, the axioms governing these terms can be thought of as specifying the behaviour of these programs.

In a sense, the production of truth conditions for natural language discourse is reduced to a computational model, rather than a set-theoretic one. A computational model is weaker than a set-theoretic one. Also, although we can produce semantics that do not appeal to a notion of set, we cannot produce semantic representations without the notion of an algorithm, or program.

The problem of representing discourse is then the problem of finding a tractable algorithm for producing the classical representations, preferably with a low computational complexity. There is no need to appeal to additional ontological notions, or non-classical interpretations of the representation language.

It could be argued that we do have a new ontology in the proposed discourse theory: that of the terms used in its representation, and the axioms that govern their behaviour. However, these terms are not the objects of natural language discourse, and so do not feature in the ontology of natural language itself. They are part of the translation machinery used to compose the appropriate classical semantics, just as phrase-structure rules are not viewed as part of the semantic ontology of natural language, even though they can be used to obtain semantic representations.

Speaking formally, this need not be at odds with other approaches to representing discourse. It is perhaps the emphasis that is different: the primary goal is seen to be the production of appropriate classical truth conditions, rather than some intermediate representation that remains to be interpreted. To find the truth conditions of discourse, the logical language of truth conditions need not contain notions of discourse structure, or assignment functions, just as it need not contain the notion of a phrase-structure rule.

6.4 The Methodology of Least Commitment

A methodological principle that we have adopted is to use the weakest theory that can be made to account for the data. One criticism that might be levelled at the use of PT is that it is actually quite a strong theory; it contains within it the λ-calculus which can encode the class of computable functions. A response to this could be that our ability to reason with the meanings of discourse depends upon some general ability to process information by way of computable functions. Using λ-calculus does not then strengthen the theory beyond what we already know is required.

However, we might still have a stronger theory than is actually required. It could be argued that the brain, with its fixed resources, is not a universal Turing machine, but is more likely to have the computational power of a bound automata, or a finite state machine. What we could seek to do is argue that the λ-expressions used never exceed what can be computed by, say, a finite state machine.

In some senses, this is to adopt a similar position to those who develop semantic theories in higher-order logics—logics that have an intractable proof theory—and claim that, as used in the semantics of natural language, all the expressions produced can be reduced to a tractable part of higher-order logic. To adopt such a position still seems to undermine the methodology of least commitment. In the case of PT, the problem arises because the apparently simple and inexpressive formalism of the untyped λ-calculus—which, after all, just characterises a syntactic notion of substitution—results in quite a powerful language. If we take this criticism seriously, then we could either produce a revised version of PT that uses a weaker language of terms, or explore the constraints on semantic representations so that their reduction to normal form is equivalent to a relatively weak computational device.

A

Dynamic Property Theory

As has been shown by Chierchia, the representation of discourse using Dynamic Montague Grammar (Groenendijk and Stokhof 1991) can be adapted to form a Dynamic Property Theory. A dynamic interpretation of generalised quantifiers is given by adding operators which allow the existential quantifier to bind outside its syntactic scope (Chierchia 1991).

Unlike the theory PT^{dt} of §5.4, Dynamic Property Theory requires us to make alterations to the basic theory and its model. However, it still has a potential advantage over Dynamic Montague Grammar in that paradoxes are not re-introduced when anaphoric reference to properties is permitted.

Essentially, this approach follows Karttunen in saying that indefinites set up discourse referents which subsequently can be referred to by anaphoric expressions (Karttunen 1976). In dynamic semantics, this is taken to mean that the existential quantifier should be able to bind outside its syntactic scope in the representation. To achieve this, Chierchia adds the operators $^{\cup}$, $^{\cap}$ and $\diamond$ to the language of terms. The first two operators are used to effectively allow what would otherwise be improper λ-reduction, where a free variable in the argument can become bound following an application of β-reduction. The third operator is for linking the sentences of discourse. As an example:

A man walked in.

would be translated as:

$$\lambda p(\Xi x(man'x \wedge walk{\cdot}in'x \wedge {}^{\cup}p))$$

Similarly, the sentence:

He looked tired.

can be represented by:

$$\lambda p(looked{\cdot}tired'x \wedge {}^{\cup}p)$$

The discourse:

A man walked in. He looked tired.

would be represented by:

$$\lambda p(\Xi x(man'x \wedge walk\cdot in'x \wedge {}^{\cup}p)) \diamond \lambda p(looked\cdot tired'x \wedge {}^{\cup}p)$$

where:

$$A \diamond B = \lambda q(A({}^{\cap}B(q)))$$

Using this definition, the final representations of the sequence of two sentences is equivalent to:

$$\lambda q(\Xi x(man'x \wedge walk\cdot in'x \wedge {}^{\cup\cap}(looked\cdot tired'x \wedge {}^{\cup}q)))$$

We require that the existential quantifier binds the x in the representation of the second sentence. In effect, this can be achieved by allowing $^{\cup}$ to cancel with $^{\cap}$. To do so in a simple-minded way would lead to improper λ-conversion (the x would have to be renamed). To avoid this, the model of PT can be altered in a manner which mirrors the model for Groenendijk and Stokhof's Dynamic Montague Grammar. The operator $^{\cap}$ abstracts over variable assignments in the model, and $^{\cup}$ applies them:

$$\begin{array}{rcl} [\![{}^{\cap}\alpha]\!]^{\omega} & = & \lambda\omega([\![\alpha]\!]^{\omega}) \\ [\![{}^{\cup}\alpha]\!]^{\omega} & = & [\![\alpha]\!]^{\omega}(\omega) \end{array}$$

where ω is the function which assigns a value to each variable, and λ is a meta-level abstraction. In our example, this interpretation allows $^{\cup}$ to cancel with $^{\cap}$, giving the expression:

$$\lambda q(\Xi x(man'x \wedge walk\cdot in'x \wedge looked\cdot tired'x \wedge {}^{\cup}q))$$

Chierchia points out that such a theory has an advantage over Dynamic Montague Grammar in that the model for $^{\cup}$ and $^{\cap}$ may require the felicity of self-application via loops in set membership, which is banned in Montague Semantics. These loops can arise if ω contains assignments of values to propositional variables. On the dynamic view, propositions can be taken to be true solely with respect to assignments, rather than to assignments, worlds and instants. So, we may have $\langle p, a\rangle \in \omega$, where p is a propositional variable, and a is the set of assignments where p is true. However, if p happens to be true at ω, then we have both $\omega \in a$ and $\langle p, a\rangle \in \omega$. This is legitimate in PT, but not in strongly typed theories. It seems that a Dynamic PT has the advantage of allowing dynamic binding of variables of arbitrary type.

In common with Dynamic Montague Grammar, Chierchia's dynamic theory takes universal quantification to be static. The sentence:

Every man walked in.

would be represented by:

$$\lambda p(\Theta x(man'x \Rightarrow walk\cdot in'x) \wedge {}^{\cup}p)$$

so that the pronoun in the continuation:

He looked tired.

is not bound. This corresponds with "box splitting" in DRT. This account would need to be embellished to cope with felicitous plural anaphoric reference.

As with Dynamic Predicate Logic (Groenendijk and Stokhof 1991), and Dynamic Montague Grammar (Groenendijk and Stokhof 1990), the semantics are such that an existential quantifier occurring in the antecedent of a conditional is interpreted as universal quantification, so the sentences:

If a man owns a book, he reads it.
Every man who owns a book reads it.

are given the same truth conditions.

B

Dependent Types and Discourse

This appendix provides some background information on an analysis of natural language within Martin-Löf's Type Theory (MLTT) (Martin-Löf 1982, Martin-Löf 1984, Sundholm 1989, Ranta 1991, Ranta 1994, Dávila-Pérez 1995).

In MLTT, there are types and elements (or "witnesses") of types. If T is a type, then:

$$w \varepsilon T$$

states that w is an element of that type.

Types can be seen as specifications, and elements of the types are then programs that meet the specification. Alternatively, types can be said to correspond with propositions, and elements of a type with proofs of that proposition. This is a form of intuitionistic logic, where a proposition is true if we can produce a proof of it. In MLTT, if the class of proofs specified by a proposition is non-empty (or "inhabited"), then that proposition is true.

Various complex types can be defined in MLTT. Those of interest for "donkey" sentences and intersentential anaphora are the "dependent types." These allow us to treat the witness for a type as providing a context for subsequent types.

In MLTT, the dynamic aspect of meaning can be modelled directly by using the dependent type operators Σ and Π. When given two appropriate arguments, the operator Σ produces a dependent-sum type. The operator Π produces a dependent-function type. We can think of these operators as the constructive versions of existential ($\exists$) and universal quantification ($\forall$) respectively (and also as conjunction and implication).

Constructive interpretations of negation, sentential conjunction, implication, relative clauses, universal and existential quantification can all be defined in terms of these two operators. In the semantics of natural language, the Σ types can be used to model existential quantification, conjunction and relative clauses. The Π types can be used to model universal quantification and implication.

It is the expressive power of the dependent types which allows them to be used both to model the complex structure of discourse and to control the accessibility of nominal antecedents. It is this uniformity of having the categories of semantic primitives in MLTT belong to the same semantic category which allows so many constructs in NL semantics to be interpreted by just two type operators.

In more detail, the expression:[104]

$$\Sigma f.(x)g$$

is a type formed from the types f, g. Viewed as a proposition, it is true if we can find an h such that:

$$h \varepsilon \Sigma f.(x)g$$

Witnesses for this type are pairs, so $h = \langle a, b \rangle$, where:

$$a \varepsilon f$$
$$b \varepsilon g[a/x]$$

Here we see the context dependence created by the Σ type: the type that b witnesses depends upon the witness a. As already mentioned, the operator Σ can be viewed as a form of existential quantification (or conjunction). Selector functions fst and snd pick the first and second elements of pairs. Such selectors can be used to pick out the antecedent of a pronoun. If a here is a witness to the representation of a nominal expression, then we can see that it becomes available for anaphoric reference in subsequent parts of the discourse.

Skipping the details of the translation procedure, the discourse:

A man walked in. He whistled.

would be represented by:

$$\Sigma(\Sigma \mathit{man}'.(x)\mathit{walked}\cdot\mathit{in}'x).(y)(\mathit{whistled}'(\mathrm{he}_0))$$

As stated previously, sentence concatenation, relative clauses and indefinites are all represented using Σ types.

If the anaphora he_0 is resolved, by replacing it by $\mathsf{fst}(y)$, then this MLTT proposition will be true if there is a witness of the form $\langle\langle m, \varphi\rangle, \psi\rangle$, where:

$$\langle\langle m, \varphi\rangle, \psi\rangle \varepsilon \Sigma(\Sigma \mathit{man}'.(x)\mathit{walked}\cdot\mathit{in}'x).(y)(\mathit{whistled}'(\mathrm{he}_0))$$

That is, m is a man, and φ is a proof that that man walked in, and ψ is a proof that that man whistled. All the nominal objects referred to by definite descriptors are available in subsequent parts of the discourse. The

[104]Here we have adopted a conventional MLTT notation for expressing abstraction. Alternative notations for $\Sigma f.(x)g$ are $\Sigma(f)(\lambda x(g))$ and $\Sigma x \varepsilon f.g$.

proof ψ is of ($whistled'(\mathrm{he}_0)$), where any occurrences of y are replaced by $\langle m, \varphi\rangle$ (the first element of $\langle\langle m, \varphi\rangle, \psi\rangle$). When $\mathsf{fst}(y)$ is substituted for the pronoun, this then becomes equivalent to $whistled'(m)$.

With the discourse:

If a farmer owns a donkey, he beats it.

we need to make use of the dependent type operator Π. The type:

$$\Pi f.(x)g$$

is inhabited by functions which take all proofs, or witnesses, w of f to a proof of $g[w/x]$. This is similar to universal quantification (or implication). As mentioned above, it can be used to represent the universal determiner 'all', and 'if ... then ...' constructions. The example can be represented by:

$$\Pi(\Sigma farmer'.(y)(\Sigma donkey'.(z)own'zy)).(x)beat'(\mathrm{it}_0)(\mathrm{he}_0)$$

The sentence is true if we can find a function h that maps objects of the form:

$$\langle f, \langle d, \varphi\rangle\rangle$$

where f is a farmer, d is a donkey, and φ is a proof that f owns d, into a proof of (or, an element of):

$$beats'(\mathrm{it}_0)(\mathrm{he}_0)$$

The anaphora are resolved if we replace them by selectors as follows:

$$beat'(\mathsf{fst}(\mathsf{snd}(x))(\mathsf{fst}(x))$$

where x becomes instantiated by $\langle f, \langle d, \varphi\rangle\rangle$—the argument of the function h—yielding:

$$beat'(\mathsf{fst}(\mathsf{snd}(\langle f, \langle d, o\rangle\rangle))(\mathsf{fst}(\langle f, \langle d, o\rangle\rangle))$$

which is equivalent to:

$$beat'df$$

For a compositional analysis, this is not the whole story. One particular problem concerns relative clauses. In a discourse containing the following:

A man who ate cheese died.

the top-level structure of the subject noun phrase is:

a (man who ate cheese)

In the semantics, the representation of the man denoted by the noun is embedded within a witness of the form:

$$\langle man', \langle cheese', \varphi\rangle\rangle$$

It is this term that will be substituted for the quantified argument of the representation of the verb 'died'. However, it is the man that died, not this structure.

To resolve this problem, we must amend the semantic rules which combine the representation of the verb phrase with that of the noun phrase so that we recurse through such structures to recover the witness to the main noun; in this case, the representation of the man himself. Dávila-Pérez achieves this using a function app (Dávila-Pérez 1995). The aim of this function is to find an appropriate selection from the witness v of the representation of the noun phrase x to use as the argument of the representation of the verb phrase y. It is defined as follows:

$$\mathsf{app}(y)(x)(v) = \begin{cases} \mathsf{app}(y)(a)(\mathsf{fst}v) & \text{if } x = \Sigma a.(y)b \\ (y)v & \text{otherwise} \end{cases}$$

In the final clause of this definition, the meaning of the verb phrase y is applied to the appropriate selection v of the quantified argument. The first clause recurses through all the Σ types of the noun phrase, represented in the second argument of app, until we end up with the underlying type of the noun. At each step in the recursion we modify the argument of the verb phrase so that it selects the witness to the underlying type.

Although this function appears in the representation of all determiners, its role is only significant with relative clause constructions, where it effectively picks out the part of the proof, or context, which is a witness to the main noun, rather than the proof which verifies the entire relative clause. As an example, the sentence:

Every man who owns a book reads it.

can be represented by:

$$\Pi(\Sigma man'.(x)(\Sigma book'.(y)(owns'yx))).$$
$$(z)(\mathsf{app}([reads'(\mathrm{it}_0)][\Sigma man'.(x)(\Sigma book'.(y)(own'yx))][z])$$

where $\mathrm{it}_0 = \mathsf{fst}(\mathsf{snd}z)$. Using the definition of app, this becomes equivalent to:

$$\Pi(\Sigma man'.(x)(\Sigma book'.(y)(own'yx))).$$
$$(z)(read'(\mathsf{fst}(\mathsf{snd}z))(\mathsf{fst}(\mathsf{fst}(z))))$$

This specifies a function which can take a man, a book and a proof of ownership, to a proof that the book is read by its owner.

Dávila-Pérez defines app using the Universe of Small Sets, although its effect can be implemented using a device similar to Cooper Storage during parsing (Dávila-Pérez 1995). In a property-theoretic treatment we can define the behaviour of app axiomatically.

C
SEMANTICS OF NL IN PT^{dt}

Here, we give a semantic analysis of a very small fragment of natural language in PT^{dt} (§5.4). For simplicity, both plurals and negation are absent from this analysis. It would be fairly straightforward to extend the analysis to cover simple cases of negation and of plural pronouns, but a more comprehensive treatment of these phenomena is beyond the scope of the current work. The main objective of this appendix is to illustrate how the theory of Chapter 5 can be applied, not to produce an empirically adequate account of all relevant linguistic phenomena. The fragment will be sufficient to analyse the kinds of basic examples that originally motivated a move away from classical logic towards Discourse Representation Theory (Kamp 1981, Kamp and Reyle 1993) and dynamic logic (Groenendijk and Stokhof 1990, Groenendijk and Stokhof 1991).

The basic categories can have the representations given in Table 4. A representation is suggested for the possessive pronouns 'his' and 'her' which uses a two place possessive relation *of*. This is generally inadequate. In the circumstances where John is Bill's manager, but not Bill's father, we would have both:

$$\mathrm{T}(\mathit{of}(\mathit{Bill}')(\mathit{John}'))$$

and:

$$\sim\mathrm{T}(\mathit{of}(\mathit{Bill}')(\mathit{John}'))$$

The possessive needs to be more intensional. We could add an extra argument to it, giving:

$$\mathrm{T}(\mathit{of}(\mathit{Bill}')(\mathit{manager}')(\mathit{John}'))$$

and:

$$\sim\mathrm{T}(\mathit{of}(\mathit{Bill}')(\mathit{father}')(\mathit{John}'))$$

However, this does not explain all of the data; we might talk of 'John's tree' to mean 'the tree that John owns', or 'John's favourite tree', for example. To represent these alternatives seems to require much pragmatic and contextual inference. The representation suggested here is

Basic Categories	Examples	Translation
Determiners (T/CN)	every a, some his, hers	$\lambda pq\langle\pi, p, \lambda x(q(H_p(x)))\rangle$ $\lambda pq\langle\varsigma, p, \lambda x(q(H_p(x)))\rangle$ $\lambda pq\langle\varsigma, \{z\epsilon p.of(\mathrm{he}_n)(z)\}, \lambda x(qx)\rangle$
Common Nouns (CN)	man, woman, donkey	*man′* *woman′* *donkey′*
Intransitive Verbs (IV)	walk, whistle	*walk′* *whistle′*
Transitive Verbs (TV)	own, beat, love	*owns′* *beats′* *loves′*
Pronouns (P)	he, she, it, him, her	$\lambda p(p(\mathrm{he}_n))$
Relative Pronouns (RP)	who, which, that	$\lambda pq\langle\varsigma, p, \lambda x(q(H_p(x)))\rangle$

TABLE 4 Basic Categories

offered merely to indicate how we might begin to extend the treatment of pronouns to other phenomena.

To treat some of the motivating examples for Discourse Representation Theory, we can use the categorial style rules given below. The notation P_A is used to denote the class of phrases of category A. In general, the numbering of the rules follows that of Montague (Montague 1973). There are some changes: pronouns are given their own category, and a new category of relative pronouns is introduced (P and RP respectively). Rule 1 is more specific than in Montague's analysis. Rules 3(a), 18, 19 are due to Dávila-Pérez (Dávila-Pérez 1995).

Determiner-Noun Rule

S2 If $\delta \in P_{\mathrm{T/CN}}$ and $\zeta \in P_{\mathrm{CN}}$ then $F_2(\delta, \zeta) = \delta\zeta \in P_{\mathrm{T}}$.
T2 $T(F_2(\delta, \zeta)) = \delta'\zeta'$

Subject-Predicate Rule

S4 If $\alpha \in P_{\mathrm{T}}$ and $\delta \in P_{\mathrm{IV}}$ then $F_2(\alpha, \delta) = \alpha\delta \in P_{\mathrm{t}}$
T4 $T(F_2(\alpha, \delta)) = \alpha'\delta'$

Transitive Verbs Rule

S5 If $\alpha \in P_{\mathrm{TV}}$ and $\zeta \in P_{\mathrm{T}}$ then $F_2(\alpha, \zeta) = \alpha\zeta \in P_{\mathrm{IV}}$
T5 $T(F_2(\alpha, \zeta)) = \lambda w(\zeta'(\alpha' w))$

Relative Clauses Rules

S3 If $\zeta \in P_{\mathrm{CN}}$, and $\varphi \in P_{\mathrm{t}}$
then $F_3(\zeta, \varphi) = \zeta$ such that $\varphi \in P_{\mathrm{CN}}$.

S3(a) If $\zeta \in P_{\mathrm{CN}}$, $\xi \in P_{\mathrm{RP}}$ and $\sigma \in P_{\mathrm{IV}}$
then $F_3(\delta, \xi, \sigma) = \zeta\xi\sigma \in P_{\mathrm{CN}}$.

T3 $T(F_3(\zeta, \xi, \varphi)) = \langle \varsigma, \delta', \lambda x(\varphi') \rangle$

T3(a) $T(F_3(\zeta, \xi, \sigma)) = \xi'\zeta'\delta'\sigma'$

Pronoun Rule

S1 If $\varphi \in P_{\mathrm{P}}$ then $F_1(\varphi) = \varphi \in P_{\mathrm{T}}$.

T1 $T(F_1(\varphi)) = \varphi'$

Conjunction Rules

S11 If $\varphi \in P_{\mathrm{t}}$ and $\psi \in P_{\mathrm{t}}$ then $F_{11}(\varphi, \psi) = \varphi$ and $\psi \in P_{\mathrm{t}}$

S12 If $\delta \in P_{\mathrm{IV}}$ and $\gamma \in P_{IV}$ then $F_{11}(\delta, \gamma) = \delta$ and $\gamma \in P_{\mathrm{IV}}$.

S13 If $\alpha \in P_{\mathrm{T}}$ and $\beta \in P_{\mathrm{T}}$ then $F_{11}(\alpha, \beta) = \alpha$ and $\beta \in P_{\mathrm{T}}$.

T11 $T(\varphi \text{ and } \psi) = \langle \varsigma, \varphi', \lambda x(\psi') \rangle$

T12 $T(\delta \text{ and } \gamma) = \lambda z \langle \varsigma, \delta' z, \lambda x(\gamma' z) \rangle$

T13 $T(\alpha \text{ and } \beta) = \lambda z \langle \varsigma, \alpha' z, \lambda x(\beta' z) \rangle$

Conditional Rule

S18 If $\varphi \in P_{\mathrm{t}}$ and $\psi \in P_{\mathrm{t}}$ then $F_{18}(\varphi, \psi) =$ if $\varphi, \psi \in P_{\mathrm{t}}$.

T18 $T(F_{18}(\varphi, \psi)) = \langle \pi, \varphi', \lambda x(\psi') \rangle$

Discourse Linking Rule

S19 If $\varphi \in P_{\mathrm{t}}$ and $\psi \in P_{\mathrm{t}}$ then $F_{19}(\varphi, \psi) = \varphi.\ \psi \in P_{\mathrm{t}}$.

T19 $T(F_{19}(\varphi, \psi)) = \langle \varsigma, \varphi', \lambda x(\psi') \rangle$

C.1 Examples

C.1.1 Worked Example Demonstrating Relative Clauses

We can represent:

A man who drank a beer laughed.

by way of the following:

$$
\begin{aligned}
&[\![\text{a man who drank a beer laughed}]\!] \\
&\quad = \langle \varsigma, [\![\text{man who drank a beer}]\!], \\
&\qquad\qquad \lambda x([\![\text{laughed}]\!](H_{[\![\text{man who drank a beer}]\!]}(x)))\rangle \\
&\quad = \langle \varsigma, [\![\text{man who drank a beer}]\!], \\
&\qquad\qquad \lambda x(\mathit{laughed}'(H_{[\![\text{man who drank a beer}]\!]}(x)))\rangle
\end{aligned}
$$

$$
\begin{aligned}
&[\![\text{man who drank a beer}]\!] \\
&\quad = \langle \varsigma, [\![\text{man}]\!], \lambda y([\![\text{drank a beer}]\!](H_{[\![\text{man}]\!]}(y)))\rangle \\
&\quad = \langle \varsigma, \mathit{man}', \lambda y([\![\text{drank a beer}]\!](H_{\mathit{man}'}(y)))\rangle \\
&\quad = \langle \varsigma, \mathit{man}', \lambda y([\![\text{drank a beer}]\!](y))\rangle
\end{aligned}
$$

$$
\begin{aligned}
&[\![\text{drank a beer}]\!]\\
&\quad = \lambda w[\![\text{a beer}]\!]([\![\text{drank}]\!]w)\\
&\quad = \lambda w[\![\text{a beer}]\!](\textit{drank}'w)
\end{aligned}
$$

$$
\begin{aligned}
&[\![\text{a beer}]\!]\\
&\quad = \lambda q\langle\varsigma, [\![\text{beer}]\!], \lambda z(q(H_{[\![\text{beer}]\!]}(z)))\rangle\\
&\quad = \lambda q\langle\varsigma, \textit{beer}', \lambda z(q(H_{\textit{beer}'}(z)))\rangle\\
&\quad = \lambda q\langle\varsigma, \textit{beer}', \lambda z(qz)\rangle
\end{aligned}
$$

Substituting the constituent representations back into the expressions in which they are contained gives:

$$
\begin{aligned}
&[\![\text{drank a beer}]\!]\\
&\quad = \lambda w(\lambda q\langle\varsigma, \textit{beer}'.\lambda z(qz)\rangle)(\textit{drank}'w)\\
&\quad = \lambda w\langle\varsigma, \textit{beer}', \lambda z(\textit{drank}'w(z))\rangle
\end{aligned}
$$

$$
\begin{aligned}
&[\![\text{man who drank a beer}]\!]\\
&\quad = \langle\varsigma, \textit{man}', \lambda y(([\![\text{drank a beer}]\!])y)\rangle\\
&\quad = \langle\varsigma, \textit{man}', \lambda y((\lambda w.\langle\varsigma, \textit{beer}', \lambda z(\textit{drank}'wz)\rangle)y)\rangle\\
&\quad = \langle\varsigma, \textit{man}', \lambda y(\langle\varsigma, \textit{beer}', \lambda z(\textit{drank}'yz)\rangle)\rangle
\end{aligned}
$$

$$
\begin{aligned}
&[\![\text{a man who drank a beer laughed}]\!]\\
&\quad = \langle\varsigma, [\![\text{man who drank a beer}]\!],\\
&\qquad\qquad \lambda x(\textit{laughed}'(H_{[\![\text{man who drank a beer}]\!]}(x)))\rangle\\
&\quad = \langle\varsigma, \langle\varsigma, \textit{man}', \lambda y\langle\varsigma, \textit{beer}', \lambda z(\textit{drank}'yz)\rangle\rangle,\\
&\qquad\qquad \lambda x(\textit{laughed}'(H_{\langle\varsigma, \textit{man}', \lambda y\langle\varsigma, \textit{beer}', \lambda z(\textit{drank}'yz)\rangle\rangle}(x)))\rangle\\
&\quad = \langle\varsigma, \langle\varsigma, \textit{man}', \lambda y\langle\varsigma, \textit{beer}', \lambda z(\textit{drank}'yz)\rangle\rangle,\\
&\qquad\qquad \lambda x(\textit{laughed}'(H_{\textit{man}'}(\mathsf{fst}(x))))\rangle\\
&\quad = \langle\varsigma, \langle\varsigma, \textit{man}', \lambda y\langle\varsigma, \textit{beer}', \lambda z(\textit{drank}'yz)\rangle\rangle,\\
&\qquad\qquad \lambda x(\textit{laughed}'(\mathsf{fst}(x)))\rangle
\end{aligned}
$$

Now we must prove that the term:

$$
{}^{\kappa}\langle\varsigma, \langle\varsigma, \textit{man}', \lambda y\langle\varsigma, \textit{beer}', \lambda z(\textit{drank}'yz)\rangle\rangle, \lambda x(\textit{laughed}'(\mathsf{fst}(x)))\rangle
$$

can be taken to form a proposition. To do this, according to the axioms of §5.4.2, we must show that the discourse term (without $^{\kappa}$) has a cat.

We shall assume that *man*′, *beer*′, *laughed*′ are properties of denotables ($\mathsf{Pty}_{\mathfrak{D}}$), and that *drank*′ forms a property of denotables when given a denotable. That is:

$$
\begin{aligned}
&\mathsf{Pty}_{\mathfrak{D}}(\textit{man}')\\
&\mathsf{Pty}_{\mathfrak{D}}(\textit{beer}')\\
&\mathsf{Pty}_{\mathfrak{D}}(\textit{laughed}')\\
&(\mathfrak{D} \Longrightarrow \mathsf{Pty}_{\mathfrak{D}})(\textit{drank}')
\end{aligned}
$$

Axiom 5.1 (§5.4.1) then allows us to derive $\mathsf{cat}_{\mathfrak{d}}(\textit{man}')$, $\mathsf{cat}_{\mathfrak{d}}(\textit{beer}')$, $\mathsf{cat}_{\mathfrak{d}}(\textit{laughed}')$ and $\forall x \varepsilon \mathfrak{d}.\mathsf{cat}_{\mathfrak{d}}(\textit{drank}'x)$.

First we look at the innermost discourse term:

$$\langle\varsigma, beer', \lambda z(drank'yz)\rangle$$

We know that $\mathsf{cat}_{\mathfrak{d}}b$ and we can deduce that $\forall x\varepsilon\mathfrak{d}.\mathrm{P}((\lambda z(drank'yz))x)$, where $y\varepsilon\mathfrak{d}$. This satisfies the precondition to Axiom 5.2, allowing us to conclude that:

$$\mathsf{cat}_{\mathfrak{d}}\langle\varsigma, beer', \lambda z(drank'yz)\rangle$$

when $y\varepsilon\mathfrak{d}$, that is:

$$\forall y\varepsilon\mathfrak{d}.\mathsf{cat}_{\mathfrak{d}}\langle\varsigma, beer', \lambda z(drank'yz)\rangle$$

This, together with the fact that $\mathsf{cat}_{\mathfrak{d}}(man')$, allows us to apply Axiom 5.3, giving:

$$\mathsf{cat}_{\mathfrak{d}\otimes\mathfrak{d}}\langle\varsigma, m, \lambda y\langle\varsigma, beer', \lambda z(drank'yz)\rangle\rangle$$

Now, from the definition of Σ and fst, we can show that:

$$\forall x\varepsilon\mathfrak{d}\otimes\mathfrak{d}.\mathrm{P}(laughed'(\mathsf{fst}(x)))$$

This means that Axiom 5.2 can be applied once more, leading to the conclusion:

$$\mathsf{cat}_{\mathfrak{d}\otimes\mathfrak{d}}\langle\varsigma, \langle\varsigma, man', \lambda y\langle\varsigma, beer', \lambda z(drank'yz)\rangle\rangle, \lambda x(laughed'(\mathsf{fst}(x)))\rangle$$

As the expression has a cat, we know that it can form a proposition when $^{\kappa}$ is applied to it:

$$\mathrm{P}(^{\kappa}\langle\varsigma, \langle\varsigma, man', \lambda y\langle\varsigma, beer', \lambda z(drank'yz)\rangle\rangle, \lambda x(laughed'(\mathsf{fst}(x)))\rangle)$$

and it is felicitous to consider its truth conditions.

The truth conditions can be unpacked as follows:

$$\begin{aligned}&\mathrm{T}(^{\kappa}\langle\varsigma, \langle\varsigma, man', \lambda y\langle\varsigma, beer', \lambda z(drank'yz)\rangle\rangle, \lambda x(laughed'(\mathsf{fst}(x)))\rangle)\\&\quad\leftrightarrow \exists x\dot{\varepsilon}^{\tau}\langle\varsigma, man', \lambda y\langle\varsigma, beer', \lambda z(drank'yz)\rangle\rangle.\mathrm{T}(^{\kappa}(laughed'(\mathsf{fst}(x))))\end{aligned}$$

The type of the existential quantified variable can be found using the axioms for $^{\tau}$ and the definition of Σ in Property Theory:

$$\begin{aligned}&x\dot{\varepsilon}^{\tau}\langle\varsigma, man', \lambda y\langle\varsigma, beer', \lambda z(drank'yz)\rangle\rangle\\&\quad\leftrightarrow x\dot{\varepsilon}\Sigma^{\tau}(man')\lambda y^{\tau}\langle\varsigma, beer', \lambda z(drank'yz)\rangle\\&\quad\leftrightarrow \mathsf{fst}(x)\dot{\varepsilon}^{\tau}(man')\ \&\ \mathsf{snd}(x)\dot{\varepsilon}[^{\tau}\langle\varsigma, beer', \lambda z(drank'yz)\rangle][\mathsf{fst}(x)/y]\end{aligned}$$

In the second conjunct we can then perform the substitution of $\mathsf{fst}(x)$ for y. To the result we can apply the axiom for $^{\tau}$ to produce a $\{\cdot\}$ expression which we can unpack using its property-theoretic definition. Finally, we can apply the vacuous instances of the axioms for $^{\tau}$ and $^{\kappa}$:

$$\begin{aligned}&\mathsf{snd}(x)\dot{\varepsilon}[^{\tau}\langle\varsigma, beer', \lambda z(drank'yz)\rangle][\mathsf{fst}(x)/y]\\&\quad\leftrightarrow \mathsf{snd}(x)\dot{\varepsilon}^{\tau}\langle\varsigma, beer', \lambda z(drank'(\mathsf{fst}(x))z)\rangle\\&\quad\leftrightarrow \mathsf{snd}(x)\dot{\varepsilon}\{z\epsilon^{\tau}(beer').\mathrm{T}(^{\kappa}(drank'(\mathsf{fst}(x)))z)\}\\&\quad\leftrightarrow \mathsf{snd}(x)\dot{\varepsilon}^{\tau}(beer')\ \&\ \mathrm{T}(^{\kappa}(drank'(\mathsf{fst}(x)))\mathsf{snd}(x))\\&\quad\leftrightarrow \mathsf{snd}(x)\dot{\varepsilon}beer'\ \&\ \mathrm{T}(drank'(\mathsf{fst}(x))\mathsf{snd}(x))\end{aligned}$$

Returning to the body of the original expression of the truth conditions, we can apply the vacuous instance of the axiom for $^{\kappa}$:

$$\begin{aligned}&\mathrm{T}({}^{\kappa}(\mathit{laughed}'(\mathsf{fst}(x))))\\ &\quad\leftrightarrow \mathrm{T}(\mathit{laughed}'(\mathsf{fst}(x)))\end{aligned}$$

So we have:

$$\begin{aligned}&\mathrm{T}({}^{\kappa}\langle\varsigma,\langle\varsigma,\mathit{man}',\lambda y\langle\varsigma,\mathit{beer}',\lambda z(\mathit{drank}'yz)\rangle\rangle,\lambda x(\mathit{laughed}'(\mathsf{fst}(x)))\rangle)\\ &\quad\leftrightarrow \exists x(\mathsf{fst}(x)\dot{\varepsilon}\mathit{man}' \ \&\ \mathsf{snd}(x)\dot{\varepsilon}\mathit{beer}' \ \&\\ &\qquad\qquad \mathrm{T}(\mathit{drank}'(\mathsf{fst}(x))\mathsf{snd}(x)) \ \&\ \mathrm{T}(\mathit{laughed}'(\mathsf{fst}(x))))\\ &\quad\leftrightarrow \exists y\dot{\varepsilon}\mathit{man}'.\exists z\dot{\varepsilon}\mathit{beer}'.(\mathrm{T}(\mathit{drank}'(y)z) \ \&\ \mathrm{T}(\mathit{laughed}'(y)))\end{aligned}$$

C.1.2 Intersentential Anaphora

Without giving the details of the derivation, the discourse:

A man walked in. He whistled.

has the representation:

$$\langle\varsigma,\langle\varsigma,\mathit{man}',\lambda x(\mathit{walked}\cdot\mathit{in}'x)\rangle,\lambda y(\mathit{whistled}'(\mathsf{fst}(y)))\rangle$$

assuming that the pronoun 'he' is co-indexed with 'the man'. If *man'*, *walked·in'* and *whistled'* are all properties of denotables, the discourse will have the following truth conditions:

$$\begin{aligned}&\mathrm{T}({}^{\kappa}\langle\varsigma,\langle\varsigma,\mathit{man}',\lambda x(\mathit{walked}\cdot\mathit{in}'x)\rangle,\lambda y(\mathit{whistled}'(\mathsf{fst}(y)))\rangle)\\ &\quad\leftrightarrow \exists y\dot{\varepsilon}\{x\epsilon\mathit{man}'.\mathit{walked}\cdot\mathit{in}'x\}.\mathrm{T}({}^{\kappa}(\mathit{whistled}'(y)))\\ &\quad\leftrightarrow \exists y\dot{\varepsilon}\mathit{man}'.(\mathrm{T}(\mathit{walked}\cdot\mathit{in}'y) \ \&\ \mathrm{T}(\mathit{whistled}'y))\end{aligned}$$

C.1.3 A Donkey Sentence

For the final example of discourse with singular pronouns, we take a donkey sentence:

If a farmer owns a donkey, he beats it.

Assuming that the constituent terms have the appropriate types, and that it has been determined that $\mathrm{it}_0 = \mathsf{fst}(\mathsf{snd}(x))$ and $\mathrm{he}_0 = \mathsf{fst}(x)$, then this will represented by a proposition with the following truth conditions:

$$\begin{aligned}&\mathrm{T}({}^{\kappa}\langle\pi,\langle\varsigma,\mathit{farmer}',\lambda y\langle\varsigma,\mathit{donkey}',\lambda z(\mathit{owns}'yz)\rangle\rangle,\lambda x(\mathit{beats}'(\mathrm{he}_0)(\mathrm{it}_0))\rangle)\\ &\quad\leftrightarrow \forall x\dot{\varepsilon}(\Sigma\mathit{farmer}'\lambda y\{z\epsilon\mathit{donkey}'.\mathit{owns}'yz\}).\mathrm{T}({}^{\kappa}(\mathit{beats}'(\mathsf{fst}(x))(\mathsf{snd}(x)))\\ &\quad\leftrightarrow \forall y\dot{\varepsilon}\mathit{farmer}'.\forall z\dot{\varepsilon}\mathit{donkey}'.(\mathrm{T}(\mathit{owns}'yz) \rightarrow \mathrm{T}(\mathit{beats}'yz))\end{aligned}$$

D

Negation and Disjunction in Discourse

This appendix offers a tentative treatment of negation and disjunction in PT^{dt} (§5.4). This is by no means complete, but it shows one way in which the discourse theory might be extended. To fit in with the thesis of Chapter 5, a more complete analysis would have to show that the new terms used here are λ-definable, or that the resultant theory is an innocent strengthening of $\mathrm{PT}^{\mathfrak{D}}$ (or $\mathrm{PT}^{\mathfrak{P}}$).

In Martin-Löf's Type Theory (MLTT), and other constructive type theories, negation is defined as follows:

$$-p =_{\mathrm{def}} p \mapsto \bot$$

so that $h\varepsilon(-p)$ means that any proof $a\varepsilon p$ can be transformed into a proof of absurdity ($\bot$), that is, $h(a)\varepsilon\bot$. There can be no proof of $\bot$, so there can be no proof a of p, hence p is false (Martin-Löf 1982, Martin-Löf 1984).

In PT^{dt}, we want to be able to combine the classical and constructive negations. Subsequently, we shall amend the behaviour to account for some of the relevant data involving double negation.

In this theory, we could try to use the follow definition of negation:

$$-t = \langle \pi, t, \nabla \rangle$$

where:

$$\nabla =_{\mathrm{def}} \lambda x(x \not\approx x)$$

But first, we need to ascertain the behaviour we require, and then see whether it can be obtained by this definition. It turns out that it is almost what is needed, except it does not produce the appropriate anaphoric behaviour with double negation.

D.1 Negation of Classical Propositions

When a term can be interpreted as a classical proposition, then we want the negation of that term to be a classical proposition:

$$\mathrm{P}({}^{\kappa}(t)) \rightarrow \mathrm{P}({}^{\kappa}(-t))$$

We also want it to obey the obvious truth conditions:

$$\mathrm{P}(^{\kappa}(t)) \rightarrow (\mathrm{T}(^{\kappa}(-t)) \leftrightarrow \sim \mathrm{T}(^{\kappa}(t)))$$

These two rules are theorems if we define $-t$ as $\langle \pi, t, \nabla \rangle$ (the proofs are trivial). If we interpret the sentence:

A man did not walk in.

as:

$$-\langle \varsigma, man', \lambda x(walk\cdot in'x)\rangle$$

this will be definitionally equivalent to:

$$\langle \pi, \langle \varsigma, man', \lambda x(walk\cdot in'x)\rangle, \lambda y(\nabla(y))\rangle$$

which, if a proposition, will have the truth conditions:

$$\forall y \dot{\varepsilon}\{x \epsilon man'.walk\cdot in'x\}.(y \neq y)$$

from which we can infer:

$$\sim \exists x \dot{\varepsilon} man'.\mathrm{T}(walk\cdot in'x)$$

D.2 Negation of Types

Given the interpretation of $-t$ as $\langle \pi, t, \nabla \rangle$, then we can show:

$$\mathsf{cat}_a(t) \rightarrow \mathsf{cat}_a(-t)$$

In the discourse:

[A man]$_i$ did not walk in. He$_i$ whistled.

it should not be possible to make the pronoun refer back to the man as indicated. In particular, this discourse should not be given the truth conditions that can be parodied by the sentence "No man walked in and whistled":

$$\sim \exists x \dot{\varepsilon}\{y \epsilon man'.walk\cdot in'y\}.\mathrm{T}(whistled'x)$$

In fact, we have the appropriate behaviour on both counts. The representation will be:

$$\langle \varsigma, \langle \pi, \langle \varsigma, man', walked\cdot in'\rangle, \nabla\rangle, \lambda x(whistled'(\mathrm{he}_0))\rangle$$

If this could be a proposition, then it would have the truth conditions:

$$\exists x \dot{\varepsilon}^{\tau}\langle \pi, \langle \varsigma, man', walked\cdot in'\rangle, \nabla\rangle.\mathrm{T}(\lambda y(whistled'(\mathrm{he}_0))x)$$

Using the simple analysis of π discourse terms given in §5.3.2, this would be equivalent to:

$$\exists x \dot{\varepsilon}(\mathsf{Id} y \varepsilon\{z \epsilon man'.walked\cdot in'z\}.(\nabla y)).\mathrm{T}(\lambda y(whistled'(\mathrm{he}_0))x)$$

where x ranges over a set which has a side condition in its definition that is always false; hence the set to which x belongs is always empty.

But, of course, this cannot be a proposition if the singular pronoun is replaced by a selector function that tries to pick an individual within the given discourse, as there would be no such denotable. The coindexing of a plural anaphora to within the scope of a negation is also blocked: if a singular or plural pronoun refers back to an antecedent within the scope of the negation we will not be able to prove the resolved pronoun is denotable, and so the entire expression will not provably be a proposition (Fox 1993).

Notice that the negation has the correct effect on the truth conditions of the discourse even if there is no infelicitous anaphoric reference, as it requires that any term representing 'a man who walked in' is not self-identical, so there can be no such man.

So far, it seems that the equation of $-t$ with $\langle\pi, t, \nabla\rangle$ is fine. However, considering double negation leads to a revision of this view.

D.3 Double Negation and Disjunction

Single negation usually blocks anaphoric reference, yet double negation seems to allow it:

> It is not the case that John does not have a car; it is parked outside.

This issue also arises in the treatment of disjunction. In this theory, we will represent disjunction by way of implication (or rather by way of a π expression) mirroring the classical equivalence:

$$(p \vee q) \rightarrow (\sim p \rightarrow q)$$

so that the disjunction of p and q will be represented by something like $\langle\pi, -p, \lambda x(q)\rangle$. The single negation here will block anaphoric reference into the first disjunct, which seems to be fine, except when the first disjunct is negated, as in:

> Either there is no bathroom, or it is in a funny place.

Here, anaphoric reference into the first disjunct should be allowed.

Both kinds of examples can be treated in the theory if we allow double negations to cancel. This has been noted in other theories (Krahmer and Muskens 1995). We might be tempted to try and follow Ranta and assert that some law of excluded middle (LEM) holds for certain types. However, this solution appears to require that we know what the "missing" discourse referents were all along. This may be acceptable when sugaring MLTT expressions into natural language, but it does not seem straight-forward when interpreting natural language.

We could set up the theory in such a way that we keep track of discourse references that have been made inaccessible by the occurrence of a negation. This can be achieved by having two sets of witness specifications for a type, one (which we are using already) that is relevant when the type occurs in a positive polarity context, the other when the type is interpreted in a negative context. Negation switches these two witness specifications. Double negation then leaves us with the original type. This simply adapts an existing proposal (Krahmer and Muskens 1995).

We will not pursue this further, instead an alternative approach will be offered, where we make use of the intermediate level of representation: the theory need not commit us to interpreting negation in discourse directly as negation in the truth conditions. Rather than keeping track of two interpretations of each type, as in the previous proposal, we can simply allow double negations to cancel when determining the truth conditions for a well formed discourse. In effect, this puts a form of LEM in the meta-level interpretation of the term representing the discourse, rather than in the representation itself.

This form of LEM can be implemented by adding additional axioms to the theory. First, however, we must consider proper names and definite descriptors.

D.4 Proper Nouns and Negation

The sentence:

John did not walk in.

can have the representation:

$$-\langle \varsigma, \{z : z \approx \mathit{john}'\}.\lambda x(\mathit{walk}\cdot \mathit{in}'(x))\rangle$$

which, if a proposition, has the same truth conditions as:

$$\langle \pi, \langle \varsigma, \{z : z \approx \mathit{john}'\}.\lambda x(\mathit{walk}\cdot \mathit{in}'(x))\rangle, \nabla\rangle$$

namely:

$$\forall y \dot{\varepsilon}\{x\epsilon\{z : z \approx \mathit{john}'\}.\mathit{walk}\cdot \mathit{in}'(x)\}.\mathrm{T}(\nabla y)$$

or equivalently:

$$\sim \exists y \dot{\varepsilon}\{x : x \approx \mathit{john}' \wedge \mathit{walk}\cdot \mathit{in}'(x)\}$$

which is fine. However, in the discourse:

John did not walk in. He laughed.

we have the interpretation:

$$\langle \varsigma, \langle \pi, \langle \varsigma, \{z.z \approx \mathit{john}'\}, \lambda x(\mathit{walk}\cdot \mathit{in}'(x))\rangle, \nabla\rangle, \lambda w.\mathit{laughed}'(\mathrm{he}_0)\rangle$$

Here the pronoun he_0 cannot refer back to 'John', as it occurs within the scope of the π expression representing negation. We must instead ensure that the ς expression representing John outscopes the negation.

This gives the following representations for these two examples:

$$\langle \varsigma, \{z.z \approx john'\}, \lambda x(-walk \cdot in'(x))\rangle$$

and:

$$\langle \varsigma, \langle \varsigma, \{z.z \approx john'\}, \lambda x(-walk \cdot in'(x))\rangle, \lambda w.laughed'(\mathrm{he}_0)\rangle$$

which, if propositions, would have the truth conditions:

$$\exists x \dot{\varepsilon} \{z.z \approx john'\}. \sim \mathrm{T}(walk \cdot in'(x))$$

and:

$$\exists w \dot{\varepsilon} \{x \epsilon \{z.z \approx john'\}.\neg walk \cdot in'(x)\}.\mathrm{T}(laughed'(\mathrm{he}_0))$$

respectively.

However, allowing proper nouns to outscope negation leads to problems when we want double negations to cancel. In the example:

Either John does not own a car or it is parked outside.

we want the negation that arise from the interpretation of the disjunction to cancel with the negation present in the first sentential clause. This would be trivial if the latter negation had wide scope over the proper noun, but this conflicts with the fact that we want proper names to outscope negation, as just discussed.

A solution to both of these problems is to make proper nouns "transparent" with respect to negation. If we always allow negation to be driven into an expression across the terms that introduce proper nouns, then proper nouns will have wide scope with respect to negation. In addition, double negations can now cancel, as the second negation can also be driven into the representation to the point where it can cancel with the first. Note that this treatment is also required for the interpretation of definite noun phrases.

The representations of proper nouns and definites have to be distinguished from those of other expressions so that negation can be given the appropriate behaviour. For the purposes of the axiomatisation given in the next section, we will say that def holds of terms corresponding to definites and proper nouns in the representation, and it does not hold of those terms that are not definites or proper nouns.

We might try to check whether a term represents a proper noun by seeing if it contains the representation of an intensional set of the form $\{x : x \approx t\}$. Unfortunately, in PT^{dt} the notation $\{\cdot\}$ is merely syntactic sugar. To simplify the presentation of our axioms, we will introduce new terms to represent proper nouns and definite descriptors.

$$D(x, s).t$$

will be used to represent 'the s such that t', and:

$$B(x, n).t$$

will be used to represent the binding of x to the rigid designator (proper name) n in t. In discourse without negation, they should have the same behaviour as:

$$\langle \varsigma, \{x : x \approx_{\mathfrak{d}} \sigma y(s)\}, \lambda x(t) \rangle$$

and:

$$\langle \varsigma, \{x : x \approx_{\mathfrak{d}} n\}, \lambda x(t) \rangle$$

respectively, where

$$x \approx_{\mathfrak{d}} y$$

provably forms a proposition only if both arguments x, y are denotable. To achieve this, the type of $\approx_{\mathfrak{d}}$ should be:

$$\mathfrak{D} \Longrightarrow (\mathfrak{D} \Longrightarrow \mathrm{P})$$

That is:

$$\mathfrak{D}(x) \mathbin{\&} \mathfrak{D}(y) \rightarrow \mathrm{P}(x \approx_{\mathfrak{d}} y)$$
$$\mathfrak{D}(x) \mathbin{\&} \mathfrak{D}(y) \rightarrow (\mathrm{T}(x \approx_{\mathfrak{d}} y) \leftrightarrow x = y)$$

This weaker form of equality is required if our treatment of felicitous discourse is to work in the interpretation of proper nouns and definite descriptors. Note that we are just interested in presenting the essential details of how definites and proper names interact with negation in discourse. To simplify the presentation, the proposed equivalences involving definites and proper names do not take account of their anaphoric content.

We are now in a position to give axioms for negation.

D.5 AXIOMS FOR NEGATION IN PT^{dt}

In place of the function $^{\tau}$, we can have two functions $^{\tau}$, $^{\bar{\tau}}$, one for each polarity. We then need the following axioms:

(i) $\mathsf{cat}_t(p) \rightarrow \mathsf{cat}_t(-p)$

(ii) $\mathsf{cat}_t(p) \rightarrow (\mathrm{T}(^{\kappa}p) \leftrightarrow \mathrm{T}^{\kappa}\langle \pi, p, \nabla \rangle)$

(iii) $(\mathsf{cat}_t(p) \mathbin{\&} s\varepsilon t) \rightarrow (\mathrm{T}(^{\tau}(-p)s) \leftrightarrow \mathrm{T}(^{\bar{\tau}}ps))$

(iv) $(\mathsf{cat}_t(p) \mathbin{\&} {\sim}\exists q(p = -q) \mathbin{\&} {\sim}\mathsf{def}(p) \mathbin{\&} s\varepsilon t) \rightarrow$
$(\mathrm{T}(^{\bar{\tau}}ps) \leftrightarrow \mathrm{T}(^{\tau}\langle \pi, p, \nabla \rangle s))$

(v) $(\mathsf{cat}_t(p) \mathbin{\&} s\varepsilon t) \rightarrow (\mathrm{T}(^{\bar{\tau}}(-p)s) \leftrightarrow \mathrm{T}(^{\tau}ps))$

(vi) $(\mathsf{cat}_t(D(x, f)g) \mathbin{\&} s\varepsilon t) \rightarrow$
$(\mathrm{T}(^{\bar{\tau}}(D(x, f).g))s \leftrightarrow \mathrm{T}(^{\tau}(D(x, f).(-g))s))$

(vii) $(\mathsf{cat}_t(B(x, n).f) \mathbin{\&} s\varepsilon t) \rightarrow$
$(\mathrm{T}(^{\bar{\tau}}(B(x, n).f)s) \leftrightarrow \mathrm{T}(^{\tau}(B(x, n). - f)s))$

These axioms give a single negation, such as $-p$, the same behaviour as the term $\langle \pi, p, \nabla \rangle$, but double negations can cancel, so $- - p$ has the same effect on the truth conditions as p.

The condition $\sim \mathsf{def}(p)$ in axiom (iv) means that we do not force the wrong, wide-scope interpretation of negation on discourse containing a definite or proper name. Axioms (vi) and (vii) then force the narrow scope interpretation in these cases.

There may be a sense in which it would be more elegant if this behaviour could be derived from the nature of the interpretation of negation.

We can examine the effect of these axioms on the discourse:

Either there is no bathroom (here), or it is in a funny place.

This will be represented by:

$$\langle \pi, - - \langle \varsigma, \mathit{bathroom}', \lambda b.\mathit{here}'(b) \rangle, \lambda x.\mathit{funny{\cdot}place}'(\mathrm{it}_0) \rangle$$

Coindexing the pronoun appropriately, this will have the truth conditions:

$$\forall x \dot{\varepsilon} \{ b \epsilon \mathit{bathroom}'.\mathit{here}'(b) \}.\mathrm{T}(\mathit{funny{\cdot}place}'(x))$$

which will be true if there is no bathroom, or if there is a bathroom it is in a funny place. If there is more than one bathroom, they must all be in a funny place.

According to these axioms, if the sentence:

Either John has no car, or it is parked outside.

is felicitous, then it will be true either if John owns no cars, or if he owns one or more cars, they are all parked outside.

In combination with the treatment of ${}^{\tau}\langle \pi, s, t \rangle$ as a pluralised type, this analysis of negation leads to the creation of plural antecedents, so that in the discourse:

No student laughed. They were very serious.

the plural pronoun can refer to the students who do not laugh. This may not always be appropriate, and it may not be the most elegant mechanism for generating plural antecedents in such examples.

Krahmer and Muskens offer a treatment of disjunction and negation in a version of Discourse Representation Theory (Krahmer and Muskens 1995). Simons and Milward have also given analyses of disjunction within discourse (Simons 1996, Simons 1998, Milward 1995). The formal theory presented here is not as comprehensive as these offerings; it is merely intended to give an indication as to how we might begin to explore problems in the semantics of discourse within the framework of PT.

References

Aczel, P. 1980. Frege Structures and the notions of proposition, truth and set. In *The Kleene Symposium*, ed. Barwise, Keisler, and Keenan. 31–39. North Holland Studies in Logic. North Holland.

Aczel, P. 1988. *Non-well-founded Sets*. CSLI Lecture Notes. Stanford: CSLI.

Ahn, R., and H. Kolb. 1990. Discourse Representation Theory Meets Constructive Mathematics. ITK Research Report Number 16, Tilburg University.

Barendregt, H. 1984. *The Lambda Calculus: Its Syntax and Semantics*. Studies in Logic and the Foundation of Mathematics, Vol. 103. Amsterdam: North Holland. Second edition.

Barker, C. 1992. Group Terms in English: Representing Groups as Atoms. *Journal of Semantics* 9:69–93.

Bartsch, R. 1973. The Semantics and Syntax of Number and Numbers. In *Syntax and Semantics Volume 2*, ed. J.P. Kimball. New York: Seminar Press.

Barwise, J. 1979. On Branching Quantifiers in English. *Journal of Philosophical Logic* 8:47–80.

Bealer, G. 1982. *Quality and Concept*. Clarendon Press.

Bealer, G. 1989. On the Identification of Properties and Propositional Functions. *Linguistics and Philosophy* 12:1–14.

Beaver, D.I. 1997. Presupposition. In *Handbook of Logic and Language*, ed. J. van Benthem and A. ter Meulen. 939–1008. North Holland.

Bennett, M.R. 1975. *Some Extensions of a Montague Fragment of English*. Doctoral dissertation, Indiana University. Thesis Distributed by the Indiana University Linguistics Club.

Bennett, M.R. 1977. Mass Nouns and Mass Terms in Montague Grammar. In *Linguistics, Philosophy, and Montague Grammar*, ed. S. Davis and M. Mithun. 263–285. Austin: University of Texas Press.

Bigelow, J.C. 1978. Believing in Semantics. *Linguistics and Philosophy* 2:101–144.

Birkhoff, G. 1967. *Lattice Theory.* Colloquium Publications. American Mathematical Society.

Black, M. 1944. The Paradox of Analysis. *Mind* LIII:263–267.

Blau, U. 1981. Collective Objects. *Theoretical Linguistics* 8:101–130.

Bunt, H. 1979. Ensembles and the Formal Semantic Properties of Mass Terms. In *Mass Terms*, ed. F.J. Pelletier. 249–277. Dordrecht: D. Reidel.

Bunt, H. 1985. *Mass Terms and Model Theoretic Semantics.* Cambridge University Press.

Burge, T. 1972. Truth and Mass Terms. *Journal of Philosophy* 69(10):263–82.

Burge, T. 1975. Mass Terms, Count Nouns, and Change. *Synthese* 31:459–478.

Carlson, G. 1977. A Unified Analysis of the English Bare Plural. *Linguistics and Philosophy* 1:413–456.

Carnap, R. 1947. *Meaning and Necessity.* Chicago: University of Chicago Press.

Carter, W.R. 1990. *The Elements of Metaphysics.* New York: McGraw-Hill.

Cartwright, H.M. 1965. Heraclitus and the Bath Water. *Philosophical Review* 74:466–485.

Cartwright, H.M. 1970. Quantities. *Philosophical Review* 79:466–85.

Cheng, C.Y. 1973. Response to Moravcsik. In *Approaches to Natural Language*, ed. K.J.J. Hintikka, J.M.E. Moravcsik, and P. Suppes. Dordrecht: D. Reidel.

Chierchia, G. 1982a. Nominalisation and Montague Grammar: a Semantics without Types for Natural Languages. *Linguistics and Philosophy* 5:303–354.

Chierchia, G. 1982b. On Plurals and Mass Nominals. In *Proceedings of the West Coast Conference on Formal Lingustics*, 243–255.

Chierchia, G. 1984. *Topics in the Semantics of Infinitives and Gerunds.* Doctoral dissertation, University of Massachusetts, Amherst. Published in 1989 by Garland, New York.

Chierchia, G. 1991. Intensionality and Context Change, Towards a Dynamic Thoery of Propositions and Properties. m.s. Cornell University.

Chierchia, G. 1998. Plurality of Mass Nouns and the notion of "Semantic Parameter". In *Events and Grammar*, ed. S. Rothstein. 53–103. Kluwer.

Chierchia, G., and R. Turner. 1988. Semantics and Property Theory. *Linguistics and Philosophy* 11:261–302.

Clarke, D.S. 1970. Mass Terms as Subjects. *Philosophical Studies* 21:25–9.

Cocchiarella, N.B. 1979. The Theory of Homogeneous Simple Types as a Second Order Logic. *Notre Dame Journal of Formal Logic* 20:505–524.

Cooper, R., R. Crouch, J. van Eijck, C. Fox, J. van Genabith, J. Jaspars, H. Kamp, M. Pinkal, M. Poesio, S. Pulman, and E. Vestre. 1994. Describing the Approaches. Framework for Computational Semantics (FraCaS), European Union funded LRE project 62-051, deliverable D8.

Cresswell, M.J. 1975. Hyperintensional Logic. *Studia Logica* 34:25–38.

Cresswell, M.J. 1985. *Stuctured Meanings.* Cambridge, Massachusetts: MIT Press.

Dávila-Pérez, R. 1995. *Semantics and parsing in intuitionistic categorial grammar.* Doctoral dissertation, University of Essex.

Dalrymple, M., M. Kanazawa, Y. Kim, S. Mchombo, and S. Peters. 1998. Reciprocal Expressions and the Concept of Reciprocity. *Linguistics and Philosophy* 21(2):159–210. An earlier version appears in Proc. of the Fourth Semantics and Linguistic Theory Conference, Salt IV, Rochester, NY, May 1994, ed. M. Harvey and L. Santelmann.

De Roeck, A., R. Ball, E.K. Brown, C.J. Fox, M. Groefsema, N. Obeid, and R. Turner. 1991. Helpful Answers to Modal and Hypothetical Questions. In *Proceedings of the European ACL 1991.* Berlin.

Dölling, J. 1990. Plurals and Collective Nouns. In *Papers from the Second Symposium on Logic and Language*, 189–201. Budapest.

Dowty, D.R. 1988. Type Raising, Functional Composition, and Non-constituent Conjunction. In *Categorial Grammars and Natural Language Structures*, ed. R.T. Oehrle, E. Bach, and D. Wheeler. 153–197. Dordrecht: D. Reidel.

Elworthy, D. 1995. A Theory of Anaphoric Information. *Linguistics and Philosophy* 18:297–332.

Feferman, S. 1984. Towards useful type-free theories 1. *Journal of Symbolic Logic* 49:61–102.

Fiengo, R., and H. Lasnik. 1973. The Logical Structure of Reciprocal Sentences in English. *Foundations of Language* 9:447–468.

Fox, C.J. 1993. *Plurals and Mass Terms in Property Theory.* Doctoral dissertation, University of Essex, Colchester, U.K.

Fox, C.J. 1994a. Discourse Representation, Type Theory and Property Theory. In *Proceedings of the International Workshop on Computational Semantics*, ed. H. Bunt, R. Muskens, and G. Rentier, 71–80. ITK, Tilburg.

Fox, C.J. 1994b. Individuals and Their Guises: A Property-theoretic Analysis. In *Proceedings of the Ninth Amsterdam Colloquium, December 1993*, 301–312.

Fox, C.J. 1998. Plurals and Mass Terms in Property Theory. In *Plurality and Quanitfication*, ed. F. Hamm and E. Hinrichs. 113–175. Studies in Linguistics and Philosophy, No. 69. Dordrecht: Kluwer Academic Press.

van Fraassen, B.C. 1966. Singular terms and truth value gaps. *The Journal of Philosophy* LXIII:481–495.

Gillon, B.S. 1992. Towards a Common Semantics for English Count and Mass Nouns. *Linguistics and Philosophy* 15:597–639.

Gilmore, P.C. 1974. The consistency of partial set theory without extensionality. *Proc. Symposia Pure Mathematics* XIII(II):147–153. Axiomatic Set Theory.

Grandy, R.E. 1973. Responce to Moravcsik. In *Approaches to Natural Language*, ed. K.J.J. Hintikka, J.M.E. Moravcsik, and P. Suppes. Dordrecht: D. Reidel.

Grandy, R.E. 1975. Stuff and Things. *Synthese* 31:479–485.

Gratzer, G. 1978. *General Lattice Theory.* New York: Academic Press.

Groenendijk, J., and M. Stokhof. 1990. Dynamic Montague Grammar. In *Papers from the Second Symposium on Logic and Language*, ed. L. Kálmán and L. Polós, 3–48. Budapest, Hungary. Akadémiai Kiadó. Also available as ITLI Prepublication Series LP–90–02.

Groenendijk, J., and M. Stokhof. 1991. Dynamic Predicate Logic. *Linguistics and Philosophy* 14:39–100.

Gupta, A. 1982. Truth and Paradox. *Journal of Philosophical Logic* 11:1–60.

Halmos, P.R. 1963. *Lectures on Boolean Algebras.* Princeton, New Jersey: D. Van Nostrand.

Heim, I. 1982. *The Semantics of Definite and Indefinite Noun Phrases.* Doctoral dissertation, University of Massachusetts, Amherst. Thesis Distributed by Graduate Linguistics Student Association.

Heim, I., H. Lasnik, and R May. 1991. Reciprocity and Plurality. *Linguistic Inquiry* 22(1):63–101.

Herzberger, H. 1982. Notes on naive semantics. *Journal of Philosophical Logic* 11:61–102.

Higginbotham, J. 1981. Reciprocal Interpretation. *Linguistic Research* 3:97–117.

Hintikka, J. 1974. Quantifiers v. Quantification Theory. *Linguistic Inquiry* 5:153–177.

Hoeksema, J. 1983. Plurality and Conjunction. In *Studies in Modeltheoretic Semantics*, ed. A.G.B. ter Meulen. 63–83. Dordrecht: Foris.

Hoeksema, J. 1987. The Semantics of Non-boolean "And". Paper presented at the LSA/ASL meeting, Stanford.

Hoepelman, J. 1983. Adjectives and Nouns : a New Calculus. In *Meaning, Use, and Interpretation of Language*, ed. R. Bäuerle, C. Schwartze, and A. von Stechow. 190–220. Berlin: Walter de Gruyer.

Hughes, G.E., and M.J. Cresswell. 1973. *An Introduction to Modal Logic.* London: Methuen.

Jubien, M. 1989. On Properties and Property Theory. In *Properties, Types and Meaning*, ed. G. Chierchia, B. Partee, and R. Turner. 159–175. Dordrecht: Kluwer.

Jubien, M. 1993. *Ontology, Modality, and the Fallacy of Reference.* Cambridge: Cambridge University Press.

Jubien, M. 1997. *Contemporary Metaphysics: an introduction.* Contemporary Philosophy. Blackwell.

Kamareddine, F. 1988. *Semantics in Frege Structures.* Doctoral dissertation, University of Edinburgh.

Kamareddine, F. 1992. Set Theory and Nominalization, Part I. *Logic and Computation* 2(5):579–604.

Kamareddine, F. 1993. Set Theory and Nominalization, Part II. *Logic and Computation* 2(6):687–707.

Kamareddine, F. 1995. Important Issues in Foundational Formalisms. *Bulletin of the Interest Group in Pure and Applied Logics* 3(2,3):291–317.

Kamp, H. 1975. Two Theories of Adjectives. In *Formal Semantics of Natural Language*, ed. E. Keenan. 123–155. Cambridge University Press.

Kamp, H. 1981. Theory of Truth and Semantic Representation. In *Formal Methods in the Study of Language*, ed. J.A.K. Groenendijk, T.M.V. Janssen, and M.B.J. Stokhof. 277–322. Mathematical Centre Tracts 135. Amsterdam.

Kamp, H., and U. Reyle. 1993. *From Discourse to Logic.* Dordrecht: Kluwer.

Karttunen, L. 1976. Discourse Referents. In *Syntax and Semantics*, ed. McCrawley. New York: Academic Press.

Keenan, E., and L.M. Faltz. 1985. *Boolean Semantics for Natural Language.* Dordrecht: D. Reidel.

Krahmer, E., and R. Muskens. 1995. Negation and Disjunction in Discourse Representation. *Journal of Semantics* 12:357–376.

Krifka, M. 1996. Parameterized Sum Individuals for Plural Anaphora. *Linguistics and Philosophy* 19:555–598.

Kripke, S. 1959. A Completeness Theorem in Modal Logic. *Journal of Symbolic Logic* 24:1–14.

Kripke, S. 1963. Semantical Considerations on Modal Logic. *Acta Philosophica Fennica* 16:83–89.

Kripke, S. 1975. Outline of a theory of truth. *Journal of Philosophy* 1(xxii):690–716.

Lakoff, F. 1970. Linguistics and Natural Logic. *Synthese* 22:151–271.

Landman, F. 1986. Pegs and Alecs. In *Towards a Theory of Information. The Status of Partial Objects in Semantics.* 97–136. Groningen-Amsterdam Studies in Semantics. Dordrecht: Foris.

Landman, F. 1987. Groups, Plural Individuals and Intentionality. In *Proceedings of the Sixth Amsterdam Colloquium*, ed. J. Groenendijk, M. Stokhof, and F. Veltman, 197–217. University of Amsterdam. ITLI.

Landman, F. 1989. 'Groups', Parts I and II. *Linguistics and Philosophy* 12:559–605, 723–744.

Langendoen, D.T. 1978. The Logic of Reciprocity. *Linguistic Inquiry* 9:177–197.

Lasersohn, P. 1998. Generalised Distributivity Operators. *Linguistics and Philosophy* 21:83–93.

Laycock, H. 1972. Some Questions of Ontology. *Philosophical Review* 81:3–42.

Laycock, H. 1975. Theories of Matter. *Synthese* 31:411–442.

Leonard, H.S., and N. Goodman. 1940. The Calculus of Individuals and its Uses. *Journal of Symbolic Logic* 5:45–55.

Levinson, S. 1983. *Pragmatics.* Cambridge University Press.

Lewis, D.K. 1970. General Semantics. *Synthese* 22:18–67.

Lewis, D.K. 1991. *Parts of Classes.* Oxford: Blackwell.

Link, G. 1983. The Logical Analysis of Plurals and Mass Terms: A Lattice Theoretic Approach. In *Meaning, Use and Interpretation of Language*, ed. R. Bäuerle, C. Schwartze, and A. von Stechow. 302–323. Berlin: Walter de Gruyer.

Link, G. 1984. Hydras: On the Logic of Relative Constructions with Multiple Heads. In *Varieties of Formal Semantics*, ed. F. Landman and F. Veltman. 245–257. Dordrecht: Foris.

Link, G. 1987. Generalised Quantifiers and Plurals. In *Generalised Quantifiers. Linguistic Approaches*, ed. P. Gärdenfors. 151–180. Dordrecht: D. Reidel.

Link, G. 1991a. First Order Axioms for the Logic of Plurality. University of Munich. m.s.

Link, G. 1991b. Plurals. In *Handbuch der Semantik*, ed. A. von Stechow and D. Wunderlich. Berlin: de Gruyter.

Lønning, J.T. 1987a. Collective Readings of Definite and Indefinite Noun Phrases. In *Generalised Quantifiers. Linguistic and Logical Approaches*, ed. P. Gärdenfors. Dordrecht: D. Reidel.

Lønning, J.T. 1987b. Mass Terms and Quantification. *Linguistics and Philosophy* 10:1–52.

Lønning, J.T. 1989. Some Aspects of the Logic of Plural Noun Phrases. University of Oslo. Cosmos Report Number 11.

Martin-Löf, P. 1982. Constructive Mathematics and Computer Programming. In *Logic, Methodology and Philosophy of Science VI*, ed. Cohen, Los, Pfeiffer, and Podewski. 153–179. North Holland.

Martin-Löf, P. 1984. *Studies in Proof Theory (Lecture Notes)*. Napoli: Bibliopolis.

Massey, G. 1976. Tom, Dick and Harry and all the King's men. *American Philosophical Quarterly* 13:89–107.

ter Meulen, A.G.B. 1980. *Substances, Quantities, and Individuals*. Doctoral dissertation, Stanford University.

ter Meulen, A.G.B. 1981. An Intensional Logic for Mass Terms. In *Formal Methods in the Study of Language*, ed. J.A.G. Groenendijk, T.M.V. Janssen, and M.B.J. Stokhof. Amsterdam: Mathematical Centre.

Milward, D. 1995. Integrating Situations into a Theory of Discourse Anaphora. In *Proceedings of the Tenth Amsterdam Colloquium*.

Montague, R. 1973. The Proper Treatment of Quantification in Ordinary English. In *Approaches to Natural Language*, ed. K.J.J. Hintikka, J.M.E. Moravcsik, and P. Suppes. Dordrecht: D. Reidel. Synthese Library.

Moravcsik, J.M.E. 1973. Mass Terms in English. In *Approaches to Natural Language*, ed. K.J.J. Hintikka, J.M.E. Moravcsik, and P. Suppes. 263–285. Dordrecht: D. Reidel. Synthese Library.

Ojeda, A. 1993. *Linguistic Individuals*. CSLI Lecture Notes. Stanford: CSLI.

Orey, S. 1959. Model Theory for Higher Order Predicate Calculus. *Transactions from the American Mathematical Society* 92:72–84.

Parsons, T. 1970. An Analysis of Mass Terms and Amount Terms. *Foundation of Language* VI(3):362–388.

Parsons, T. 1975. Afterthoughts on Mass Terms. *Synthese* 31:517–21.

Partee, B., and M. Rooth. 1983. Generalised Conjunction and Type Ambiguity. In *Meaning, Use and Interpretation of Language*, ed. R. Bäuerle, C. Schwartze, and A. von Stechow. 361–383. Berlin: Walter de Gruyter.

Pelletier, F.J. 1974. On Some Proposals for the Semantics of Mass Terms. *Journal of Philosophical Logic* 3:87–108.

Peyton-Jones, S. 1986. *The Implementation of Functional Programming Languages.* Prentice Hall.

Quine, W.V.O. 1960. *Word and Object.* Cambridge, Mass.: MIT Press.

Ramsay, A. 1990. *The Logical Structure of English.* London: Pitman.

Ranta, A. 1991. Intuitionistic Categorial Grammar. *Linguistics and Philosophy* 14:203–239.

Ranta, A. 1994. *Type Theoretic Grammar.* Oxford University Press.

Roberts, C. 1987. *Modal Subordination, Anaphora, and Distributivity.* Doctoral dissertation, University of Massaschusetts.

Roberts, C. 1988. Distributivity. In *Proceedings of the Sixth Amsterdam Colloquium*, ed. J. Groenendijk, M. Stokhof, and F. Veltman. University of Amsterdam. ITLI.

Roeper, P. 1983. Semantics for Mass Terms with Quantifiers. *Noûs* 17:251–265.

van der Sandt, R. 1988. *Context and Presupposition.* London: Croom Helm.

Scha, R. 1981. Distributivity, Collective and Cumulative Quantification. In *Formal Methods in the Study of Language*, ed. J.A.G. Groenendijk, T.M.V. Janssen, and M.B.J. Stokhof. 4830–512. Mathematical Centre Tracts 136. Amsterdam.

Scha, R. 1984. Distributive, Collective and Cumulative Quantification. In *Truth, Interpretation, and Information*, ed. J. Groenendijk *et al.* 131–158. GRASS 2. Dordrecht: Foris.

Scha, R., and D. Stallard. 1988. Multi-level Plurals and Distributivity. In *Proceedings of the ACL Meeting, June 1988*, 17–24.

Schwarzschild, R. 1991. *On the Meaning of Definite Plural Noun Phrases.* Doctoral dissertation, University of Massachusetts, Amherst.

Schwarzschild, R. 1992. Types of Plural Individual. *Linguistics and Philosophy* 15:641–675.

Scott, D.A. 1970. *Constructive Validity*. Lecture Notes in Mathematics, Vol. 125. Berlin: Springer-Verlag.

Scott, D.A. 1973. Models for various type-free calculii. In *Logic, Methodology and Philosophy of Science IV*, ed. P. Suppes *et al.* 157–187. North Holland Studies in Logic and the Foundations of Mathematics. North Holland.

Simons, M. 1996. Disjunction and Anaphora. In *Proceedings of Semantics and Linguistic Theory (SALT) VI*, ed. T. Galloway and J. Spence. Rutgers University, April. CLC Publications, Cornell University.

Simons, M. 1998. *"OR" Issues in the Semantics and Pragmatics of Disjunction*. Doctoral dissertation, Cornell University. CLC Publications.

Smith, J.M. 1984. An Interpretation of Martin-Löf's Type Theory in a type-free theory of propositions. *Journal of Symbolic Logic* 49.

Stalnaker, R. 1984. *Inquiry*. Cambridge, MA: MIT Press.

Strawson, P.F. 1950. On Referring. *Mind* 59.

Strawson, P.F. 1959. *Individuals*. London: Methuen.

Strawson, P.F. 1964. Identifying Reference and Truth-Values. *Theoria* 3:96–118.

Sundholm, G. 1989. Constructive Generalised Quantifiers. *Synthese* 79:1–12.

Thomason, R. 1980. A Modeltheory for Propositional Attitudes. *Linguistics and Philosophy* 4.

Turner, R. 1987. A Theory of Properties. *Journal of Symbolic Logic* 52(2):455–472.

Turner, R. 1988. Properties, Propositions, and Semantic Theory. In *Proceedings of Formal Semantics and Computational Linguistics*. Switzerland.

Turner, R. 1989. Two Issues in the Foundation of Semantic Theory. In *Properties, Types and Meaning*, ed. G. Chierchia, B. Partee, and R. Turner. Dordrecht: Kluwer.

Turner, R. 1990. *Truth and Modality for Knowledge Representation*. Pitman.

Turner, R. 1992. Properties, Propositions and Semantic Theory. In *Computational Linguistics and Formal Semantics*, ed. M. Rosner and R. Johnson. 159–180. Studies in Natural Language Processing. Cambridge: Cambridge University Press.

Turner, R. 1997. Types. In *Handbook of Logic and Language*, ed. J. van Benthem and A. ter Meulen. 535–586. Elsevier.

Westerståhl, D. 1987. Branching Generalised Quantifiers and Natural Language. In *Generalised Quantifiers. Linguistic and Logical Approaches*, ed. P. Gärdenfors. Dordrecht: D. Reidel.

Author Index

Formal Index

General Index